To: Ryan
Love, Grandma

2007

# Your Iguana's Life

# Also Available from PRIMA PETS™

*The Allergy Solution for Dogs* by Shawn Messonnier, D.V.M.

*The Arthritis Solution for Dogs* by Shawn Messonnier, D.V.M.

*Your Beagle's Life* by Kim Campbell Thornton

*Your Bearded Dragon's Life* by Liz Palika

*Your Border Collie's Life* by Kim D.R. Dearth

*Your Boxer's Life* by Kim D.R. Dearth

*Your Cat's Life* by Joanne Howl, D.V.M.

*Your Chihuahua's Life* by Kim Campbell Thornton

*Your Dog's Life* by Tracy Acosta, D.V.M.

*Your German Shepherd's Life* by Audrey Pavia

*Your Golden Retriever's Life* by Betsy Sikora Siino

*Your Lab's Life* by Virginia Parker Guidry

*Your Poodle's Life* by Virginia Parker Guidry

*Your Rottweiler's Life* by Kim D.R. Dearth

*Your Yorkshire Terrier's Life* by Elaine Gewirtz

**LIZ PALIKA**
Edited by reptile expert Dr. Richard C. Paull

# Your IGUANA'S *Life*

## Your Complete Guide to Caring for Your Pet at Every Stage of Life

**PRIMA PETS**

An Imprint of Prima Publishing
3000 Lava Ridge Court • Roseville, California 95661
(800) 632-8676 • www.primalifestyles.com

© 2000 by Prima Publishing

All rights reserved. No part of this book may be reproduced or transmitted in any form or by any means, electronic or mechanical, including photocopying, recording, or by any information storage or retrieval system, without written permission from Prima Publishing, except for the inclusion of brief quotations in a review.

**DISCLAIMER:** While the publisher and the author have designed this book to provide up-to-date information in regard to the subject matter covered, readers should be aware that medical information is constantly evolving. The information presented herein is of a general nature and is not intended as a substitute for professional medical advice. Readers should consult with a qualified veterinarian for specific instructions on the treatment and care of their pet. The author and Prima Publishing shall have neither liability nor responsibility to any person or entity with respect to any loss, damage, or injury caused or alleged to be caused directly or indirectly by the information contained in this book.

YOUR PET'S LIFE and PRIMA PETS are trademarks of Prima Communications, Inc. The Prima colophon is a trademark of Prima Communications, Inc., registered in the United States Patent and Trademark Office.

All products mentioned in this book are trademarks of their respective companies.

Interior photos© by Liz Palika and Isabelle Français
Color insert photos© by Isabelle Français

**Library of Congress Cataloging-in-Publication Data**
Palika, Liz
    Your iguana's life : your complete guide to caring for your pet at every stage of life / Liz Palika
      p.  cm.
    "Your pet's life series."
    ISBN 0-7615-2623-4
    1. Iguanas as pets.  I. Title.

SF459.I38 P36 2000
639.3'9542—dc21
                                                                           00-061144

00 01 02 03 DD 10 9 8 7 6 5 4 3 2 1
Printed in the United States of America

## How to Order

Single copies may be ordered from Prima Publishing, 3000 Lava Ridge Court, Roseville, CA 95661; telephone (800) 632-8676 ext. 4444. Quantity discounts are also available. On your letterhead, include information concerning the intended use of the books and the number of books you wish to purchase.

Visit us online at www.primalifestyles.com

# Contents

Introduction .................................................. vii

Chapter 1: So, You Want an Iguana ....................... 1

Chapter 2: Welcome Home! .............................. 27

Chapter 3: Mmmm, Good! It's Feeding Time ............. 49

Chapter 4: Medical Care for Your Iguana ................. 73

Chapter 5: Iguana Health Concerns ...................... 95

Chapter 6: Iguana Body Language and Behavior .......... 117

Chapter 7: Can You Train Your Iguana? ................. 135

Chapter 8: Routine Care ................................ 155

Chapter 9: Breeding Your Iguana ........................ 173

Chapter 10: An Iguana in the Family .................... 201

Chapter 11: When Your Iguana Grows Old ............... 225

Chapter 12: The Future of Iguanas and Other Reptiles .... 243

Appendix A: Resources. . . . . . . . . . . . . . . . . . . . . . . . . . . . . . . . . . . . . . . . . 261
Appendix B: Glossary. . . . . . . . . . . . . . . . . . . . . . . . . . . . . . . . . . . . . . . . . 265
Appendix C: The Iguana Family Tree . . . . . . . . . . . . . . . . . . . . . . . . . . . . . . 269
Index. . . . . . . . . . . . . . . . . . . . . . . . . . . . . . . . . . . . . . . . . . . . . . . . . . . . . 281

# Introduction

My husband and I have been rescuing turtles and tortoises for almost 20 years. We take in abandoned, unwanted, neglected, or abused animals, evaluate their health, nurse them back to health when need be, and then find new homes for them. Over the years we have placed hundreds of turtles and tortoises in new homes. And many that we feel have been through enough already will live out the rest of their lives with us.

Every once in awhile we have been asked to take in other reptiles, too, and sometimes we do—especially if we have an empty cage or enclosure at the time—but our primary focus has been turtles and tortoises.

About eight years ago, however, something changed. About mid-afternoon one Friday I received a telephone call from a friend who managed a pet store. The store had just been sold and the new owners were making some changes. One of those changes was to get rid of Conan, the store's longtime mascot.

Conan was a then six-year-old Green Iguana. He had been to hell and back with that store, having been stolen from the store during a burglary, mistreated by the thieves, and brought back to the store by the police injured and sick. Now he was facing the loss of the only home he'd known. The manager knew my husband and I had soft hearts and called us, hoping we would take in her store's pet. After hearing Conan's story, of course we said yes.

So the next afternoon we drove to her store to meet the fabled Conan. He was perched on his extra-large cat tree (complete with carpet). A large male (especially for his relatively young age) with a big dewlap, he was obviously comfortable with the movement of customers around him. My husband rubbed the iguana's forehead and the lizard relaxed, closing his eyes. He was very calm and quite tame.

Other than his healing tail (he had lost the tip of it), Conan didn't show any scars from his bad time with the burglars—my friend said he had recovered from that trauma well. But she said he was still very jumpy when he heard glass breaking; the burglars had come in through the front plate glass window. Recently someone had dropped something made of glass in the store and when it shattered on the floor, Conan jumped off his cat tree and hid under a display shelf. So he did remember his adventure.

Over the last eight years, Conan has become a part of our family, and even though my husband has occasionally threatened to turn him into a pair of boots (especially when Conan acts up during breeding season), this lizard has a home with us for the rest of his life. He's quite a character and we enjoy his company.

## Conan in the Public Eye

Conan has introduced many other people to the idea of iguana ownership—the good and the bad. Now 14 years old, six feet long, and weighing over 20 pounds, Conan is a large lizard. Many people who buy tiny baby Green Iguanas in the pet store have no idea how big iguanas can get, and when they see Conan it can be quite a shock!

We use many of our rescued pets to give educational talks to adults and children, primarily talking about reptiles as pets. We emphasize the special care reptiles need, how long they live, and how much is involved in keeping a reptile. Our goal is to help people make an informed decision when getting a reptile. I would love it if our rescue work slowed down considerably!

Conan became a part of our program right away. He was comfortable being around a lot of people and seemed to enjoy the attention. We made him a portable stand with a six-foot-long log mounted on a high table, so that he perched above people's heads. As arboreal lizards, iguanas feel safe when they're up high. During our talks, Conan is usually quite still on his log and most people think he's a prop. However, when he blinks an eye or turns his head, I will see people's eyes get wide, they nudge one another, and then someone will ask, "Is that real?" When I say yes and scratch Conan's head, mouths get wide, chins drop, and people make comments about dinosaurs.

## What It Means to Own an Iguana

Buying or adopting an iguana should not be an impulsive decision. These lizards grow quite large (although not all will reach Conan's size) and live for 15 to 20 years. Having a large lizard as a pet will require some effort on your part, including making some changes around your house. A large iguana needs some space of his own, heat, lighting, a place to relieve himself, and a water bowl big enough to splash in. You will need to spend time with him, feed him and clean up after him. You will also have to make arrangements for his care when you travel or go on vacation.

We have taken in many iguanas since Conan's adoption, although all were temporary residents. Conan made it quite plain that his is a one-iguana home; he will readily attack any other iguana. Rescued iguanas must therefore be housed away from Conan and adopted out to new homes as soon as possible.

> Buying or adopting an iguana should not be an impulsive decision. These lizards grow quite large and live for 15 to 20 years.

Keeping an iguana, and getting to know an iguana, is much different than owning a dog or a cat. Dogs and cats have been domesticated for thousands of years and our relationship with them is long-term and ongoing. Iguanas are not domesticated, and I get the feeling sometimes that I am merely being tolerated, perhaps only because I am the bearer of good food. When I rub Conan's forehead and look into one of his eyes, I see intelligence and awareness there. Sure, his intelligence isn't in physics or calculus, but there is intelligence and awareness of himself and his surroundings. Living with an iguana can certainly be a walk on the wild side!

## In This Book

In this book I hope to give you all the information you need to choose the right iguana for you—if, of course, an iguana is the right pet for you. I will also show you how to care for your iguana so that he can live a long, healthy, happy life with you.

Be aware, however, that in the field of reptile care nothing is set in concrete. Ask a dozen reptile owners, experts, breeders, or keepers any question about care and you will get at least a half a dozen different answers. What we know about reptiles is changing quickly, especially as more and more reptiles are being kept, bred, and raised in captivity.

In this book I have tried to give you information that is known and accepted as true by more than one reputable source, plus the knowledge my husband and I have learned firsthand with our own pets and through our rescue work. If there seems to be some disagreement, I will share both sides with you and you can make the decision yourself. After all, you are ultimately responsible for your pet's well-being.

# Chapter 1

# So, You Want an Iguana

### In This Chapter
- What Kind of a Pet Is an Iguana?
- Will an Iguana Fit Into Your Life?
- Finding the Right Iguana for You

Did you see the movies *Jurassic Park, The Lost World* and *Godzilla?* Are you fascinated by dinosaur fossils? Does the idea of those monstrous creatures roaming our planet send chills down your spine? When you look at an iguana, that reptilian head with spines down the dorsal ridge, the heavy dewlap, and the large scales on the cheeks—do you see a dinosaur? Most of us probably envision all dinosaurs as meat-eating carnivores, and our herbivorous iguana doesn't fit that description. Still, many reptile owners have reptiles because they are about as close to dinosaurs as they can expect to get.

Iguanas are not dinosaurs, of course, and in fact, some experts now think that today's birds are more closely related to dinosaurs than living lizards are. How disappointing! But even if they aren't related to dinosaurs, iguanas are very much a part of the natural world, a bit of wildness and wildlife that we can share our lives with. The dog slumbering at your feet and the cat purring on your lap might be wonderful pets, but that iguana on the log perch is nowhere near as domesticated.

## What Is an Iguana?

Simply put, we can say that an iguana is a large lizard from Mexico, and Central and South America. Scientifically, an iguana is in the genus *Iguana* and species *iguana*. Green Iguanas, which are the ones we keep as pets, are *Iguana iguana*. That certainly makes it easy to remember, doesn't it?

> Unlike many other reptiles (especially most other lizards), the iguana is an herbivore, which means it eats plant matter.

Physically, the Green Iguana looks like what it is: a lizard. It has a long body, slightly rounded (rather than flattened), with a very long tail, and feet and legs adapted to climbing bushes and trees. As with all reptiles, iguanas are cold-blooded (or ectothermic), which means they cannot create their own body heat and must rely on the environment to warm themselves.

Unlike many other reptiles (especially most other lizards), the iguana is an herbivore, which means it eats plant matter. The iguana's teeth and jaws are perfectly suited to this, with strong, wide jaws with many very small teeth.

## Reptile Eggs

Most amphibians return to the water to lay their soft eggs. But about 330 million years ago, something wonderful happened: an amphibian began laying hard-shelled eggs. The hard-shelled reptile egg, which contained yolk to nourish the growing embryo, could be buried in the dirt or hidden away from the water. This was a major step up the evolutionary ladder for land-based creatures.

## Where Did Iguanas Come From?

The Green Iguana *(Iguana iguana)* is found from central Mexico south (primarily in the coastal regions) to southern Brazil. Iguanas can be found in Columbia, Costa Rica, El Salvador, Guyana, Honduras, Peru, Suriname, Paraguay, and in the Lesser Antilles. They are found primarily at lower elevations, rarely more than about 2,500 feet above sea level.

Hurricanes and other storms have also carried iguanas to other locations. Florida has iguana populations that were first thought to be made up of discarded or escaped pets. However, after several hurricanes in the area, experts now believe that the populations are made up of both pets and storm survivors.

## What Does an Iguana Look Like?

An iguana has a characteristic lizard shape, with a body that is long in proportion to the length of his legs. A row of spines runs down the back from the head to the tail, with the longest spines

## Iguana Relatives

Green Iguanas do have some relatives from other areas. The most famous are probably the Galapagos Iguanas. There are two types, with one type of iguana living on land with the other being primarily aquatic. Neither of these species can legally be kept as pets. Other iguana relatives include the Rock Iguanas that are found in the Caribbean Islands. These prehistoric-looking iguanas are classified by CITES as "Endangered." Interstate and foreign sales are banned without federal permits from USFWS for both seller and buyer. Rhinoceros Iguanas, also from the Caribbean, have been bred in captivity recently and may be sold as pets.

The Fiji Islands are home to the beautiful Fiji Banded Iguana. These iguanas are endangered in their native habitat but are being bred successfully by some zoos. More than 50 genera and 700 species make up the iguana family, but none are as popular (or as readily available) as pets as the Green Iguana.

growing on the neck and shoulders. The spines are not sharp like a porcupine's quills, and can be bent or broken. These spines are made partially of keratin (the same substance that makes up your fingernails).

The legs and feet of an iguana are made for climbing. The legs are sturdy and muscular, and rather short for a lizard of this size. The feet have long toes tipped with tough, hard claws that can grasp the bark of a tree with ease.

The iguana's tail is usually twice the length of his body. It is thick and muscular where it attaches to the body, and narrows to a fine tip. The tail is a counterbalance when climbing or used for propulsion, but it is also a formidable weapon. When threatened, an iguana will turn sideways and lash out with his tail. It is strong enough to break the skin or leave a nasty welt. Even though the tail can be used as a weapon, it can still be damaged. If a predator grabs the tail, it will detach from the body, the blood vessels closing on their own. The tail will then continue to twitch so that the predator will pay attention to the tail instead of the escaping iguana. If the iguana is in good health, he may regrow a little of his tail—although it is usually never as good as the original tail.

The iguana's head is roughly triangular, like a wedge, with a slightly pointed but basically rounded nose. Males have a larger head than females. The eyes are gold, orange, brown, or gray and are set on the sides of the head, with small ridges above them. Like most diurnal lizards, iguanas see very well during the day but do not see well at night. Iguanas have heavy jowls, and as the male iguana matures, his jowls get larger. A single large scale is located below the ear on each jowl. This scale has several names: the tympanic plate, the subtympanic shield, or, more commonly, the helmet scale.

> When threatened, an iguana will turn sideways and lash out with his tail. It is strong enough to break the skin or leave a nasty welt.

Iguana's have what is called a "third eye." This parietal eye is on the top of the head and is covered with a round scale. This is not an eye like an eyeball, but it does sense light and shadow. Some experts believe the third eye helps the iguana gauge how much sunshine he's had and keeps him from overheating. It also seems to be able to help the iguana detect flying birds of prey, somehow sensing movement above him.

Under the iguana's head is a dewlap—a flap of skin. During hot weather, the iguana can extend the dewlap and the blood circulating through it will cool, enabling the iguana to cool off, too. The dewlap is also used to communicate dominance and sexual readiness; I'll discuss that in more detail in later chapters.

The iguana's skin is covered with scales just like a snake's, but the scales are rougher than most snakes. Each scale is a small

## Regional Variations

Although the Green Iguana (<u>Iguana iguana</u>) is one species, there are some regional variations in body characteristics, including color. Some of these include:

Suriname: Brighter green coloring, blue and turquoise colors, rounded nose, and shorter spines

Venezuela: Red, pink, and rose coloring on males during breeding season

Costa Rica and Central America: Gray, grayish brown, and grayish green body coloring

Mexico: Brown to gray body coloring on adults, orange on breeding males

Peru: Gray-green, accentuated male primary sexual characteristics.

---

piece of thickened skin. The color of the skin and scales varies, as does the size and thickness of the scales. Most hatchlings are bright green, but the colors and patterns will change as the hatchlings grow up and mature. Colors range from bright green through darker green, gray, gray-brown, orange, and blue-gray. Stripes and blotches are usually darker and can be dark green, brown, gray, or black. The tail usually has broad, dark, vertical stripes. The belly can have thin, fine, dark stripes and often the shoulders are striped. During breeding season, the males will show their breeding colors, usually on the legs and face; these can be bright orange, green, red, and brown.

## How Big Does It Grow?

There are a lot of variations in the length and stockiness of an adult iguana. Genetics plays a big part in ultimate size—how big were your pet's parents and grandparents? Nutrition is also important; a well-fed iguana will grow more rapidly than an undernourished one. Environment, too, is important. Is the iguana being kept under the right conditions—with correct heat, light, photoperiods, and in a cage that suits him?

The potential for most iguanas is four to five feet long, including the tail, but some have reached six feet in length. Some South American iguanas have even been known to grow to seven feet long. Just as not all people reach six feet or more in height, not all iguanas will reach six feet or more in length.

Males are generally larger than females, both in weight and in length.

## Iguana Personality

As with people and other pets, iguanas differ in personality and temperament. Some are calm and steady, others curious and active. Some are nervous, easily upset, and quick to whip that tail, while others have never been known to react with a tail whip. Some are very quick to react when young, but calm down significantly when they mature. Many older iguanas have been described as grouchy.

> As with people and other pets, iguanas differ in personality and temperament. Some are calm and steady, others curious and active.

Although each iguana has his own unique personality, there are some generalizations we can make. Captive-bred and farm-raised iguanas, on the whole, do seem to be more at ease with people and are calmer. Wild-caught iguanas are generally more reactive, nervous, and more apt to flee when frightened.

How the iguana has been handled sometimes affects the iguana's personality and temperament. An iguana handled calmly and gently will be more likely to respond that way. But not always. Some iguana owners have more than one iguana, handle each the same way, and one will be calm while the other is flighty.

Although iguanas are not usually described as affectionate (especially the way a dog can be), many do tolerate handling and even cuddling. Most recognize one person as "their person" and react to that person. Some iguanas will even solicit attention from their one person—usually ignoring other people.

Conan, for example, is very much my husband's iguana. He will let me rub his forehead, and, if my husband is out of town, I am allowed to feed him. However, I cannot do anything else. I am not allowed to trim his toenails, peel off shedding skin, wash dirty spots, or anything else. Meanwhile, Conan allows my husband to do anything that needs doing without any protests at all. Conan made his choice and my husband is his special person.

## How Long Do Iguanas Live?

According to Frank L. Slavens, curator of reptiles at the Woodland Park Zoological Gardens in Seattle, Washington, and author of *Reptiles and Amphibians in Captivity: Breeding and Longevity*, the record life span is 19 years, 10 months for a male iguana. However, James Hatfield reported in *Green Iguana: The Ultimate Owner's Manual* that Don Burnham of California had an iguana named "Iggy" who lived for 29 years!

Right now, most experts, if asked how long iguanas can live, would answer with a shrug, "We don't know." As we learn more about their nutritional and environmental needs, iguanas will live longer.

## The Iguana's Place in the Wild

Iguanas are arboreal lizards, meaning they live in trees. Iguana researchers have found iguanas in the wild living in a four-foot-tall shrub, high in the rainforest canopy, and in between. Iguanas are found primarily where they can eat the tree leaves and bask in the sun.

Iguanas are diurnal, which means they are active during the day. They become active when the sun is up and they have had a chance to bask in the sun to warm up. During the day, the iguana will eat, drink, relieve himself, and, if it's the appropriate time of the year, reproduce. By nightfall, the iguana has found a protected spot for the night and won't move again until the next morning.

In the wild, iguanas always run the risk of being killed by a predator. Any number of predators (including people) will catch and eat iguanas. In fact, many native people consider the iguana a staple of their diet. The iguana's green and gray coloring helps the lizard hide in the trees. Iguanas also use their climbing ability to remain in the treetops as much as possible. In fact, they drink rainwater or condensation off leaves instead of going down to the ground to drink. On the ground, iguanas are much more vulnerable to attack by predators.

However, if an iguana is on the ground, he will protect himself by standing tall, inflating himself to look bigger, whipping with his tail, and then running away. In the trees, to escape from danger, iguanas have been known to jump down long distances from limb to limb, tree to tree, tree to ground, or tree to water, where they can easily swim away.

Unfortunately, iguana populations have declined significantly in many areas, and not just because of predators. Habitat destruction and the lizard's value as both food and leather have reduced many iguana populations.

**Did You Know?**
There are approximately 6,300 known species of reptiles. In comparison there are 4,000 known species of mammals.

## Iguana Farming

Luckily, some iguana researchers have recognized the value of this lizard and iguana farms have been established. Although the idea of raising iguanas on a farm may sound distasteful to some pet owners—after all, we have been taught that puppy and kitten farms are horrible places to raise animals—iguana farming can be a very positive thing.

In Columbia, iguana farms have been promoted so that rural farmers can earn much-needed money without resorting to growing illegal drugs. In both Columbia and El Salvador, iguana farms provide employment, earning potential, and social opportunities for the farmers and their workers. By raising iguanas commercially for the pet trade, for meat, and for leather, wild populations are just a little bit safer, too.

In addition, because iguana populations are threatened in many areas, the iguana farms have an agreement to release a certain number of iguanas into the wild each year; usually five percent of their farm-raised hatchlings.

## The Iguana's Place in Captivity

Thousands of iguanas have been imported into the United States during the last two decades. James W. Hatfield III, author of *Green Iguana: The Ultimate Owner's Manual,* tabulated the import records available from the U.S. Fish and Wildlife Service from 1988 through 1995. During that eight-year period, more than 1,398,000 iguanas were imported from Columbia, more than 1,117,000 from El Salvador, more than 143,000 from Guatemala, and more than 143,000 from Suriname. When totals from Mexico, Peru, and other countries were also included, Hatfield found that over three million iguanas had been imported into the United States in eight years!

With those numbers, it might be assumed that we would be up to our elbows in iguanas. Unfortunately, most of those iguanas died. Experts believe that 90 percent of all iguanas imported died within their first year. Why? There are lots of reasons. Wild-caught adult iguanas often fail to adjust to captivity and die. Wild-caught iguanas are also usually loaded with internal and external parasites, and if not treated, the stress of those parasites added to the stress of captivity will rapidly kill them. Although farm-raised (that is, captive-bred) iguanas are usually well-adjusted to captivity and are healthier, sometimes the stress of shipping will kill those iguanas, as well.

The biggest killer of iguanas, though, are pet owners. New iguana owners often buy their pet before they know how to care for him; before they have a cage set up and before they know how to choose a healthy iguana. The result, unfortunately, is often death for the iguana.

> The biggest killer of iguanas, though, are pet owners.

However, times are changing. Fewer and fewer wild-caught iguanas are being imported, and the vast majority of imported pets are farm-raised. In addition, more people are successfully breeding and raising iguanas at home. Home-raised iguanas are much calmer around people, are relatively tame, and may not have to go through the stress of shipping. In addition, books like this one are providing iguana owners with good, solid information about how to keep an iguana healthy and happy for many years. The future is looking brighter for iguanas in captivity.

## What Kind of a Pet Is an Iguana?

Iguanas are not the same kind of pets as dogs and cats—in both good and bad ways. Your neighbors will never call and complain about your iguana barking all day, but you can never train an iguana the way you can a dog, either. Your iguana will not shed hair all over the house, but the iguana will not be as cuddly as a dog or a cat. The iguana, when given the chance, will climb all over the furniture, just like your cat does, but the iguana won't shred your furniture.

Having an iguana as a pet is different. This reptile can provide companionship, but it's a different kind of companionship than you would get from a dog or a cat or a horse. When an iguana is in the room with you, he knows where you are and what you're doing. He may not be in your lap, but he's very much aware of you. Because the iguana will rarely come begging for attention as a dog does, when you pet your iguana and he obviously enjoys it, you will feel special and privileged. You have an iguana and he likes you!

> People will look at you differently because you have an iguana, especially once your iguana gets big.

People will look at you differently because you have an iguana, especially once your iguana gets big. When people come to our house and see Conan, their eyes get wide and I see them looking at us differently. We are the same people they knew a few minutes ago, but somehow, in their minds, we have changed because now we are the people who have the big iguana.

An iguana will interact with you but on his own terms. An iguana will watch you and be aware of you and will provide companionship, but in his own way. Having an iguana as a pet may require you to make some changes in your home, some compromises, but the only compromise your iguana will make is that of being a pet.

If you also have furry pets—and many iguana owners do—you may have to change your expectations about pet ownership when you have an iguana.

## Will an Iguana Fit Into Your Life?

A dog or a cat will learn your rules, and, for the most part, adhere to them. An iguana, however, will teach you the rules, and—for the most part—you will be required to adhere to them!

Reptiles lack the enlarged cerebral hemispheres of the brain found in mammals. Because that portion of the brain controls reasoning and learning, most reptiles don't have the learning power that more warm-blooded creatures have. Now, that doesn't mean iguanas are dumb; far from it. Reptiles—including iguanas—are very smart when it comes to the things that are important to them, and when possible, are very quick to bring those needs to your attention. For example, a large iguana can make a big fuss if his water bowl is empty!

## Is an Iguana the Right Pet for You?

Many people like having reptiles as pets because they are different and unusual. If you treasure the odd, the uncommon, or the unusual, well then, an iguana might be for you. I have to admit, when we take Conan out for one of our educational talks on reptiles, he does attract a lot of attention!

If you are the snuggly, cuddly type, keep in mind that most iguanas will only tolerate so much handling and then will have had enough. Don't expect an iguana to relish the petting that a dog will thrive on. However, if you like to watch animals and would be content to watch your iguana as well as interact with him, then an iguana might very well be the right pet for you.

Before you decide that an iguana is the right pet for you, though, make sure you can supply an iguana with the things he will need.

- Cage: Iguanas need room to grow and to move around. A hatchling could live in a 40-gallon glass aquarium tank, but an adult will need much more room. A cage the size of a small bedroom is perfect, but not everyone can give an iguana that much space. At a minimum, the cage should be twice the iguana's total length, at least as wide as the iguana is long and from floor to ceiling in height.
- Environmental conditions: Iguanas need heat, light, access to the sun (or fluorescent lights), and a place to relieve themselves.
- Time: Iguanas are not nearly as demanding as dogs, but do require some of your time. You will need to spend time every day feeding and cleaning, plus a thorough cage cleaning once a week. In addition, your iguana will need daily handling to become (or remain) tame.
- Finances: Iguanas themselves are not expensive, but that large cage will probably set you back a pretty penny unless you have good carpentry skills. The other cage furnishings, including the heat and lighting, will also cost you some money. Daily expenses won't be much—herbivores are not expensive to feed—but if your iguana gets sick, veterinary bills can add up quickly. Make sure your budget can handle routine and emergency bills.

## What Does Your Family Think?

If you live alone, then obviously no one else needs to approve of your choice of a pet (except maybe your landlord). However, if you live with other people, their thoughts about iguanas must be taken into consideration. After all, the iguana will affect them even if he is your pet.

If someone in your family objects to the iguana, life could be difficult, especially if the iguana disrupts the family routine in any way. If the family member takes his (or her) anger out on your iguana (and some people do), that is unfair and potentially dangerous to your pet.

## Do You Have Allergies?

Many people who cannot live with furry animals can live with animals covered by scales. However, before you bring home an iguana, visit with a friend's iguana. Pet him, hold him, and enjoy his company for awhile. How are your allergies? Any reactions?

I am allergic to dogs and cats, but the iguana doesn't cause any allergic reactions for me at all.

If you have children in the family, can you protect the kids and the iguana from each other? The children could (intentionally or unintentionally) torment the iguana, especially if they want the iguana to play. In self-defense, an iguana could bite a child or whip the child with his tail—both of which could cause injury.

Before you bring an iguana home, make sure your significant other (and other family members) approve. It is far better to prepare your significant other for the realities of iguana ownership before you bring the pet home, rather than trying to sneak the lizard in, hoping he (or she) won't notice.

## Do You Have Other Pets?

Obviously, you can't ask your dog or cat what they think about the idea of an iguana roommate, but you should think about the realities of keeping a predator (dog or cat) and a prey animal (the iguana) in the same house. A dog or a cat could easily maim or kill a small iguana, and while a large iguana could probably defend himself against a well-fed house cat, a large dog could kill even a big iguana.

My husband and I have three dogs, three cats, and Conan, as well as quite a few other reptiles. Conan's cage is a small bedroom with a heavy-gauge screen door instead of the regular bedroom door. The cats and dogs cannot get in, and even if one should sit outside the door looking in, Conan knows he's safe and isn't stressed by their presence. When we bring Conan out, the dogs are in a down stay (they are *very* well trained) or the dogs are outside, and the cats are in another room. This works for us, but you will have to look at your own household and decide how you can protect your pets from one another so that all can be safe and secure.

## What Makes an Iguana Happy?

It really doesn't take a lot to make an iguana happy.

- Cage: A large, roomy cage outfitted properly for an arboreal lizard is a necessity. This is your iguana's home, refuge, and place of security.
- Territory: Although some people own more than one iguana, sometimes several iguanas, most prefer to live solitary lives.
- Good food: A good, nutritious diet is necessary for his good health.
- Security: Part of your iguana's security is his cage, but you must also consider the rest of the home. He should feel protected from other pets, rowdy kids, and a blasting stereo or television.
- Sunshine and fresh breezes: Your iguana should have access to an outside cage or a protected windowsill where he can bask in the sun and enjoy the breeze.

## What Makes an Iguana Unhappy?

Unfortunately, some things do make iguanas upset or insecure. When an animal (human or iguana) is under stress, the immune system reacts and the animal is more prone to catching a disease or suffering from stress-related illnesses. Stress alone can cause a reptile to stop eating, and eventually he will die. What stresses an iguana?

- The wrong cage: A hatchling can live in a small glass tank, but a larger iguana needs more than that. A cage that is too small or too confining will stress the iguana.
- The wrong environment: Iguanas are tropical lizards and need warmth. If the environment is too cool, food won't digest properly and the iguana will stop moving.
- Too much activity: To a prey animal like the iguana, activity is always a potential threat. Although most iguanas can tolerate normal household movements, some cannot and need a quieter environment. Too much activity is stressful.
- Mirrors or reflective glass: Male iguanas in particular react angrily to mirrors or reflective glass, especially during breeding season. Most iguanas do best in a one-iguana home and the reflection is, to your iguana, a trespassing iguana. Males will posture to that reflection, and because the reflection is posturing back, will continue to do so until they are exhausted. After all, the reflection is not giving up! Make sure the cage is not reflected in a mirror or a window.
- Teasing: Protect your iguana from teasing. Kids, pets, and even other adults can be cruel in the name of having fun.

## Maybe an Iguana Isn't the Right Pet for Me

Iguanas are not the right pet for everyone. My sister kept one for awhile and

**Did You Know?**
Not many American presidents owned reptiles while in office. Theodore Roosevelt, however, was an animal lover and had a lizard named Josiah (of unknown species).

## A Place in Heaven

On the way home from picking up Conan (five feet long!) at the pet store where he had been the mascot for several years, my husband and I stopped by my parents' home to show them our "dinosaur." My mom had a fairly typical reaction, "Oh my gosh! What are you going to do with that?" My dad, however, looked at my husband and said, "Paul, you have a place reserved for you in heaven. What other man would put up with a woman who brought home THAT!"

decided this wasn't the right pet for her. We found him a new home and now she has a terrarium with several White's Treefrogs. They are easier to care for and are better pets for her. However, once you have an iguana, it isn't always easy to find him a new home. Therefore, I would much rather you thought through iguana ownership first, before you bring home an iguana.

If you decide an iguana isn't the right pet for you but would still like to have a reptile, what should you do? Well, the Internet is a great source of information; talk to people who own other types of pets. Stop by the local pet store that carries reptiles and talk to them. Don't buy the first thing you see, however. Make this decision rationally and do your research first. Look at Appendix A in this book, which lists Resources, and read some of the books and magazines listed. There is a lot of information available to you.

## Finding the Right Iguana for You

After reading all this information about iguanas, what do you think? Are you intrigued? Does this sound like a pet you could care for? Remember, this is at least a 15-year commitment.

## Green Iguanas Grow Very Quickly

A Green Iguana weighs, on the average, about half an ounce when hatched. By three years of age, that hatchling can grow to three pounds in weight and three feet in length, including the tail!

Before you go shopping for an iguana, try to meet several different iguanas—pets belonging to other people. See if you can notice their unique personalities, their physical differences, and how they relate to their owners. Ask these iguana owners what they do with their pets and how they interact with them. Make sure you will be very comfortable with this type of pet before you add one to your family.

## Young, Old, Male, Female?

So let's get down to the nitty-gritty. You've decided that an iguana is the right pet for you. What now? Would you prefer to raise a baby iguana? They are cute! If you get a baby iguana, you can raise him the way you want, teaching him as much as you want (or as much as he is willing to learn), and the baby will grow up knowing you and trusting you. That is certainly a big plus.

Unfortunately, the mortality rate for baby iguanas in captivity is quite high. If you choose a healthy, young iguana and care for him properly, your success rate should be much higher. My husband and I have raised three baby iguanas, carefully choosing very healthy ones, and all three thrived and grew up to be healthy adults. The information in this book will certainly help you, but you need to know there is a risk in getting a baby.

If you decide to adopt an adult iguana, you will at least be past the fragile infant stage. However, there are problems here, too. When you get an adult iguana, you are facing the same problems you might have when you buy a used car. He could be a gem or he could be a lemon! But you can stack the odds in your favor by asking some questions. How was the iguana treated and cared for before you got him? Was he treated well and nurtured, or was he ignored? You might end up with someone's treasured pet who simply cannot keep him anymore, or you might have an angry, neglected, malnourished, unhealthy iguana. If you decide to choose an adult, choose carefully and get to know the iguana (and his owners) if you can, before you decide to bring him home.

The sex of your future pet should be decided before you get one, too. Male iguanas are generally bigger than females, usually quite significantly so. Males are also brighter in color, especially during breeding season. Males can also be significantly more aggressive, again, especially during breeding season. However, many veterinarians are willing and able to neuter male iguanas, and this can reduce aggressive behavior. Making a generalization (and there are always exceptions), females are usually calmer, less aggressive, smaller, and less colorful.

## Pet Stores

So you've decided that an iguana will be the right pet for you. Now, how do you find one? The most obvious place is a pet store. Pet stores that carry reptiles (not all do) usually have baby Green Iguanas. However, every pet store is not equal as far as the personnel's knowledge about to how to care for these babies. Very young Green Iguanas that have just been shipped in from Cen-

## Selecting an Iguana

Your entire future relationship with your pet iguana depends upon choosing the right one. Here are some tips:

- Avoid adult wild-caught iguanas; find a captive-bred iguana instead. Wild-caught iguanas are rarely as healthy as captive-bred animals, and often have trouble adapting to captive life. Especially avoid wild-caught adult iguanas.

- Avoid the frantic iguana, the one dashing here and there, beating himself against the glass. Don't assume you can tame him; this one will always be wild. Choose instead the iguana who is relatively calm.

- Choose the healthy-appearing iguana, with bright eyes, green skin, and an alert appearance. The healthy iguana will have a rounded belly, padded thighs, and a plump tail. Avoid the iguana who is thin, listless, and lethargic.

- Don't choose the iguana with lumps and bumps on the body or under the jaw, or the one with swollen toes, limbs, lower jaws, or thighs.

- Look at the vent area. Don't choose the iguana who appears to have diarrhea or feces caked around the vent.

tral or South America (or from the pet store's distribution center) will need careful handling. They need water, good food, and warm temperatures. If that care is not provided, these babies will die.

Ask where the iguanas in the store came from. Are they from local breeders? More and more people are breeding iguanas now and these babies are occasionally showing up in pet stores. Or are the iguanas being shipped in from farms in Central America?

Take a look around the pet store before you decide to buy an iguana. The animal cages should be clean, with feces picked up and with clean food and water bowls. If the cages are filthy, don't buy the lizard out of sympathy—go somewhere else—because unfortunately, the babies will probably die.

The food provided for the baby iguanas should be appropriate—a commercial juvenile iguana food soaked in water served alongside finely chopped vegetables. If iceberg lettuce has been given to the lizards, go elsewhere—iceberg lettuce has fiber, moisture, and very little else, and chances are, those lizards are malnourished.

If the cages are clean, the food provided for the iguanas looks fresh and good, and the baby iguanas look healthy, ask to see one or two. A healthy baby iguana will be bright green and will appear active and alert. The eyes should be clear and there should be no discharge from the nose. Make sure the baby looks unhurt, with an intact tail, no broken toes or toenails, and no obvious wounds. It will be normal for the baby iguana to try and escape from your hands when you first hold him, but then he should calm down. Don't buy an iguana who continues to struggle and doesn't accept handling.

> A healthy baby iguana will be bright green and will appear active and alert.

## Reptile Dealers

Reptile dealers can be wonderful to do business with or can be absolutely horrible. Many times their prices are lower than a pet store's because there are fewer middlemen. And some reptile dealers really love their animals and think of them all as their babies. However, some are not in the business because they love animals, and they treat their animals as a commodity. Yes, this is a business, and the goal of business is to be successful, but anyone in the animal business must care about the animals they are responsible for. Therefore, before you decide to do business with a particular reptile dealer, ask around and get some referrals. How

## A Healthy Iguana

A healthy iguana will have:
- A bright, alert attitude
- Alert, clear eyes with no discharge
- A dry nose with no discharge
- A clean vent (anal area)
- A plump tail and thighs
- A rounded belly with no lumps
- A firm jaw that closes completely, with no swelling, abrasions, or drooling
- A complete tail and 20 claws.

has this person dealt with his customers? Does he follow through with promises? Does he deliver what he says he will? Are his animals healthy and well cared for? Don't be afraid to ask questions, either.

## Iguana Rescue Groups

There are people all over the country who are trying to save iguanas who were unwanted in their previous homes. Very often people get a baby iguana and don't realize how big he can get, and when he does grow up, they are unprepared to care for him. Sometimes the iguana was an impulse decision, not well thought out, and again, the people are not prepared to care for the iguana. For whatever reason, in every community, there are usually iguanas who need help.

As I said in the introduction to this book, my husband and I have been doing reptile rescue work for over 20 years, beginning with turtles and tortoises and eventually taking in other reptiles, too, including iguanas. You can find an iguana rescue group in your area by calling the local animal shelter. You can then see what they have and what condition the iguanas are in. Very often the iguanas need help, perhaps because they were malnourished or have broken toes or a missing tail. There is no reason not to get an iguana who needs some help, as long as you are fully aware of the problem and are sure you can deal with it.

If you decide to adopt an iguana from a rescue group, be prepared to be asked a lot of questions. They are going to want to make sure that iguana doesn't end up in another bad home. You will be asked about your iguana knowledge, your ability to care for the lizard, and whether you already have a cage and supplies. Don't take offense at the questions; it's all to protect the iguana.

Rescue groups usually survive on donations, so be prepared to offer a donation for their work.

## Humane Societies and Shelters

A few years ago you would have never seen an iguana at a local humane society, animal control facility, or shelter. The popularity of iguanas, however, has changed that. Although many shelters refer iguana owners to the local iguana rescue group, some shelters are prepared to take in one or two iguanas. There is no problem with adopting an iguana from a shelter, as long as you're careful. Just as with a pet store, the cage should be clean and the food appropriate and fresh. Just as with a rescue group, you may be getting an iguana with problems, so ask a lot of questions and make sure you can handle the problems the iguana may have.

# The Right Iguana for You

Don't be in a hurry to buy or adopt an iguana. Don't take the first one you see. This is a big decision—a 15- to 20-year commitment. Take your time, look at a variety of iguanas, talk to people, and then make a well-thought-out, informed decision. You won't regret it!

# 2

# Welcome Home!

### In This Chapter
- Preparing for Your Iguana's Arrival
- What Supplies Will Your Iguana Need?
- Making Your Iguana Feel Welcome and Secure

Adding a new pet to the household can be an exciting time. After all, you have high hopes that this new pet will become a good friend and companion. However, the first few days after you bring your pet home can be nerve-wracking, confusing, and downright scary if you aren't prepared.

This chapter will make sure you are as ready as you can be. You will need to set up or build a cage, furnish it, and make sure your iguana has the right kind of light and heat. I will also talk about how to bring your iguana home, what to do (and not do) those first few days, and how you can make your iguana feel welcome. A little preparation now will ensure that you're ready to bring home your special new pet.

# Preparing for Your Iguana's Arrival

When you bring home your iguana, you cannot put him in the backyard or on the living room floor until you have a cage ready. That would be a disaster waiting to happen. You must have a place ready and waiting for your new pet. The cage must be furnished with all the things your iguana needs, including basking logs, food and water dishes, light, and heat. This all takes time (and money), so it must be done before you bring home your new iguana.

## The Cage

Think of the cage as your iguana's home. Sure, he is living in your home, too, but the cage is where he will spend most of his time. That means the cage should be roomy and set up for iguana comfort, and should make your iguana feel secure and relaxed.

The first thing to think about is its size. The ideal cage is actually a spare bedroom—preferably with a doggy door to an outside cage where the iguana can bask in the sun. However, very few pet owners can afford to give their iguana a room of his own. So what is the next best solution?

A reasonable cage should be twice as long as the iguana, at least as wide as the iguana is long, and should go from floor to ceiling. That means your four-foot-long iguana needs a cage that is eight feet long, four feet wide, and as tall as the room where he is housed.

If a cage this large seems excessive, keep in mind that iguanas in the wild live in forests, high up in the tree canopies. They have room to establish territories, forage for food, and hide from predators. In a small cage, iguanas feel vulnerable and exposed, and stress levels build to un-

## It's All an Illusion

We found that Conan would protest, thrash his cage, and try to escape if confined to a cage smaller than he wanted. However, when given free run of a small bedroom (8′ × 10′) with a doggy door through the window to his outside cage, he would relax. He rarely ever moves around the room, in fact. It seems to be the illusion of freedom that's important to him.

acceptable levels. An iguana forced to live in too small a cage will begin fighting the cage, beating up against the walls, and trying to escape. Eventually, he will hurt himself, or even worse, will give up, succumb to the stress, and die.

A hatchling iguana can be kept in a 40-gallon or larger aquarium tank for the first year or so, but not much longer than that. Not only will the hatchling rapidly become too big for the tank, but iguanas rarely seem to figure out see-through glass or acrylic. Many will continue to beat up against the sides of the tank, bruising their nose, often to the point where it is permanently damaged.

If your baby iguana does this, you should change his cage. A large plastic storage container, one that is opaque plastic, a minimum of three feet long by 18 inches wide and 18 inches tall will suffice for a baby iguana. Although this seems confining (and it is), it is better for the baby who can't figure out see-through glass.

As soon as the iguana is big enough, he should be transferred to a wire cage. The wire material that makes up the sides can be metal bars (as in a bird cage) or hardware cloth (half-inch squares). If at all possible, the wire should be coated with vinyl; this is easier on the iguana's nose and feet and is easier to keep clean. These open cages also provide better air ventilation than do solid-sided tanks.

## Do It Yourself

If you have good carpentry skills, you can build your own iguana cage. You can use two-by-fours or two-by-threes for the support, vinyl-coated hardware cloth for the sides, and plywood for the solid sides and bottom. Some people have used rounded half logs instead of two-by-fours so that the cage is a little more attractive.

Build the door(s) to the cage larger than you think you'll need. Make sure you will be able to remove the cage furnishings through the door easily for cleaning. Make sure, too, that you can climb in or step into the cage for cleaning or to remove the iguana.

The design of the cage is up to you. Just make sure it is secure, safe, and easy to clean. In addition, make sure any finishes or paints are non-toxic, and don't put your iguana into the cage until all fumes from building materials have thoroughly dissipated.

One wall of the cage (usually the back wall) should be solid. This provides security for the iguana, and, in addition, can cut down drafts or breezes. The top of the cage should be wire bars or hardware cloth that is not vinyl coated because this is where your heating elements and lights will be. The bottom can be set up like the bottom of a bird cage, with a tray that pulls out. This can make cleaning the cage much easier. In addition, one wall (front or side) should have a very large door—big enough for you to step or reach in to pick up your pet. If the entire side or front can be a door, that's even better.

There are some companies that make cages specifically for iguanas. ZooMed, in San Luis Obispo, California, makes iguana cages of several different sizes with PVC-coated wire sides, pull-out bottom trays, and wheels so that the cage can be more easily moved. Other companies also make iguana cages. Please don't try to use a big bird cage for an iguana. It won't work; bird cages are not made for iguanas and your iguana will either hurt himself or escape from the cage—or both.

## Where Will You Put the Cage?

The location of the cage is just about as important as the cage itself. You should have easy access to it, since you will be going to the cage several times each day to feed, water, and clean, as well as to just say hi to your pet. There should be family activity around the cage, but not too much. Put the cage in the family room if the iguana won't be bombarded by loud stereo music and surround-sound television. If the family room is routinely loud and boisterous, put the cage in a room that is visited by family members often but isn't quite as loud.

Do not put the cage where it will be in full sun without shade. Although your iguana will enjoy some sun, he must have a way to get out of the sun if he overheats. A hatchling iguana in a glass tank shouldn't be in the sun or even outside at all—those glass tanks heat up very quickly.

Try not to isolate the cage too much. If the iguana is out of the way, it will be too easy to forget about him. He won't get as much attention and people could easily forget to pet him, feed him, give him fresh water, or clean his cage.

Sometimes iguana owners tell me the cage is in an out-of-the-way place because it doesn't fit in with the décor of the house. I always answer the same way: "If the décor is more important than the well-being of your pet, then don't get an iguana—or any pet." When

> **Did You Know?**
> Be patient while your lizard gets to know you, but at the same time don't allow him to bite you or thrash you with his tail.

you take on the responsibility of a pet, you assume the responsibility of doing the best you can for that pet. With an iguana, much of his well-being is centered around his cage.

## Furnishing the Cage

Your iguana doesn't need much in the way of cage furnishings. In fact, the simpler his cage is, the easier it is to keep clean. He should have a couple of logs to bask on, and these should be wider than his body so that he can relax on them without having to hold on. A real log, complete with bark, is fine as long as you can keep it clean. Some iguana owners use plastic pipe (six or eight inches in diameter) covered with indoor-outdoor carpet. Some cages come with flat shelves and these are fine, too, except that iguanas (when given a choice) do seem to prefer rounded logs.

One of the perches should be located under a basking light. (I'll talk about those later in this chapter.) The other log can be placed elsewhere in the cage. This way the iguana can take his choice of a log under the heat or one away from the heat. As a cold-blooded creature, this gives him a means of regulating his temperature.

If your cage is floor to ceiling (the preferred height), you can also place a taller log on a diagonal, running from the floor to the uppermost perch. Your iguana can climb the bars or screen sides of his cage, but a log will give him an additional means of going up.

If the floor of the cage has a pull-out tray, you can put newspaper on the bottom of the tray. This is cheap and is easy to pick up and throw away. Newspaper will also work if you don't have a pull-out tray, but just a regular cage floor. Just make sure you can get to the bottom of the cage easily, especially

## Caution: Harsh Substrates

Be careful about using sand, pea gravel, large pieces (other than shredded) of bark or other harsh substrates. Iguanas aren't always careful about what they eat, and should your iguana ingest pieces of these substrates, they could cause significant intestinal damage.

if you're designing and building your own cage, so you can replace the newspaper every day. If you don't want to use newspaper (some people are concerned about the long-term effects of newsprint ink on their pets), you can use layers of paper towels. This is a little more expensive but is just as easy to clean.

Some people prefer a cage substrate that is a little nicer to look at, and alfalfa pellets or shredded bark make an attractive covering for the cage floor. Alfalfa pellets (rabbit food) have the advantage of also providing good nutrition. When used in a baby iguana's cage, if the baby eats some with his food, it's good for him. Alfalfa pellets should be replaced as soon as they get damp, however, because wet pellets will develop mold very quickly. Shredded bark is very attractive and smells good, too, but is a little more difficult to clean. You may find that you want to try some different substrates and see what works best for you, for your iguana, and in the cage.

## The Toilet Area

Iguanas are one of the few reptiles that actually housetrain themselves. Most will choose one spot where they prefer to eliminate, and once chosen, will rarely eliminate anywhere else.

Unfortunately, many iguanas prefer to relieve themselves in water. Our big guy, Conan, is one of these lizards. So to accommodate him, we have a mortar mixing pan—a big, flat, shallow plastic tub—on the floor of his outside cage. He can get to the outside cage through the doggy door in the window of his room. (So he's spoiled!) This way it's easy to take the tub out and clean it.

You can use something similar by putting a shallow plastic container—like a sweater box—on the floor of your iguana's cage. Make sure the container is big enough so that your iguana can get into it and position himself so that he can relieve himself in the box. Put a couple of inches of water in the box. When your iguana relieves himself, take the container out, flush the water down the toilet, and then take it outside to clean it. (Do NOT clean it in the kitchen sink!)

Not all iguanas require a water toilet, however. Some iguanas will relive themselves in a box with kitty litter (Use clay litter; not clumping. Clumping litter is too easily swallowed.), wood shavings, or shredded bark. Just put a shallow container of the material on the floor of the cage and clean it whenever it gets soiled.

## What Supplies Will Your Iguana Need?

Unlike some reptiles that need elaborate environments, iguanas have relatively simple needs. The cage is the most important, of course, but heat and light are vital to your iguana's good health, too.

### Heat

As I've already mentioned, reptiles are ectothermic or cold-blooded. This means they cannot produce their own body heat and must rely on heat sources in the environment. Certain body processes work better at certain temperatures. Enzymes, for example, require heat to perform their chemical conversions. Because reptiles cannot produce the heat needed for these and other body processes, outside sources of heat are needed.

The need to maintain body heat is one of the most important factors in any reptile's life. A rock in the sunshine, an asphalt street, or a dark-color log will all absorb heat, and reptiles can often be seen taking advantage of this.

If a reptile is unable to find or maintain enough body heat, bodily processes will slow down. Instead of digesting, food in the digestive tract can rot, poisoning the reptile. In addition, other functions will slow down. Activity levels will drop off and stop, breeding behaviors will cease, and the reptile will become almost motionless. Some species will hibernate when they're too cool, but iguanas do not hibernate. Sustained cool temperatures will kill an iguana.

One portion of your iguana's cage right above one basking log should reach at least 88° to 90°F; 94° to 96°F is even better. Other portions of the cage must be lower temperatures, with one end of one log even going as low as room temperature. This range of temperatures (called a heat or thermal gradient) allows the iguana to choose the temperature he needs at any particular time. By moving back and forth between the different temperature ranges in the cage, the iguana can warm up or cool off as he needs to.

Overheating will occur if the iguana cannot get away from the heat. If the entire cage is heated (rather than one end

> **Did You Know?**
> It's very easy for a young lizard to be squished and injured (even killed) and it's just as easy for a lizard to escape from a child. Supervise children the first few times they try to handle your new pet.

or one spot), the iguana may shows signs of anxiousness, pacing, and fighting the cage walls. He may begin panting, breathing through the mouth, until he overheats and stops moving. Death can follow very quickly. Therefore, although heat is necessary, so are cooler spots in the cage so that the iguana can regulate his temperature as he needs to.

Use one or two thermometers to verify these temperatures. Don't guess at them! Temperature is too important to be casual about.

A variety of heating devices are available.

- Incandescent lightbulbs: These are the most popular and most inexpensive way of providing both light and heat. A white incandescent bulb is fine for daytime use, as long as it is turned off at night. Never leave a white bulb on for 24 hours a day. Your iguana does need nighttime darkness. At night you can use a red or black bulb.
- The wattage of the bulb depends upon how much heat you need to provide and how far away from the basking log the fixture is. When setting up the cage (before your iguana is in it), place a thermometer on the basking log and turn on the light. In a few minutes, check the temperature. If it's too cool, you need a higher watt bulb or a different heat source.
- Because incandescent lightbulbs get hot, always set up the bulb outside of your iguana's cage. Make sure he cannot touch the bulb or the fixture, or he could be burned. For safety's sake, make sure, too, that nothing else can touch the bulb.
- Ceramic heat emitters: These heating devices screw into a lightbulb socket and produce heat without producing any light. Therefore they can be used 24 hours a day. Heat emitters usually last much longer than lightbulbs, so although

## Be Careful!

Do not use an inexpensive lamp for your iguana's cage. Use ceramic lightbulb sockets (instead of plastic ones) for both lightbulbs and heat emitters. Most plastic lightbulb sockets are not made for continuous use and will overheat, possibly melt, and could even start a fire. Ceramic lightbulb sockets are a bit more expensive, but are much safer in the long run.

   they are more expensive to buy, they are usually a better bargain in the long run.
- Just as lightbulbs come in different powers (watts), so do heat emitters. Again, you will have to use a thermometer on the basking log to decide how much power you need to produce the temperature your iguana needs.
- Heat emitters can burn your iguana if he touches them, so they, too, should be set up outside of your iguana's cage. When lightbulbs burn out, it's very obvious because they no longer produce light. However, heat emitters don't show that they are no longer working, so it's important you check the temperature in your iguana's cage often. Your heat emitter could stop working, and unless you check it, your iguana could easily get chilled.
- Hot rocks: These are simulated stones or bricks with heating elements inside. They are made to be buried in cage substrate so that the reptile can lie on the substrate to warm up. This is called belly heat. These are very good for some reptiles, but should not be used with iguanas. Iguanas in the wild bask in the sunshine to warm up, and do not use belly heat. Iguanas have softer belly scales than many other reptiles and have been known to burn themselves (sometimes severely) on hot rocks.

- Undercage heaters: These heaters are installed under the floor of a glass or plastic tank so they heat up the substrate, again, providing belly heat. These heaters can be used for hatchlings less than a year old that are still being kept in a tank. Make sure the heat is only being provided at one end of the tank and the other end is cooler. However, these are not the best choice for adults.
- Make sure you monitor the temperature in the iguana cage at least once a day—and preferably more—even after the cage has been set up awhile. Have more than one thermometer in the cage and watch both the hot and cool temperatures. The warm spot should heat up to at least 90°F, with 94° preferable. The cooler end of the cage can go down to 72°F or so, but not much lower than that.
- Thermometers that register 24-hour low and high temperatures are invaluable. You will be able to see exactly how cool the cage gets at night and how warm it gets during the day. Knowing this, you can then make any necessary changes to your iguana's habitat.

## Light

Are you slower to get moving in the morning when it's gray and cloudy out? Do you seem to have a little more spring in your step on a bright, sunny morning? If either (or both) of these situations apply to you, you are reacting to light. Iguanas do too. Light affects every part of an iguana's life, including appetite, digestion, sleeping, activity levels, and reproduction.

Natural sunlight produces heat, just as incandescent lightbulbs do, but it also produces ultraviolet rays. If you stay outside too long without any sunscreen, you will get burned by the ultraviolet rays of the sun. However, these ultraviolet rays are not all bad. UVA rays are needed by plants to grow and flourish. Grow lights that are sold for use in greenhouses (or for houseplants) produce UVA rays.

UVA is also beneficial to reptiles by increasing the appetite and stimulating activity. In addition, UVA rays seem to be necessary for psychological well-being, although it isn't understood why.

Iguanas also use (and need) the other type of ultraviolet rays—UVB rays—so that they can synthesize vitamin $D_3$. Iguanas and most other reptiles cannot store $D_3$ in their bodies, and must have exposure to UVB rays to metabolize it. Since vitamin $D_3$ is necessary for calcium absorption and metabolism, a deficiency may result in metabolic bone disease, rickets, or other illnesses.

If your iguana can bask in natural sunlight several times a week, you won't have to worry about a shortage of vitamin $D_3$. A few hours a week is sufficient as long as the sunlight is not filtered through glass or plastic. That means it's not shining in through a closed window or through the clear walls of a cage. Glass and plastic shut out the UVB rays. Screen is fine and doesn't stop or interfere with the UVB rays.

If your iguana can't get outside regularly, or your climate prevents him from basking outside during the winter, you will need to provide a fluorescent light specifically made for reptiles that provides UVB rays. Incandescent lights do NOT provide any UV rays, and fluorescent lights made for home or office use are not the same as those made for use with reptiles. You can't make any substitutions here—this is too important for your iguana's health! The lights should be set right above your iguana's favorite basking log, no higher than 12 inches away.

> **Did You Know?**
> Give your lizard at least a couple of days to get used to the household and his new cage before you try to handle him much.

## Photoperiods

Photoperiods are the rhythm of light and dark created by the rotation of the Earth. One cycle of daylight and nighttime is one photoperiod. As the days get longer in summer and shorter in winter, the photoperiods change. These changes key certain behavior changes in some species. For some species that hibernate, the shorter days and longer nights prepare the animal for hibernation.

Iguanas don't hibernate, but the shorter days do prepare adult iguanas for the upcoming breeding season, which usually occurs in December through February or March in North America.

For your pet, a cycle of 14 hours of light and 10 hours of darkness will be fine. Later, if you decide to breed your iguana, you will need to adjust the photoperiods so that you provide shorter daylight hours during the winter. Timers available at your local hardware store (such as those used to set up nighttime security lights) can be used to turn your iguana's lights on and off.

Fluorescent lights made specifically for iguanas and reptiles are sold at pet stores selling reptiles, or you can find them at pet e-commerce sites. Pets.com has a reptile section and a variety of fluorescent lights at reasonable prices. They are packaged for shipping and can be sent anywhere.

To make sure your iguana is getting the full benefit of the lights, these lights should be replaced every six months even if the bulb hasn't burned out.

### What Else Does Your Iguana Need?

Okay, you've got the cage set up with a couple of basking logs. You have a toilet spot on the bottom of the cage and you have a heat light and a fluorescent light, both mounted above one of the basking logs. What else does your new pet need?

Well, he's going to need food and water dishes. These should be shallow and relatively flat. If the dish is too deep, the iguana will have a difficult time getting to the food. In fact, many people feed their iguanas on paper plates. These are inexpensive, flat, and you just throw them away. However, if you don't like paper plates, a flat, shallow ceramic dish will work just fine.

You may also want to get your iguana a large, floor-to-ceiling cat tree. A carpeted or sisal cat tree can be placed somewhere in the house where people often are, or near a window where your iguana can look out at the world. Then, when you let him out of his cage, he has a place where he can hang out and feel safe. Most iguanas can climb the carpeted or sisal cat trees with no problem. You haven't seen anything quite as funny as a large iguana lying in a cat bed on a cat tree about six feet up, with his tail hanging out.

## Bringing Home Your Iguana

Once the cage is completely set up, you can bring home your new iguana. Have a travel cage (a plastic dog crate will work) that's big enough so that your iguana's body is not curved or bent (his tail can be curved inside the crate). If you don't have access to a carrier, have a sturdy cardboard box of the appropriate size. Poke some air holes in the box so your iguana won't suffocate.

Once you put him in the carrier or box, don't let him out on the way home, even if he is thrashing around. He probably won't enjoy the car ride and may make a fuss, but he's less apt to hurt himself in the carrier or box than he will be if you let him out in the car. In addition, if he gets out in the car he could hurt you or cause you to lose control of the car. So keep him in the carrier or box and make sure it is securely closed.

When you get him home, make sure the lights are on and there is fresh food and water in his dishes before you let him out of the carrier. When everything is all set, close the door to the room where his cage is. Carefully open the carrier door. Your iguana will probably come out on his own. If he does, grasp him under the chest with one hand and under the hips with the other. Never, ever grab the iguana by the tail! It may detach.

If your iguana doesn't come out of the carrier on his own, carefully and slowly reach in and try to grasp the iguana under the chest. If the iguana is frightened and goes to the rear of the carrier or tries to bite, don't force the issue. If the cage is big enough, place the carrier on the floor of the cage with the carrier door propped open. Let the iguana come out on his own. If the cage isn't big enough, put a towel over your hand and arm and gently pull the iguana out of the carrier, being very careful not to damage legs, toes, and toenails.

Once the iguana is out of the carrier, carefully place him in the cage on the basking log under the heat. Close the cage door securely and leave the iguana alone.

## What to Do the First Night

What should you do with your iguana on his first night home? Nothing. Absolutely nothing. Let him get used to his cage and the household around him. Let him see, hear, and smell the people, pets, and things around him, but make it a point to keep the household as quiet and relaxed as possible. Don't let the kids, dogs, or cats harass him, tease him, or try to make him move. He's going to play statue for awhile, so let him.

## Staring Is a Threat

As your iguana is getting used to his new home, make sure you don't get into the habit of staring at him. You're going to want to watch him—after all, he's new and fascinating. However, staring is a threat.

Staring, in your iguana's terminology, can be taken as a dominance issue—a threat to his new home and position—or it could be the first step in an attack by a predator.

So let everyone in the family know that they can look at the iguana briefly, or out of the corner of their eyes, but they should not stare at him. If you catch the family dog or cat staring, interrupt them, too. In their case, it is the first step in an attack by a predator.

## What Not to Do

Don't try to handle him; that will be incredibly stressful. Don't invite the neighbors over to see him; he needs to get used to you first. Don't even make him explore his cage; let him play statue. He's very aware of what's going on—he's watching, listening, and smelling, and for the first few days that is enough.

## Making Your Iguana Feel Welcome and Secure

Let your iguana have at least a week to get used to his new cage and home. Change his food and water and clean his cage, but otherwise don't mess with him. No petting, no grooming, no trimming toenails, or anything else. Just let him relax a little.

At the same time, try to keep everything else somewhat calm around his cage. He's going to have to get used to your normal household routine, but if you can let him do so gradually, that will help his adjustment.

## What Are You Going to Name Him?

We named Conan because he was such a prehistoric, macho lizard. The name Conan just fit him like the proverbial glove.

The most common names for iguanas seem to stem from the word iguana. There are lots and lots of Iggys, Little Ig, Big Ig, Iggums, Igster, Igwana, and other plays on the word. A lot of iguanas have names relating to dinosaurs, such as Dino, Rex, or Saur.

Lots of iguana have names relating to their green color: Emerald, Greensleeves, Jade, L'il Green, Big Green Guy, Mr. Green, Miss Green, Kelly Green, Green Pea, Sprout, and Leprechaun.

Some iguanas were named for science fiction characters, especially aliens, which is something I find appropriate, since iguanas are often so alien in their approach to life. Kira, Keylar, Dax, Kes, and Jadzia are all both female iguanas and female *Star Trek* characters. Spock, Doctor, Kirk, Bones, Odo, and Worf are all male iguanas and male *Star Trek* characters.

When naming your iguana, choose a name that will suit your iguana's personality without emphasizing his bad points. Don't name him Killer if he's aggressive. With that name he will never calm down; after all, it's hard to say "Killer" sweetly. Instead, name the aggressive, forward iguana a sugary sweet name like "Bubbles."

Make sure, too, that you won't be embarrassed by the name five to 10 years from now. Make sure you can say the name without blushing or stuttering. After all, this is your pet's permanent name—you are going to teach him to respond to it—so choose a name you can actually use and won't be embarrassed to say in front of others.

## Gentle Handling

Over the next few weeks, you can begin handling your new iguana. The key words here are "gentle" and "calm." Keep in mind that even if you bought a farm-raised baby iguana, this is still a wild animal. Unlike domesticated dogs that have had relationships with people for thousands of years, the iguana is not a domesticated animal. You are not taming this creature, but instead are teaching him to trust you. To do this, you have to be trustworthy, so keep things calm and gentle.

Start by hand-feeding your iguana. Try to figure out which foods he really likes and begin feeding him small bits of these foods. Many iguana are attracted to bright-colored foods, such as strawberries, cherry tomatoes, red, pink, or yellow rose blossoms, or yellow hibiscus flowers.

If you offer something by hand and your iguana dashes away, you may be moving too quickly. Try to move more slowly next time. If your iguana closes his eyes, he's making you disappear. (If he can't see you, you aren't there.) Let him sniff the special food. He may just decide to open his eyes and take it.

When you can hand-feed him some special foods, begin touching him very gently, rubbing his back next to the spines or along the rib cage. Many iguanas enjoy having their head rubbed or

**Did You Know?**
Be prepared for your new pet BEFORE you bring it home!

the skin under the jowls rubbed. Don't pet him until he gets anxious just rub or pet a few strokes and then stop.

## In and Out of the Cage

You will need to be able to put your iguana in his cage without wrestling with him and take him out without him thrashing. When you can hand-feed your iguana a special treat, and when he will allow you to touch him and rub him, then it's time to start working on this.

Begin by offering a treat. As he eats it, begin rubbing him as you have been doing. Then slip one hand under his chest so that a finger or two or three (depending upon how big he is) are between his front legs under his chest. Pull him out of the cage and then place the rest of his body on your forearm and tuck his tail between your arm and your body. His head should be above your hand, which is between his front legs and under his chest. His body is on your forearm with his back legs on either side of your arm. His tail is behind you, between your arm and your body. In this position he is secure, held close you to, and cannot whip you with his tail.

When you are picking him up off his basking log, disengage his toes from the log very carefully. His toes are surprisingly flexible and easy to damage. As you pick him up with one hand, you can disengage his toes with the other hand.

Never, ever pick up or grab your iguana by one of his legs. His legs could be dislocated, broken, or otherwise hurt quite easily, especially since he will take that grabbing as an attack and struggle against you. Don't grab him by the tail, either, even though the tail seems like such a convenient handle. If you grab him by the tail, it will probably break off. Although this doesn't hurt him fatally, it will hurt your growing relationship. In addition, the tail that grows back will never be as large or as nice as his original tail.

If he tries to thrash, just hold him calmly (don't get angry!) and talk to him in a calm, soothing voice. When he relaxes, rub him a little and then put him back in his cage. That's enough for one session.

Once he comes out of the cage more calmly, you can gradually keep him out for longer periods of time. However, pay attention to things that stress him, and in the beginning, try to avoid those things. He's got enough to adjust to in the beginning. For example, if he becomes very alert when your cat comes into the room, put the cat away when you bring the iguana out. He can see the cat when he's safely in the cage; he doesn't need to worry about her when he's out of the cage. Later, when he has more confidence, he can learn to deal with the cat.

# 3

# Mmmm, Good! It's Feeding Time

### In This Chapter
- What Is Good Nutrition?
- Foods for Herbivores
- How Do You Feed an Iguana?

For as long as iguanas have been around (a long time!) they have foraged for themselves. In the wild, iguanas will perch in a tree where they can eat its foliage, blossoms, and fruit, and where they can bask in the sun. Iguanas aren't dumb!

There is an iguana living in a park near my house in San Diego. My dog spotted him first, and when she went nuts over something in the tree, I looked and saw this half-grown Suriname Iguana high in a maple tree. He (he looks like a young male, although I'm not sure) is either an escaped or abandoned pet, since iguanas aren't found here naturally. Now, each day on our walks, we look for this iguana. I've never been able to get close enough to catch him, but I have been able to observe him, and one of the things that has fascinated me is his choice of foods. He has apparently staked out a territory that encompasses several trees, some shrubs, and one neighbor's backyard. He has been seen eating leaves, flowers (including the neighbor's roses), and some fruits, including avocados. One neighbor even saw him on the ground eating dandelions. He appears to be quite healthy, and although I put out the word to the neighbors that if anyone catches him I will take him, he does appear to be doing quite well on his own.

## What Is Good Nutrition?

The food that is eaten by any body (mammal or reptile) supplies energy for activity, substances for organ function and food metabolism, and disease resistance. Correct nutrition is needed for a strong immune system, reproduction, and normal growth. Although an animal eating a poor diet may survive for a period of time, unless the diet is corrected, the animal will eventually fail to thrive and could die.

There are eight basic building blocks of nutrition present in the food your iguana eats. They are:

- Water
- Enzymes
- Protein
- Carbohydrates
- Fats
- Fiber
- Vitamins
- Minerals

## A Malnourished Iguana

A malnourished iguana will look much like a dehydrated one. The skin will be wrinkled, the bones will appear prominent, and the eyes will be sunken.

To treat a malnourished or starving iguana, soak some alfalfa pellets (rabbit food) in Pedialyte or Gatorade. Blend in a blender until smooth and then place in the iguana's mouth with a small spoon or a large syringe (with the needle removed). If the iguana will not swallow, your veterinarian's help will be needed to force-feed the iguana.

Each of these building blocks has its own purpose (or purposes) and its own function, but does not work alone. All are needed for good nutrition. Of course, the amounts needed may vary, depending upon the iguana's age, state of health, stress levels, activity level, and whether or not he is breeding.

## Water

Water is the most abundant substance on the planet, and is necessary for life as we know it. The body of your iguana is about two-thirds water. The blood is about 80 percent water, muscles are over 70 percent, and the brain is about 75 percent water. Water is required for normal functioning of every cell in the body. Respiration, digestion, metabolism, and elimination all require water. Water is needed to dissolve and transport nutrients. Water keeps all things in balance. Only oxygen is more important to life.

A certain amount of water is lost each day through respiration and elimination, and must be replaced. A certain amount of water is taken in via the food your iguana eats. Some fruits—especially watermelon, cantaloupe, and strawberries—are very high in moisture content. But your iguana will still need to drink water.

Your iguana will readily drink out of a relatively flat, shallow bowl. Obviously, a shallow bowl will empty quickly, so you will need to refill it often. However, a deeper bowl will be difficult for your iguana to use. If you set up a tub in the bottom of your iguana's cage as a toilet area (as I discussed in chapter 2) this, too, will need to be cleaned regularly so that your iguana doesn't try to drink water soiled with feces.

> The body of your iguana is about two-thirds water. The blood is about 80 percent water, muscles are over 70 percent, and the brain is about 75 percent water.

Many iguana owners have also taught their pets to drink from a spray bottle. Have the spray bottle full of clean water and gently mist your iguana's face. When he opens his mouth or licks his mouth, gently spray the water into his mouth. He will probably swallow and continue opening his mouth. When he turns his head away, he's had enough.

## Enzymes

Enzymes have many functions in your iguana's body and he could not survive without them. Enzymes are made up of two parts: One is a protein molecule and the other is called a coenzyme. The coenzyme is a vitamin or the chemical derivative of a vitamin. Enzymes work by initiating a chemical reaction so that other substances can do their job.

Digesting and metabolizing food requires a complex system of enzymes to make sure that thousands of different chemical reactions happen as they should. In the digestive processes, an enzyme is capable of breaking down one specific substance. For example, an enzyme designed to break down carbohydrates does not metabolize fats. Breaking down foods means the nutrients in the food become available for use by the body.

Because enzymes are made up of proteins and other substances, usually a vitamin, the number of enzymes available to the iguana depends upon the iguana's diet.

## Protein

After water, protein is the most plentiful element in an animal's body, representing approximately 50 percent of each cell. Proteins are incredibly diverse, and serve as the building blocks of claws, skin, muscle, tendons, cartilage, and other connective tissues. Proteins are among the most important elements of food for growth, development and repair of body tissues, sexual development, and metabolism. Proteins are also vital parts of the bloodstream, the immune system, the digestive system, hormone production, and much, much more.

Carnivorous reptiles get their protein by eating meat. Although herbivores don't have the same protein needs as carnivores, proteins are still required for many body functions. Most experts recommend that herbivorous reptiles eat a diet containing 12 to 14 percent protein. Herbivores must get their proteins from the plants they eat. Different plants have different protein contents. Romaine lettuce, for example, has only traces of protein, while kale has 2 grams of protein per

> **Did You Know?**
> A well-fed, healthy lizard will have a round but not obese belly; a fat tail; bright, shiny, alert eyes; and energy to be active when needed.

cup. Yellow winter squash, pumpkin, and soybeans are also good sources of plant proteins.

Inadequate protein levels can lead to weight loss, muscle tissue loss, and a weak immune system. Too much protein can lead to hyperuricemia, where uric acid is deposited in internal organs, leading to a potentially fatal case of gout.

## Carbohydrates

Carbohydrates are the major element of most plants, accounting for 60 to 75 percent of the weight of most plants, once you remove the water. Like proteins, carbohydrates have more than one use in the body. Probably most important, carbohydrates supply energy for bodily functions and are needed to assist in the digestion of other foods. They are also needed to regulate protein and are one of the most important sources of energy for muscular exertion.

## Fats

Dietary fats, called lipids, are a group of compounds that are not soluble in water and that have a number of different functions in the iguana's body. One of the most important functions is that they carry the fat-soluble vitamins A, D, E, and K. Fats are also a source of energy. And fats are involved in a number of different chemical processes in the body and are necessary for growth, healthy blood, and normal kidney function.

Fatty acid requirements have not yet been established for iguanas, but a diet with 0.2 percent linoleic acid is recommended. A lack of fat has been linked to small clutch sizes during reproduction.

## Fiber

Fiber is the cellulose in the plants that your iguana eats. Fiber promotes good intestinal health by absorbing water and aiding in the formation and elimination of feces.

## Vitamins

Vitamins are organic compounds found only in plants and animals. With a few exceptions, your iguana's body cannot synthesize vitamins; they are only supplied in the food he eats. Vitamins work together with other compounds (usually enzymes) to perform different functions, including digestion, metabolism of food, growth, reproduction, and cellular reproduction and oxidation, to name just a few. Vitamins are responsible for thousands of different chemical actions.

**Vitamin A:** This is fat-soluble vitamin has two forms: carotene and vitamin A. Carotene, which is found in plants, must be converted to vitamin A before it can be used by the body. Preformed vitamin A is the result of that chemical conversion, and is found in animal tissues. Because A is fat-soluble, excess is not excreted through the urine but instead is stored in the liver, fat tissues, lungs, and kidneys.

Vitamin A is an important antioxidant, helping in growth and body tissue repair. It also helps keep the immune system strong. And vitamin A is also needed for good eyesight.

A vitamin A deficiency will cause slow or retarded growth, reproductive failure, and skin disorders. In addition,

> **Did You Know?**
> Your pet needs a varied diet, just as people do, for good, balanced nutrition.

secondary infections and eye disorders are common in an individual with a vitamin A deficiency. Too much vitamin A has been associated with bone deformities, joint pain, and bleeding.

Vitamin A is found in leafy green vegetables, yellow and orange vegetables, fish oils, and animal liver. Most commercial reptile food manufacturers add vitamin A to their foods.

**The B vitamins:** There are a variety of B vitamins. This group is called the vitamin B complex, and includes $B_1$ (thiamine), $B_2$ (riboflavin), $B_3$ (niacin), $B_5$ (pantothenic acid), $B_6$ (pyridoxine), $B_{12}$ (cyanocobalamin) and $B_{15}$ (pangamic acid). The B complex also includes biotin, choline, folic acid, inositol, and para-aminobenzoic acid (PABA). The B vitamins are water-soluble so excess is not stored in the body, but instead is excreted through the urine.

The B vitamins help provide energy by assisting in the conversion of carbohydrates to glucose, which is the body's fuel. The B vitamins also help metabolize proteins and fat. These vitamins are needed for normal functioning of the nervous system, for good muscle tone, and healthy skin. In addition, each of the B vitamins has individual functions, all of which are vital to good health.

Because the B vitamins often work together, a deficiency of one could cause a chain reaction. Therefore, if a B supplement is given, it should be a B complex supplement and not just one B vitamin alone.

The B complex vitamins are found in many grains, including whole-grain breads. They can also be found in brewer's yeast.

**Vitamin C:** Vitamin C is often called the "wonder vitamin" because it has such a beneficial effect on the body. It helps form blood corpuscles, aids in a healthy immune system, fights bacterial infections, helps healing, and much, much more. Vitamin C is water-soluble and excess is excreted in the urine.

## Sources of Vitamins for an Iguana

Vitamin A: Leafy green vegetables, carrots
Vitamin B complex: Brewer's yeast, whole-grain cereals, whole-grain breads
Vitamin C: Fruits and vegetables, leafy green vegetables
Vitamin D: Sunshine, fluorescent reptile lights, supplements
Vitamin E: Leafy green vegetables, soybeans, nuts, seeds
Vitamin K: Alfalfa, kelp, supplements

Your iguana is able to synthesize vitamin C internally and get it from his food, especially dark green vegetables and fruits.

**Vitamin D:** Often known as the "sunshine vitamin," your iguana can get vitamin D from the sun's rays if he is able to bask in the sun several times a week. The D vitamins are necessary for normal growth and healthy bones and teeth. The D vitamins work in conjunction with vitamin A, and a deficiency in either vitamin can lead to bone deformities, rickets, or other bone diseases or deformities. Vitamin D is fat-soluble and excess is stored in the liver, brain and skin.

There are three forms of vitamin D: $D_1$, $D_2$, and $D_3$. Mammals use the first two forms and reptiles need vitamin $D_3$. Of particular interest to iguana owners, since iguanas are prone to metabolic bone disease, vitamin $D_3$ is necessary for proper calcium-phosphorus metabolism by aiding in the absorption of calcium in the intestinal tract and the assimilation of phosphorus.

**Vitamin E:** Vitamin E is fat-soluble and is vital to healthy blood. As an antioxidant, it protects both the pituitary and adrenal hormones from oxidation. Tocopherols are a form of vitamin E, and are often added to commercial reptile foods as preservatives.

## Vitamins That Work Better Together

Just eating foods that contain vitamins is not always enough. Many vitamins work so closely together that they are much more effective when eaten together than when consumed separately.

Here are some of the vitamins (and minerals) that work well together.

- Vitamin A works best when eaten with foods containing:

  Vitamin B complex
  Vitamin D
  Zinc

- Vitamin B complex works best when eaten with:

  Vitamin C
  Vitamin E
  Calcium and phosphorus

- Vitamin C works best when eaten with a wide variety of vitamins and minerals.

- Vitamin D is more effective when eaten with foods containing:

  Vitamin A
  Vitamin C
  Calcium and phosphorus

- Vitamin E is most effective when eaten with:

  Vitamin A
  Vitamin B complex
  Vitamin C

**Vitamin K:** This fat-soluble vitamin is necessary for blood clotting and normal liver functions.

As you can see, most of the vitamins work closely together, and no one vitamin should be emphasized without the others. An excess or toxicity of any one vitamin can affect the functioning of all of the other vitamins.

## Minerals

Minerals are present to some extent in the tissues of all living things. Minerals make up part of the bones, teeth, muscles, blood, and nerves. Minerals work with vitamins, enzymes, and one another to perform their functions. For example, calcium and phosphorus are so closely related and their functions so intertwined they could actually be called one mineral: calcium-phosphorus. But they are really two minerals that function best together.

Many other vitamins and minerals work together. The B complex vitamins need phosphorus for their best metabolism. Iron needs vitamin C for best absorption, and zinc helps vitamin A to be released from the liver. A deficiency of any one mineral can have chain reaction effects on many systems of the body.

**Calcium and phosphorus:** As I just mentioned, calcium and phosphorus are two different minerals that work closely together. Calcium is needed for muscle contraction, neuromuscular transmission, and blood coagulation. Calcium is also needed for some of the body's enzyme reactions.

Because it is present in every cell, phosphorus plays a part in many chemical reactions in the body. It is part of the digestive process, the production of energy, cell reproduction, and much, much more. Working together, calcium and phosphorus are vital to creating and keeping bones strong and healthy.

A phosphorus deficiency will inhibit calcium metabolism, resulting in calcium deficiencies. A calcium deficiency can cause metabolic bone disease, an entirely too common problem in captive iguanas.

**Other minerals:** Other vital minerals include copper (works with iron and helps oxidize vitamin C); iodine (important to the thyroid gland); magnesium (works

> **Did You Know?**
> Commercial reptile foods should be a part of your pet's diet but natural foods are important, too.

## Minerals That Work Best Together

Just as the vitamins are more effective when eaten with certain other vitamins (and minerals), minerals often work better when eaten with other minerals or with certain vitamins.

- Calcium is more effective when eaten with:

  Vitamin A
  Vitamin C
  Vitamin D and $D_3$

- Copper is most effective when eaten with:

  Cobalt
  Iron
  Zinc

- Iron is most effective when eaten with:

  Vitamin B complex
  Vitamin C
  Calcium
  Copper
  Phosphorus

- Phosphorus is most effective when eaten with:

  Vitamin A
  Vitamin D and $D_3$
  Protein

with other vitamins and minerals, including C and E, calcium and phosphorus); and zinc (works with B complex vitamins and enzymes).

## Maintaining a Balance

When looking at your iguana's nutritional needs, it's important to remember that no one vitamin, mineral, or nutritional element (such as protein or carbohydrate) functions alone. Each has its own part to play in the system and each is also dependent upon the others.

# The Process of Digestion

The building blocks of nutrition are vitally important, but how do they end up in a form the iguana's body can use? The answer is digestion, a marvelous process.

First, the iguana eats some food. The food is swallowed and passed into the stomach. Enzymes in the digestive tract cause the chemical breakdown. Each enzyme is capable of breaking down only one type of substance. For example, an enzyme capable of breaking down proteins cannot break down fats. Enzyme action takes place in the mouth with the saliva, in the stomach, and in the intestinal tract.

Absorption is the process where nutrients are taken up by the intestines and passed into the bloodstream to facilitate cell metabolism. The nutrients picked up include glucose from carbohydrates, amino acids from protein, and fatty acids from fats.

Metabolism is the process that involves all of the chemical changes that nutrients undergo from the time they are absorbed until they become a part of the body or are excreted. Metabolism is the conversion of the digested nutrients into building material for living tissue or energy to meet the body's needs. The process of metabolism requires thousands of enzymes be maintained to make sure the thousands of chemical reactions occur as they should. These enzymes often require a coenzyme to function, and this coenzyme is often a vitamin or mineral.

Enzyme reactions require heat. In mammals, that heat is provided by the body. Metabolism itself also creates heat, but the

> No one vitamin, mineral, or nutritional element functions alone. Each has its own part to play in the system and each is also dependent upon the others.

body heat must happen first. In reptiles, those enzyme reactions won't take place unless heat is provided from outside the reptile's body.

## Foods for Herbivores

As I've already mentioned, iguanas are herbivores, which means they eat plants. In the wild, iguanas eat the leaves, blossoms, and fruits of the trees and plants found in their native habitat. That means the iguanas in southern Mexico might eat a particular diet while the iguanas in central Brazil eat a totally different diet. This adaptability is one characteristic of herbivores. It also makes it easier for iguana owners to provide for their pets, because we sure can't travel to Central or South America to bring back iguana food!

In fact, if you have room for a small garden, you can grow your own food for your iguana. Zucchini is a standing joke; it is easy to grow and produces lots and lots of fruit! Strawberries are easy to grow, as are tomatoes. Just be careful about any insecticides and fertilizers. Use them sparingly and according to directions.

### No Lettuce!

Look at the list on page 63 of foods recommended for iguanas—do you see lettuce on that list? No, it's not there. Lettuce, particularly iceberg lettuce, has no nutritional value whatsoever! It's only use is to coax an injured or ill iguana to eat (because the silly lizards DO like it), but it should not be a part of your pet's regular diet.

# Safe, Nutritious Foods for Iguanas

- Alfalfa: fresh, hay, dried, meal, or pellets
- Apple: fresh, no core or seeds
- Banana: peeled fruit
- Barley: leaves, hay, meal or flour, sprouted seeds
- Beans, green or yellow wax: leaves, stems, sprouts
- Beets: stems, flowers, grated roots
- Blackberries: fruit
- Blueberries: fruit
- Bok choy: leaves
- Broccoli: heads, grated stems
- Brussels sprouts: heads
- Cactus: dethorned pads, leaves, blossoms
- Carrots: root, chopped or grated
- Clover: leaves, blossoms, hay
- Collard greens: leaves
- Corn: kernels off the cob
- Dandelion: leaves, blossoms
- Grapes: fruit
- Grass: fresh, clean without fertilizers or insecticides
- Hibiscus: flowers, leaves
- Kale: leaves
- Legumes: cooked beans
- Millet: leaves, meal or flour, hay
- Mustard: leaves, flowers
- Nasturtium: leaves, flowers
- Okra: fresh or frozen, thawed
- Parsley: fresh leaves
- Papaya: fruit
- Pea: pods, fruit
- Pumpkin: fruit, chopped, grated
- Soybean: leaves, hay, meal or flour
- Spinach: fresh leaves
- Squash: blossoms, fruit
- Strawberries: fruit
- Sunflower: seeds, unsalted, meal or flour
- Swiss chard: leaves
- Timothy: hay
- Tomato: fruit only
- Turnip: leaves, grated root
- Vegetables: Cooked, frozen or canned, mixed
- Wheat: sprouted seeds, fresh leaves, bran, or flour
- Zucchini: fruit or blossoms

# Nutritional Values of Some Foods

Knowing what you are feeding your beardie can help you decide what to feed. As a sample, here are the nutritional values of some foods commonly fed to beardies.

| Food | Calories | Protein | Carbo-hydrates | Fiber | Vita-min A | B complex | Calcium | Phos-phorus |
|---|---|---|---|---|---|---|---|---|
| Alfalfa sprouts 1 cup | 10 | 1 gram | 1 gram | 0.5 gram | 51 IU | 13 mg | 10 mg | 23 mg |
| Banana 1 fruit | 105 | 2 grams | 27 grams | 1 gram | 92 IU | 2 mg | 7 mg | 22 mg |
| Bread whole grain, 1 slice | 257 | 10 grams | 47 grams | 1 gram | trace | 5 mg | 104 mg | 212 mg |
| Broccoli 1 cup | 24 | 2.6 grams | 4.6 grams | 1 gram | 1,356 IU | 62 mg | 42 mg | 58 mg |
| Carrots 1 cup | 48 | 1 gram | 11 grams | 1 gram | 3,0942 IU | 15 mg | 30 mg | 48 mg |
| Collard greens 1 cup | 35 | 3 grams | 7 grams | 1 gram | 6,194 IU | 2 mg | 218 mg | 29 mg |
| Grapes 1 cup | 58 | 0.5 gram | 15 grams | 1 gram | 92 IU | 4 mg | 13 mg | 9 mg |
| Prickly pear cactus 1 large pad | 42 | 1 gram | 10 grams | 2 grams | 53 IU | 1 mg | 58 mg | 25 mg |
| Pumpkin 1 cup | 49 | 2 grams | 12 grams | 2 grams | 2,651 IU | 2 mg | 37 mg | 74 mg |
| Soybean curd (tofu) 3.5 ounces | 72 | 8 grams | 3 grams | 1 gram | less than 0 | 0 | 100 mg | 176 mg |
| Squash, winter 1 cup | 129 | 4 grams | 32 grams | 3 grams | 8,610 IU | 2 mg | 57 mg | 98 mg |
| Strawberries 1 cup | 45 | less than 1 gram | 10 grams | less than 1 gram | 41 IU | 2 mg | 21 mg | 28 mg |
| Tomato 1 cup | 24 | 1 gram | 5 grams | 0.5 gram | 1,394 IU | 10 mg | 8 mg | 29 mg |

## Allowing Your Iguana to Graze

Many iguana owners like to let their iguana graze (or more correctly, browse) in the backyard. This is a wonderful way for your iguana to add some different foods to his diet as well as bask in the sun. However, take care, because the backyard does have some dangers.

Check the list of poisonous plants on page 66 and make sure your landscaping is safe. Make sure, too, that the neighbor's cat or dog can't get into your yard and your iguana can't get out. Last, but certainly not least, make sure no dangerous chemicals have been used in your yard. Fertilizers, herbicides, pesticides, and insecticides can all kill your iguana.

> Make sure no dangerous chemicals have been used in your yard. Fertilizers, herbicides, pesticides, and insecticides can all kill your iguana.

## Commercial Iguana Foods

Commercial pet foods have been around for most of the past century, but commercial reptile foods are still relatively new. Some have been tested by feeding trials—feeding numbers of animals the food and observing the results—while others are tested by making a nutritional analysis of the ingredients. Both, actually, are necessary so that you can really understand what is in the food, what its nutritional value is and how it will affect your iguana.

Until great numbers of iguanas have been fed these foods, grown up, lived and died, we really won't know how iguanas respond to the commercial foods. After all, these foods aren't available to the iguanas living in the treetops of the Brazilian jungles!

# Poisonous Plants

Some plants are not safe to feed your iguana. Listed below are those plants known to be harmful to herbivorous reptiles. Many are house plants, or common yard or landscaping plants, so make sure you check this list before offering leaves to your iguana.

- Amaryllis
- Anemone
- Apple (seeds)
- Avocado (leaves, not fruit)
- Azalea
- Belladonna
- Bird of paradise
- Bottlebrush
- Boxwood
- Buttercup
- Calla lily
- Cherry (seeds)
- Common privet
- Crocus
- Croton
- Cyclamen
- Daffodil
- Diefenbachia
- Dogwood
- Eggplant (foliage)
- English ivy
- Foxglove
- Hemlock
- Holly
- Horse chestnut
- Hyacinth
- Impatiens
- Iris
- Jasmine
- Jimson weed
- Larkspur
- Lily of the valley
- Milkweed
- Mistletoe
- Morning glory
- Mushrooms
- Oleander
- Peach (seeds)
- Pennyroyal
- Philodendrons
- Poison ivy
- Poison oak
- Poison sumac
- Pokeweed
- Potato (foliage)
- Privet
- Rhododendron
- Sage
- Snapdragon
- Sweetpea
- Tomato (foliage)
- Tulip
- Wisteria
- Yew

The most common form of iguana food is dry kibble. Dry food usually has a moisture content of 10 to 12 percent or less, and contains grains and grain products. Other vegetables are usually added, as are vitamins and minerals. Dry foods are easy to store, last for several months, and are reasonable in price. When soaked in water first, there is a pleasing fruity odor and most iguanas will at least try the food.

There are a couple of canned iguana foods on the market. Canned foods have a higher moisture content, usually about 70 to 80 percent. These foods, being higher in moisture, do not need to be soaked in water before feeding. They are usually palatable to most iguanas.

## Feeding Commercial Foods

If you decide to feed your iguana commercial foods, make sure you read the directions carefully and feed the correct amount for the age and size of your iguana.

If you decide to feed a dry food, always soak the food in water before offering it to your iguana, even if the label says the food can be offered dry. Iguanas who eat dry food that is not soaked first get very thirsty and drink large amounts of water; bloating is not unusual and can be life-threatening. In addition, kidney problems have been known to occur in iguanas eating only a diet of dry, unsoaked food.

The most common use of commercial reptile foods is as an addition to the iguana's diet. Although many of the foods are labeled "Nutritionally complete," very few experienced iguana owners feed only commercial iguana foods. Commercial iguana foods can be a good addition to an iguana's diet, because most have added vitamins and minerals. But an iguana also needs fresh foods.

## Supplements

If you are feeding your iguana a good diet rich in dark green leafy vegetables, with some fruit and commercial iguana food on the side, do you need to include a vitamin-mineral supplement? Probably not. Your iguana should be getting everything he needs from his diet.

However, your iguana's food is only as good as the soil in which it is grown. If the vegetables are being grown in soils that are depleted of minerals, then that food will not be passing those minerals on to your iguana. The same applies to the ingredients of the commercial foods.

Therefore, it's usually a good idea to give a young, rapidly growing iguana a vitamin-mineral supplement marketed specifically for iguanas three to four times a week. Your adult iguana will probably do fine with a supplement two to three times a week. An ill or injured iguana should have a supplement three to four times a week to help him heal and to boost the immune system. An old iguana should be supplemented three to four times a week, because the old iguana's digestive system will become less efficient as he ages.

Keep in mind that over-supplementation can be just as deadly as too little. Try to give your iguana a good, balanced diet and then use the supplement as a way of making up for any chance shortfalls in the food.

## Caution!

Feed broccoli, kale, spinach, cabbage, and bok choy in small amounts, because they can chemically interfere with calcium absorption. They have also been suspected of causing thyroid dysfunction. However, they are good nutrition, so don't eliminate them altogether.

# Different Foods at Different Ages

Just as with humans, iguanas have different nutritional needs at different times in their lives. A rapidly growing baby, for example, needs more protein than a full-grown adult. The dietary guidelines that follow will help you balance your iguana's diet for the growth stage he is in. In addition, the best diet will offer certain foods along with other foods. The ingredients or nutrients of these particular foods will serve your iguana best in this way.

## A Sample Juvenile Iguana Diet

A young iguana grows rapidly, and has special needs. Here's a good diet for a youngster:

- 40 percent calcium-rich green vegetables: alfalfa, collard greens, mustard greens, dandelions, spinach greens, cabbage, bok choy, Swiss chard, kale, beet greens, green beans, broccoli
- 40 percent other vegetables: grated squash, zucchini, bell peppers, sprouts, grated carrots, canned or frozen mixed vegetables, tomatoes, okra, sweet potatoes, clean rose blossoms, clean hibiscus blossoms
- 20 percent other foods: whole-grain cereals, whole-grain bread, commercial iguana food, tofu

- Twice a week: bananas, apples, melons, peaches, strawberries, grapes, papaya, raspberries, soaked, dry kibble dog food, crumbled hard-boiled egg

## A Sample Adult Iguana Diet

Here is a good diet for a healthy adult iguana:

- 40 percent calcium-rich green vegetables: alfalfa, collard greens, mustard greens, dandelions, spinach greens, cabbage, bok choy, Swiss chard, kale, beet greens, green beans, broccoli
- 50 percent other vegetables: grated squash, grated carrot, grated pumpkin, grated beets, sprouts, frozen or canned mixed vegetables, peas, lima beans, avocado
- 10 percent other foods: fruits, berries, commercial iguana foods, a rose blossom or two, a couple of hibiscus flowers
- Twice a week: crumbled hardboiled egg, tofu, whole-grain breads, whole-grain cereal

## How Do You Feed an Iguana?

Most iguanas will not eat until they have warmed up in the morning. A noon feeding is perfect for most iguanas, but if you have to go to work every day, fix the meal before you go. Then your iguana can eat when he's ready.

Do not feed your iguana late in the evening. When he cools off for the night, his food will not digest well and he could end up with a tummyache. He needs warmth to digest his food.

Feed your iguana in one spot where he can have easy access and you can easily clean up the mess. Iguanas can be messy eaters! If your iguana likes strawberries, for example, he may shove everything else out of the way until he's eaten all of the strawberries. Then he may eat his greens. In the meantime, he's made a mess. This one spot may be in his cage, or you may decide to feed him somewhere else. Where ever you decide to feed him, make sure he can have some peace and quiet while he eats.

Determining how much to feed is an ongoing process. Your iguana will eat more when he's actively growing and when the weather is warm. He will eat less when it's cooler, during breeding season, and in between growth spurts. Watch how much he eats, give him a little more if his plate is always clean, and cut back a little if he's leaving food uneaten.

> Most iguanas will not eat until they have warmed up in the morning.

Although some experts say iguanas should be fed three to four times a week, my own observations show me that herbivores eat every day. Plant matter is less dense in nutrients than meat, and it takes longer to digest. While a meat eater might go a day or two between meals, herbivores need to take in food more often. Feed your iguana every day. If he doesn't eat a lot, that's OK—at least you offered it to him.

## Evaluating the Results

You can easily tell if your feeding program is working.

- Does your iguana look healthy? Does his skin look bright, clean, and clear?
- Does his skin look filled out and smooth?
- Are his stools good?
- Are your iguana's eyes bright and alert?
- Does his weight look good? Not too fat or too skinny?
- Is your iguana's activity level normal for him?

# 4

# Medical Care for Your Iguana

### In This Chapter

- Finding a Veterinarian
- A Healthy Iguana
- What to Do in an Emergency

When you bring a pet into your family, you also assume the responsibility for his care and well-being. As we've already seen, for iguanas that means the right cage, UVB fluorescent light, photoperiods, heat, and a good diet. However, just as we sometimes need to see a physician, your iguana may sometimes need to see a veterinarian. But not all veterinarians like to treat iguanas or know how. In this chapter I'll discuss how you can find a good vet in your area. In addition, I'll look at how you can keep your iguana healthy, and will talk, too, about iguana first aid.

## Finding a Veterinarian

Not all veterinarians are skilled at treating iguanas, or reptiles in general. Some, in fact, would prefer to not see iguanas at all! Not that they necessarily dislike iguanas, but iguanas are very different from dogs and cats. They require different care, and often, different tools and medications. In addition, iguanas can be very difficult, and, at times delicate patients.

You need to find a veterinarian who is skilled and knowledgeable before you need his services. If you wait until you have an emergency, you may not have the time to look around for the right vet, and your iguana may end up being treated by someone who is not as skilled as you might like. For example, my husband and I had to call our veterinarian early one Sunday morning when Conan, our very large male, attacked a much smaller female iguana. He bit her severely several times and she needed to have stitches. Because our vet knew us and knew our pets, he was willing to come in to his clinic on a Sunday. However, if we had not established a relationship with him, he may have sent us to the local emergency clinic and the vet on duty may (or may not) have had any experience with iguanas. Therefore, do some homework now.

The first thing to do is to come up with the names of a few vets who do treat reptiles. Some veterinarians who treat exotic animals (including reptiles) will advertise that fact in their Yellow Pages ads. If you have friends with reptiles, they might be able to refer you to a good vet. Local herpetological clubs also maintain listings of reputable vets.

The Association of Reptilian and Amphibian Veterinarians is a group of vets who have an interest or specialty in reptiles. This association may be able to help you find a vet near you. Write to them at ARAV, c/o Wilbur Amand, D.V.M., P.O. Box 605, Chester Heights, PA 19017.

When you have the names of a few vets in your area who will treat iguanas, make an appointment with each of them. Be prepared to pay for an office visit (you will be taking their time), and go prepared with a list of questions.

- Have you personally owned reptiles?
- Do you see many iguanas?
- Have you successfully treated many iguanas?
- Is your office staff trained to handle and care for iguanas?
- Do you have heated cages for iguanas who are undergoing medical procedures?
- Are you continuing your medical education in regards to reptile medicine?
- What are your policies regarding emergencies?
- Are you available after hours?
- Do you accept credit cards or payment plans?

Once you and the vet have had a chance to talk, ask yourself what you think of him (or her). Did the vet seem to be interested in you and your pet? Was he encouraging? Or did he try to discourage you from becoming a client? Did he (or she) appear caring, up to date, and willing to work with you?

A good veterinarian is your partner in your iguana's health. Having a veterinarian you can call, not just in emergencies, but whenever you have concerns, will help you care for your iguana in the best way possible.

## Establish a Working Relationship

Once you've found a vet, make an appointment and take your iguana in to see him. Let your vet meet your iguana

## Anesthesia

Isoflurane is the anesthesia of choice for most veterinarians who specialize in reptiles. This gas has a quicker induction and faster recovery rate than many other anesthesias, and is quite safe. It does, however, require special equipment. When interviewing veterinarians, ask if isoflurane is available.

when he's healthy. The vet will probably weigh him, measure him, and examine him thoroughly—all the while taking notes—so that when there is a future problem, he will have some baseline facts about your pet to look back at. He may also request you bring in a fecal sample so that he can check for parasites. He may ask if he can run a blood panel. If your budget can afford it, do so, again so that there is a normal baseline on record. This can be very important later, so do it if you can.

Many people complain that veterinarians are there only to "bleed them dry" with outrageous bills. I'm sure there are some vets who overcharge their clients, just as some other professionals do. But I'm a firm believer that what goes around, comes around, and those vets won't keep their clients very long. However, do remember that veterinarians are in business, too, and have bills of their own to pay.

Veterinary bills are not determined by how much your pet cost, either, so just because your iguana only cost $29.95 doesn't mean his care should cost less than that for a $500 purebred dog. In fact, some medications and treatments for iguanas cost more than treatments for dogs and cats. Veterinary care for your iguana should be reasonably priced, but it won't be cheap.

## A Healthy Iguana

A healthy iguana has an attitude. His bearing just screams, "I'm here!" When you pick him up, unless he was sound asleep and you woke him up, he should be bright and alert. He should feel substantial; even small iguanas should feel heavy and compact.

Your iguana's eyes should be bright and clear with no discharge. His nose should be dry with no discharge and no crusty material. His mouth should be clean (unless you interrupted a meal, of course), and the jaws should be firm. There should be no softness or swelling along the jawline.

Your iguana's ears are not really obvious (as are a cat or dog's) but he does have them. The ears are located behind his jaw, above the jowls. There should be no discharge or swelling from them.

Your iguana's skin should be free of cuts, scrapes, or other injuries, and should be free of any unexplained swellings. There should be no ticks embedded between the scales.

If your iguana is getting ready to shed, his skin may look whitish and dull. Most iguanas shed their skin in pieces, chunks at a time, until they have lost all the old skin. Make sure all of the old skin is off, including each toe and all of the spines.

A healthy iguana will also have normal feces. What is normal for one iguana isn't necessarily normal for another, so you will need to be observant. Often the first signs of illness are changes in the feces, so pay attention to what is normal for your iguana.

Keeping track of your iguana's weight is also important. Any weight loss is significant, unless it's a breeding age

> **Did You Know?**
> It's true for reptiles as well as for people; preventive health care will keep your pet healthy longer.

## Shedding

Your iguana will shed periodically, and when he does, he will scratch or rub off all of the older layer of skin, until it's completely off. This process (which scientists call ecdysis) will happen from the time your iguana hatches until he dies.

Very young, rapidly growing iguanas shed more frequently, as if to keep up with their growth. As the iguana matures and his growth slows down, shedding will also slow down. Mature iguanas may only shed a few times a year.

When the skin begins to show white or blue overtones, a soak in a warm bathtub (shallow water, please!) will help the skin come off easier. In addition, a few rough textured items in the cage (such as logs with bark still attached) will give the iguana something to rub against to loosen the skin.

If your iguana appears to have completed a shed, but some skin is still attached, use some mineral or baby oil to help loosen that skin. Trouble spots are often the toes, the tip of the tail, and the spines. If left attached, this old skin can cause problems and even restrict blood flow to the toes. With some oil on your fingers, gently rub the retained skin, loosening it, and working it off. Very few iguanas protest this massage; it probably feels good!

male during breeding season. Appetites often drop off then. But otherwise, the iguana's weight should gradually increase as a juvenile and remain relatively stable during adulthood.

## Preventive Medicine

Keeping your iguana healthy is the best preventive medicine there is. There are no vaccinations for iguanas yet, and none in the foreseeable future. However, iguanas can live a long life without them; it's just up to us to make sure they can.

## The Details

Part of preventive medicine for your iguana includes his proper care. Proper care includes a good, nutritious diet. Other details of good care include heat, correct lighting, photoperiods, and sunshine when possible. All of these details are part of what keeps an iguana healthy. Most veterinarians working with reptiles estimate that most of the sick reptiles they see are ill because of improper diet and/or inadequate light or heat.

> Most veterinarians working with reptiles estimate that most of the sick reptiles they see are ill because of improper diet and/or inadequate light or heat.

## Cleanliness

My grandmother often used that old cliché, "Cleanliness is next to godliness." I hated hearing it as a child, but I sure do understand it now. Cleanliness is vital to your iguana's good health.

In the wild, your iguana lived in the treetops. He basked on branches, ate leaves and flowers, and eliminated off the branch, where his feces fell to the ground below. He never came into contact with his feces.

In his cage, he is forced to eliminate much closer to his living area. Of course, you set up a toilet area for him and clean it often—preferably after each time he uses it. If he is forced to come into contact with his feces, he will NOT like it, will smear it all over and could threaten his own health, especially if it fouls his food or water.

In chapter 8 I'll talk more about cage cleaning and how to do it, so right now I'll just say that cleaning the cage regularly is a vital part of keeping your iguana healthy. Cleaning the cage includes scrubbing the basking logs, the walls of the cage, where he eats, and the floor of the cage.

## Salmonella

A few years ago, there were several newspaper headlines blaming iguanas for the deaths of some babies due to salmonella poisoning. A few cities and animal control departments cried out for justice, saying that iguanas were poor pets and should be outlawed. Luckily, that hubbub died down and iguanas are still allowed as pets. Unfortunately, however, iguanas CAN carry salmonella and people CAN be infected with it. It is a real danger.

Iguanas are not the only means of infection, though. In most cases, people are infected with salmonella from improperly refrigerated foods, or foods contaminated during processing. Even contaminated water can carry salmonella. However, salmonella can also be carried by reptiles, and is more frequently found in aquatic turtles, box turtles, snakes and a few lizards, including iguanas.

Salmonella is not to be taken lightly. Although most healthy adults can fight off an infection without showing any symptoms, young children, elderly people and those with a compromised immune system can become very ill. Some of the symptoms of salmonella include nausea, cramps, vomiting, bloody diarrhea, and fever. In rare cases, serious bone infections, meningitis, and encephalitis are potentially deadly side effects. If you or someone in your family becomes inexplicably ill, make sure you tell your physician that you do have a reptile in the home so that he or she can test for salmonella.

While many infected reptiles will show no symptoms of the dis-

## Salmonella Prevention

We have never had a salmonella scare with either Conan or any of the rescued iguanas we've taken in over the years. However, we work hard to make sure we don't have a problem. Cages are cleaned regularly, water is replaced daily, dishes are cleaned daily, and we always wash our hands after handling any reptile. Salmonella is very scary and can be deadly; however, good hygiene can prevent disasters.

ease, others whose immune systems are weakened due to injury, illness or environmental stress may become ill and die. Veterinarians can test to see if a reptile is carrying salmonella. Unfortunately the treatments, which may include fluids and antibiotics, are rarely successful. Many veterinarians recommend euthanasia.

## Preventing Infection

You can prevent salmonella infections or the transmission of the disease by practicing good hygiene.

- Keep cages and cage furnishings very clean.
- Make sure feces are disposed of often in a closed garbage bag. Do not add iguana feces to the backyard compost heap.
- Never wash the cage, cage furnishings, or food and water dishes in the kitchen sink. Use the deep sink in the basement, the bathtub, or the hose outside. Do not use the kitchen cleaner materials, either; have a separate sponge or scrubber for your iguana's things.
- Use a strong bleach-and-water solution to disinfect cage furnishings, bowls, and the cage.

In addition, always wash your hands after handling your iguana or anything in the iguana's cage. Teach the kids to do the same. The antibacterial hand gels work very well and some iguana owners have gotten into the habit of keeping a bottle of one of these cleaners right next to the iguana's cage so that it is easy to remember to use it.

Teach the kids, too, that they should never kiss the iguana. Not only does kissing put them at risk of contacting salmonella, but it puts the iguana at risk of catching something from them.

## Spaying and Neutering

Most pet owners today understand that spaying or neutering their cats and dogs is a good idea. After all, we've been inundated with photos of homeless cats and dogs at the shelters, waiting for adoptive homes that may never come.

Iguana owners, however, don't face quite the same problem. Although some shelters and iguana rescue groups may have several iguanas waiting to be adopted, the situation is not quite as dire. Iguanas are not running loose, visiting the neighbor's iguana, and producing lots of babies. (Unless you live in southern Florida, that is, where this is happening.) The reality is that in most of North America, iguanas cannot survive and reproduce outside without our help.

But you should still consider spaying your female iguana and neutering your male. Unspayed females can and often do lay eggs, even if they haven't been around a male and even though the eggs are unfertile. Continued egg laying does take a lot out of the female's body. She is using up nutrients that could otherwise be used to keep her healthy. Proteins and calcium are used in great quantities to produce eggs. In addition, if she doesn't have the right place to lay her eggs (a deep box of warm potting soil) she could become egg-bound. This is when the eggs are retained in her body, and sometimes surgery is required to remove them.

A female that is spayed has a hysterectomy. The ovaries and the reproductive system are removed. Although not many vets are spaying female iguanas as elective surgery yet, more are beginning to do so. Ask your vet about it, and if he (or she) is not comfortable with the surgery, ask for a referral to a vet who is.

In male iguanas, the surgery is called neutering or castration. Some mature males become quite aggressive during breeding season—so much so that they have even been known to attack their owners (see the box on page 84). Some are even aggressive to female iguanas, hurting or even killing them during breeding attempts. Neutering the male iguana will curb this behavior as well as making him unable to breed. If you have no plans to breed your iguana, or if he shows a great deal of aggressiveness during breeding season, talk to your vet about neutering your pet.

## What to Do in an Emergency

No matter how careful you are, there will be accidents. Perhaps your iguana will catch a claw on something and break the claw or toe. Maybe you will trip over him, or he'll fall. Accidents happen but you can be prepared—or as prepared as humanly possible.

When you come upon your iguana and see that something is wrong, be

### Did You Know?
A calm, well-mannered lizard who is used to being handled is much easier to bring to the veterinarian's office than a lizard who is rarely handled.

## Male Aggressiveness

During breeding season—usually December through March in North America—male iguanas often become the definition of macho. Eager to defend their turf, they will charge anyone who ventures near, and often will chase or attack the trespasser. In the wild that trespasser would be another male iguana. In captivity it could be one of your other pets, your kids, or the adults in the family.

Women who are menstruating are often targets of this aggression, and although experts aren't sure why, it is surmised that the iguana can sense or smell the woman's pheromones. I've been lucky; even though Conan has shown aggressive behavior during breeding season, he has never tried to attack me.

Although most male iguanas respect their male owner as a very large male, and therefore won't attack him, attacks sometimes still happen. When Conan was just coming into maturity, he tried to attack my husband. When he charged toward him, Paul simply picked Conan up off the floor and held him suspended. All of the confidence and fight went out of that big lizard; you could see him wilt, and as a result, this was the last time he tried to attack Paul.

It's very obvious when an attack is imminent. The iguana will stand tall, sometimes even on his tip toes, and will inflate his body so that he looks bigger

calm. When you're calm, you will be able to think and make better decisions.

## Restraining Your Iguana

A hurt iguana is not going to cooperate with your efforts to help him. In his mind, he is now particularly vulnerable to attack by predators, so he will fight you. While handling the iguana might normally require light restraint (to keep him from inadvertently clawing you), handling a hurt or ill iguana is a totally different story.

than he really is. His color usually brightens—Conan turns really bright orange—with the color usually appearing on the face, legs, and lower sides. The dewlap will be fully extended. The iguana will slightly turn his head and body, so that you can appreciate him in his full glory, and he will bob his head up and down. He will slowly move his tail from side to side very stiffly. If appropriate attention is not given him, he will then open his mouth wide and charge.

It's amazing how quickly these big lizards can move! Some iguana owners have admitted that they run from their lizard during these charges, because they are really frightening. Although running might prevent a bite, many iguanas will stop an attack if faced straight on and yelled at in a deep, authoritative tone of voice. Not that the iguana understands the tone of voice or words—it is your bearing and refusal to acknowledge the attack that often stops it.

It's important to remember that during breeding season, your iguana is operating under the influence of hormones and instincts. He's not thinking, he's just doing. So protect yourself. Handle the iguana as little as possible, make sure you don't put yourself in a vulnerable position, and always watch your lizard.

A nice thick towel can be a life-saver in these situations. You can catch a frantic iguana by tossing the towel over him and then grasping the iguana through the towel. You can use the towel to wrap him snugly but firmly, making sure his legs are folded back along his sides. Then just expose the area that is hurt.

You may even be able to get away with just covering the iguana's head with the towel. Just make sure he can breathe! We have sometimes been able to immobilize Conan simply by putting a hand over his eyes.

Most iguanas, when hurt, will not calm down just with the eyes covered, however. They will fight. Respect your iguana's

## An Iguana First-Aid Kit

Keep the following items in your first aid kit:

- Gauze pads (variety of sizes) for cleaning, wiping, or to put pressure on a wound
- Gauze or elastic wrap to hold a gauze pad or a splint in place
- Butterfly tape to hold a wound closed
- Bandage tape to hold a gauze pad, splint or butterfly in place
- Cotton-tipped swabs to clean wounds or apply medications
- Nutrical nutritional supplement
- Betadine to wash a wound
- Hydrogen peroxide to clean wounds
- Scissors—round tip and sharp tip
- Iguana nail trimmers
- Tweezers, large and small
- Saline eyewash to flush eyes
- Kwik Stop or other styptic powder to stop bleeding
- Popsicle sticks for temporary splints
- Gloves to protect you from iguana bites
- Towel to wrap your iguana

Check your first aid kit often, replacing used materials and throwing away expired items. In addition, you should have a plastic pet carrier large enough for your iguana and store it someplace that is easily accessible.

ability to harm you, either by whipping you with his tail or by biting. A large iguana can actually take a chunk of flesh from your arm or sever a fingertip. Therefore, treat his fright with respect, don't assume that he will not hurt you, and be careful.

Restraining your iguana is not without risk to your iguana, as well. If your iguana struggles too forcefully, he can hurt himself. If he is suffering from metabolic bone disease, he could even break his own bones. You must be careful to hold your iguana firmly but not so hard that you injure him. There's a fine balance here.

## Bleeding

There are several types of bleeding, and how the bleeding is treated depends upon the type of bleeding and its severity.

If the skin isn't broken, there can be bleeding under the skin. This can result in a bruise if the bleeding is small or a hematoma if the bleeding continues. A bruise is usually not a significant problem. However, a hematoma can be a problem that your vet should see. At the first sign of bleeding under the skin, put a very small ice pack (one or two ice cubes) on that spot for just a few seconds at a time. You want the chill to help slow the bleeding without chilling your iguana and sending him into shock. If the bleeding appears to continue, call your vet.

Bleeding from small scrapes, scratches, and small cuts is usually not a danger. Wipe the wound off and apply pressure with a gauze pad. When the bleeding stops, wash it off with a little hydrogen peroxide. Check the wound often to make sure it's healing well and not infected.

If the bleeding is continuous and oozing, this is more serious. Put pressure on the wound with a couple of layers of gauze pads, using your hand to maintain the pressure. You will want to get your iguana to the vet right away, because he could quickly bleed to death.

Bleeding that comes out in spurts is very dangerous. This means a major blood vessel has been cut and your iguana is in danger of bleeding to death. If the wound is on the tail or a limb, you can make a tourniquet out of gauze wrap or a shoelace. Wrap it around the limb, then tie a small stick or a pencil to the knot and twist to tighten. Be careful—tighten enough to slow the bleeding but be careful you don't break the iguana's bones. Get your iguana to the vet right away; he's in danger of dying!

Tourniquets must be loosened every 10 to 15 minutes or the tissue in that limb will die from lack of blood flow. You can loosen the tourniquet, allow the blood to flow for a few minutes, and then tighten it again.

Internal bleeding is less obvious and is very dangerous. If your iguana has jumped from a high place, or fell, or was in an accident of some kind, watch his behavior. If he stops moving, acts restless, or breathes through his mouth, get him to the vet's office right away. Other symptoms of internal injuries include pale gums, a distended abdomen, bloody feces, bloody vomit, or blood in the saliva.

## Choking

It is important, when feeding your iguana, to make sure the food is chopped up to an appropriate size. Iguanas will try to swallow anything, and food that is too big could cause an iguana to choke, especially a baby iguana.

If your iguana seems to be choking or gagging, open his mouth and see if you can see anything. If there is a bit of food in the back of the mouth or throat, pull it out. Tweezers can help.

> Iguanas will try to swallow anything, and food that is too big could cause an iguana to choke, especially a baby iguana.

If you can't see anything, use the iguana version of the Heimlich maneuver. With your iguana on his side on a flat surface, give a sharp compression of the abdomen right below the ribs. Make it firm but not so firm that you damage internal organs. In addition, watch where the ribs are so that you don't break any!

If this doesn't work, get him to the vet right away. His life is in danger.

## Burns

Iguanas can be burned if they get too close to an incandescent light, or if the light falls onto or into the cage. Iguanas can also burn their belly if you use a heat rock (rock or brick with a heating element inside) in the cage (see chapter 2 on using heating elements safely). Iguanas allowed free run of the house can burn themselves if they get into the kitchen while you're cooking, or if they get too near lamps.

If you suspect your iguana has been burned, immediate veterinary care is needed. Make a very small ice pack (one or two cubes) and repeatedly put this on and off the burn while on your way to the vet's office. (Put it on to cool the burn but take it off so the iguana doesn't chill too much.)

## Animal Bites

If your iguana was bitten by another iguana, the wounds will probably be through the skin—often horseshoe shaped—but will not be too deep. Wipe the wound clean and pour hydrogen peroxide over the wound. Sometimes these wounds can be closed with butterfly bandages but often need to be stitched closed. Your vet may recommend antibiotics as many times these bites will be infected with bacteria. Without antibiotics, they often become abscesses.

If your iguana was bitten by a cat, the wound will be smaller and will have two or four punctures from the canine teeth. If your iguana is small, there may be some crushing damage but if your

> **Did You Know?**
> If your lizard is bleeding, is unconscious, or needs emergency care; don't hesitate. Get your lizard to the vet right away.

iguana is larger, few cats are strong enough to cause any crushing damage on a big iguana. Your vet will probably recommend not stitching these wounds, suggesting instead that they be thoroughly cleaned and kept clean, and that you give your iguana antibiotics. Cat bites frequently get infected.

Dogs can cause a lot of damage to iguanas. Medium to large dogs can crush the iguana as they bite, and worse yet, may shake the iguana as they bite. Your iguana could have crushing injuries, broken bones, internal bleeding and injuries, as well as skin punctures, and more. If a dog gets hold of your iguana, take the lizard to the vet immediately, even if you don't see any outward problems. A broken rib or internal bleeding may not show any immediate outward signs.

## Broken Tail

Iguanas with a long, tapering tail are quite handsome. Unfortunately, by the time most iguanas have reached full maturity, their tail has probably been damaged in some way. That long tail is just too fragile. In many species of lizards, the tail is designed to separate from the lizard's body. The tail will just lay there and twitch for a few moments—long enough to distract a predator—while the lizard escapes.

In captivity, the tail may detach if a dog or cat grabs the tail, or if another iguana does. If you try to grab the iguana by the tail when he's determined to go another direction, the tail could detach. The tail might also break if it's caught in a cage door, or if it is whacked hard up against an immovable object.

In any case, this is usually not an emergency. The lizard's body handles it quite well. The blood vessels will seal off, the tail portion will continue to twitch for awhile, and eventually a new tail will grow in place of the broken section. Often the new tail is darker.

## Exposure to Cold

Anything under about 75°F counts as freezing to your iguana. In the wild, he would be living in a tropical climate. Other than south Florida, the United States doesn't offer that climate, so your iguana is living in a climate much cooler than he's designed for.

The seriousness of cold exposure depends upon several things. If your iguana is a baby (a healthy baby) and the heat light above his cage burns out while you're at work, he will probably be just fine. If you lose electrical power in the middle of a blizzard and power is out for days, light a fire in the fireplace and move your iguana's cage close to the fire; temperatures that cold could be a serious problem.

When exposed to cold temperatures, your iguana will first slow down. He won't move as much as normal, his digestion will slow, and circulation and other body functions will slow.

If your iguana is just slightly chilled, you can warm him up slowly. Do not place him on a heating pad or under a high wattage incandescent bulb. That's too rapid a change and will cause him to go into shock—he may even die. Instead, use lukewarm water bottles wrapped in lightweight towels to warm him slowly. A 40- to 60-watt incandescent light can supply gentle heat. Call your veterinarian; he or she may wish to see your iguana, depending upon the circumstances.

**Did You Know?**
Don't hesitate to call your vet if you have questions about your pet's health. Don't be embarrassed—that's why he's in business!

If your iguana got severely chilled, wrap him up with a warm water bottle and take him immediately to the veterinarian's office. Your vet will probably want to start intravenous fluids and treat your iguana for shock.

## Broken Bones

Broken bones always require a fast trip to the veterinarian's office. If you see a broken bone protruding through the skin, or suspect a broken bone, stabilize the limb if you can with a temporary splint and gauze wrap, then transport your iguana immediately to the vet's office.

## Dehydration

When iguanas have access to water, they rarely suffer from dehydration. However, accidents can happen. If your iguana tips over his water on a very hot summer day, he could become dehydrated. The symptoms of dehydration are sunken eyes and wrinkled skin that doesn't return to its original position when pinched. In addition, a dehydrated iguana will feel light when you pick him up.

You can treat mild dehydration at home by giving your iguana Gatorade or infant Pedialyte. Dehydrated reptiles often will not drink—they are no longer thirsty—and must be given the liquids through an eyedropper or a syringe (with the needle removed). Make sure you don't drown your iguana when giving him fluids; give him a few drops at a time and give him a chance to swallow before you give any more.

If your iguana is dehydrated, unresponsive, and you cannot get fluids into him, take him to the vet's office right away. Your vet will give him IV fluids and treat him for shock.

## When to Call the Veterinarian

Many reptile owners hesitate to call their veterinarian. I don't know why, and when asked, many can't say why. But reptiles, including iguanas, can be surprisingly delicate. If injured, they can quickly go into shock and die. Many of these deaths from shock could have been prevented if veterinary care had been provided quickly. If your iguana is injured, bleeding, is burned, has broken a bone, or just simply looks "wrong," call your vet!

# 5

# Iguana Health Concerns

### In This Chapter
- Parasites That Can Plague Your Iguana
- Threats to Your Iguana's Health
- Nursing Your Iguana Back to Health

Iguanas are, on the whole, quite healthy. If given the appropriate environment (cage, heat, and light, including sunshine and/or UVA and UVB light) and a good diet, these lizards can live for many years without any problems at all. In fact, most of the health problems iguanas have stem from inadequacies in the animal's care or environment. Finding these problems sometimes takes a bit of detective work.

Other problems can plague iguanas, too, including external and internal parasites. To keep your iguana healthy, use this chapter as a reference for yourself and your veterinarian. Keep it handy and refer to it whenever your iguana's health seems not quite right.

## Parasites That Can Plague Your Iguana

Parasites are, as the name suggests, organisms that live and feed on another creature. External parasites live on the surface of the skin. Internal parasites live either in the digestive tract (the most common) or in other organs. Most parasites do not intend to harm the creature on which they feed; after all, if the creature died, so would they. However, parasites do harm their host, by directly destroying tissue or depleting the blood supply, by using up the nutrients available in the food that is eaten, or by causing secondary infections.

> Parasites do harm their host, by directly destroying tissue or depleting the blood supply, by using up the nutrients available in the food that is eaten, or by causing secondary infections.

All reptiles and mammals have internal parasites. So if this is a normal thing, why should pet owners worry about it? Well, first of all, many wild animals die from their parasites—if not outright, then because of secondary problems. A heavy load of parasites may stress the immune system so much that the animal dies of a disease. Technically, the disease killed the animal, but it might not have succumbed had it not been carrying a heavy load of parasites. Parasites can cause other problems, too, including malnutrition.

In captivity, parasite loads (populations) can increase tremendously because the animal is being kept in a smaller place than it would live in naturally. In the wild, iguanas live in the trees and their feces drop far below them. In captivity, they are often exposed to their feces over and over again, and, depending upon the internal parasite involved, can become re-infested again and again. In addition, a reptile may be infested with more than one type of internal or external parasite, with the combination causing many different problems.

Some general symptoms of parasites might include:

- Failure to grow and thrive
- Failure to reproduce
- Lethargy
- Failure to gain weight or weight loss
- Refusal to eat or lack of appetite

## Don't Share Parasites!

The importance of good hygiene has been stressed several times in previous chapters, but I can't emphasize it enough. As a warning to you, humans are also vulnerable to infestations by many of the same parasites that plague iguanas. Many of these parasites are transmitted through poor hygiene practices when feces come into contact with water or food. Keep cage furnishings clean, never wash them in the kitchen sink, and always wash your hands after handling your pet.

Here are some ways to prevent the sharing of parasites between your iguana and yourself, and your iguana and other pets.

- Clean up feces often; at least daily, and more often is better.
- Food and water dishes must be emptied and washed daily.
- If your iguana doesn't eat, don't offer his food to another pet.
- Quarantine any new pet for at least 30 days.
- Always, always wash your hands after touching your iguana, the iguana's cage, or anything in the cage.

**Did You Know?**
By paying close attention to your pet's daily routine, habits and actions, you can more quickly see differences that might signal a health problem.

## The Parasite Life Cycle

All parasites require a host to live on. They do not and cannot live their life cycle without one. In addition, many parasites require more than one host during their life cycle. For example, hookworms are a very common parasite in the sunbelt states, and can infect people as well as dogs, cats, reptiles, and wildlife. Adult hookworms, in a host, produce eggs. These eggs are passed out of the host via the feces. The eggs, in the soil where the feces were deposited, hatch and release larvae. The larvae are picked up by new hosts (or the old one again) by invading a cut in the skin or by being ingested with grass or water.

## Diagnosing Parasites

External parasites can be recognized simply by looking at them. Figuring out exactly what type of mite your iguana has may require a look through a microscope, but ticks and mites can be recognized on or off the reptile. Internal parasites, however, require your veterinarian's help.

A fresh fecal sample is required to diagnose internal parasites. It's best if the sample is taken from very fresh feces, but if you cannot get it to your vet immediately, seal the sample in an airtight plastic bag (removing as much air as possible) and store it in the refrigerator. If you still haven't gotten to the vet by the next morning, discard this sample and take a new one when you can go to the vet's office. Samples that are too old will not give an accurate diagnosis.

Your vet can use a direct smear of the fecal material—smearing a small amount of feces on a glass slide—along with a stain such as methylene blue. Protozoans or eggs may be visible in the sample. Your vet may prefer to do a fecal flotation, because parasitic worm eggs will float in some solutions, enabling the slide placed at the top of a flotation to pick up the eggs.

# External Parasites

External parasites are unsightly, can damage your iguana's scales, and can threaten your iguana's health.

## Ticks

The most common external parasites are ticks. Ticks are blood-sucking parasites that often carry disease. They use their beak to dig into the skin and suck up blood. An infestation of ticks can deplete an iguana of his blood supply quite rapidly.

Ticks can be seen on the iguana's skin, often in spots where the skin and scales are softer, such as under the legs and necks. Ticks that are full of blood will look obviously swollen—sometimes bigger than a pencil eraser, depending upon the species of tick. Ticks not inflated with blood can be significantly smaller, sometimes just dot-like. An iguana with ticks may try to scratch them off or may have trouble shedding, especially in the area where the ticks are or have been.

Ticks can be removed one by one, by grasping them with tweezers close to the iguana's skin and gently pulling them out. To kill the tick, burn it or drop it in a jar of alcohol and then screw the lid on tightly. Do not flush it down the toilet; it may survive its trip downstream. Do not try to squash it between your fingers, either, because you will then be exposed to any diseases the tick may be carrying.

Clean the wound with some hydrogen peroxide and apply an antibiotic ointment. Watch as it heals to make sure it doesn't get infected.

## Mites

Mites are teeny, tiny little parasites no larger than the period at the end of this sentence. However, these tiny pests can cause a lot of damage because where there is one, there are thousands more. Mites also suck blood and although one single mite may not eat much, thousands can rapidly drain your iguana dry.

You may see mites on your iguana. They look like tiny red, brown, or black specks moving around. You may also see them on your hands after handling your iguana, or you may see them on the newspaper on the floor of the cage.

If you find one mite, which your vet can confirm, you need to thoroughly clean the iguana, the cage, the furnishings, and everything around the cage. Mites reproduce very quickly and just a couple will rapidly turn into zillions. Take your iguana into the bathroom and put him in the tub, but with no water. Rub baby oil all over your iguana (all over!) and then leave him in the tub with the bathroom door shut while you clean his cage.

Take the cage apart and clean the entire cage, furnishings, and bowls with a strong 30 percent bleach solution. Let everything air-dry with the bleach on it. Do not rinse—just let things dry.

When the cage has been put back together, go back to your iguana, and, using a mild soap, wash him off. Get as much of the baby oil off as possible, but don't be concerned if you don't get it all.

You may need to repeat this a couple of times to kill all the mites. However, if it seems as if this cleaning regimen is doing no good at all, you need to talk to your veterinarian about a mite insecticide. Make sure you use the product according to directions, because these products are toxic and can harm your pet if they are not used properly.

# Internal Parasites

Internal parasites are much harder to find than external parasites, and your vet will have to help you. Internal parasites can do a great deal of harm to your pet's health, so regular check-ups at the veterinarian—complete with fecal exams—are always a good idea.

Parasites may harm their hosts by:

- Sucking blood and causing blood loss (hookworms)
- Causing nutritional deficiencies (roundworms and others)
- Absorbing intestinal contents directly (tapeworms)
- Destroying the host's cells (coccidia)
- Obstructing the intestinal tract (roundworms)
- Obstructing the liver bile ducts (roundworms, tapeworms)
- Producing toxic substances (several)
- Triggering allergic reactions (several)
- Causing intestinal tract inflammation and infection (several)
- Suppressing the immune system (all)

## Diagnosing Parasites

Some specific symptoms of an internal parasite infestation might include:

- Mucus or blood in the feces
- More frequent than normal defecation
- Worms visible in the feces
- Change in appetite

- Change in behavior; loss of vigor
- Vomiting
- Death

## Roundworms

Although roundworms are more common in carnivorous reptiles, they can be found in iguanas, too. Roundworms live in the digestive tract and can absorb most of the nutrients your iguana eats, so even with a good diet your iguana could be malnourished. Roundworm larvae can migrate throughout your iguana's body, where they can cause secondary infections. Roundworm eggs can be identified in the feces. Treatment usually consists of giving Panacur (fenbendazole) at a dosage of 25 mg per kilogram of body weight (a kilogram is about 2.2 pounds), given orally once every two weeks for two to three treatments.

## Hookworms

Hookworms are, unfortunately, very common in reptiles. Hookworms live in the digestive tract, anywhere from the stomach to the rectum. They attach themselves to the intestinal wall and feed on blood. Blood in the stools is often the first symptom. Treatment usually consists of giving the iguana Panacur (fenbendazole) at a dosage of 25 mg per kilogram of body weight, orally, once every two weeks for two to three treatments.

## Tapeworms

Tapeworms in large numbers can cause malnutrition, intestinal dysfunction, and obstruction of the bowel or intestinal tract. To treat them, the usual course is Droncit (praziquantel) given orally

## Giving Your Iguana Oral Medication

Oral medications are those which the iguana must swallow: pills, capsules, or liquids. If medications are prescribed, your iguana obviously needs them and must take them. So how do you get them down his throat?

If you iguana is still eating, it's easy. For liquids, stand close to your iguana. Have the medication all measured and ready in one hand and a treat for your iguana in the other. Hold the treat (a strawberry, a slice of tomato, or a rose blossom) in front of your iguana and tempt him to take it. When he opens his mouth, squirt the medication in the back of his mouth. (Don't squirt it across his mouth so that it comes out the other side!) A syringe with the needle removed works really well for this. Let him take the treat and eat it. For pills or capsules, hide the medication in the treat and hand-feed him.

If your iguana is not eating, wrap him in a towel with his legs flat against his sides and his head exposed. If your iguana is very small, use the side of a spoon to GENTLY open his mouth. Pop the medication in the back of his mouth and then pop a tiny bit of food in his mouth, too, so that he swallows. If your iguana is large, pull down GENTLY on his dewlap, up near his chin (not down near his throat) so that he opens his mouth on his own. Give him the medication and a bit of food.

or by injection at 5 mg per kilogram of body weight. A second treatment should follow in two weeks.

## Pinworms

Pinworms are usually transmitted through contact with contaminated water. Cage cleanliness is very important to prevent them! These worms live in the lower digestive tract. Treatment consists of giving Panacur at the same dosage as for hookworms and roundworms.

## Protozoans

Protozoan parasites are relatively common in reptiles. Cleanliness is vital to preventing these infestations. Coccidia is one of the most common protozoans and is usually passed in food or water contaminated by feces. Diagnosis is based on fecal examination. Treatment is usually Albon (sulfadimethoxine) at 50 mg per kilogram of body weight for three days, no medication for three days, and then repeating the treatment for three more days.

## Flagellates

These protozoans are found in reptile intestinal tracts so often that many experts believe they are normal intestinal flora. However, large numbers accompanied by diarrhea, anorexia, blood in the feces, or other intestinal disorders should be treated as a problem. Treatment is usually one dose of Flagyl (metronidazole) orally, 25mg to 50 mg per kilogram of body weight, with a follow-up dose in three days.

# Threats to Your Iguana's Health

Iguanas, by nature, hide their health problems as much as possible until they are too sick to do so anymore—and then it's often too late to do anything. So iguana owners must be masters of the details. Look at every little thing and make note of any changes. Those details could be the key to your iguana's good health.

## Abscesses

These infected wounds are often caused by an injury or bite. Bacteria in the wound causes a buildup of pus. Closed abscesses will require veterinary care to open and drain, and antibiotic treatment will be necessary.

## Anorexia (Loss of Appetite)

Male iguanas will stop eating—or at least slow down—during breeding season. Females will stop eating just before laying their eggs. Iguanas will not eat as much when their temperature is too cool, either. But an iguana kept at the correct temperature should eat well consistently.

Loss of appetite could also be caused by:

- Changes in the cage or environment
- External or internal parasites
- Intestinal obstruction (foreign body)
- Liver disease
- Kidney disease

> Male iguanas will stop eating—or at least slow down—during breeding season.

Oral or force-feeding may be necessary until you and your veterinarian can accurately determine what is causing the anorexia.

## Bacterial Diseases

These diseases are fairly common in reptiles, including iguanas, and are often caused by opportunist bacteria that infect an iguana with a weak immune system. Your veterinarian will need to decide which bacteria (and what kind) is causing the problem and what antibiotic should be used to treat it. In addition, any environmental conditions leading to the infection will need to be corrected.

## Constipation

Iguanas do not necessarily defecate every day. Much depends upon what the iguana is eating and how much. However, the normal defecation cycle is probably every other day to every three days. You need to learn what is normal for your iguana and then watch for changes.

Constipation can be caused by:

- Internal parasites
- Anorexia
- Kidney disease
- Imminent egg laying
- Chronic metabolic bone disease

The first thing to do is to soak the iguana in a lukewarm bath. Repeat daily (or twice daily) for three days. If the warm baths don't work, veterinary care is needed.

## Dermatitis

Skin infections can be caused by bacteria or fungus, and are usually the result of something in the iguana's environment. This could be too much humidity, parasites, contaminated water, or a number of other problems. The dermatitis can be treated but the environmental problem must be corrected, too.

Small blisters are caused by blister disease, which, in turn, is caused by incorrect husbandry. Dirty, damp cages can cause this disease, which begins with small blisters that can rapidly turn into large sores and ulcers. This can kill an iguana in a short period of time.

> Skin infections can be caused by bacteria or fungus, and are usually the result of something in the iguana's environment.

## Mouth Rot (Stomatitis)

Mouth rot, which is a good name for this disease, is very difficult to cure. Deep pockets of pus develop in the mouth, along with significant swelling. Symptoms include drooling, increased salivation, and redness of the tissues in the mouth. Pneumonia often accompanies mouth rot.

Soft diets that rely too much on fruits are blamed for some cases of mouth rot. But some experts believe mouth rot is probably the precursor to metabolic bone disease.

## Diarrhea

Diarrhea is a symptom that something is not right. It could be caused by bacteria, contaminated food or water, salmonella, a poor diet, or parasites. Diarrhea lasting more than two days must be treated by a veterinarian, because your iguana could become dehydrated and die. In addition, the environmental problem must be taken care of.

## Egg-Binding (Dystocia)

Female iguanas that are nine inches long from nose to vent are large enough to lay eggs. If they have not been with a male, the eggs, obviously, will not be fertile.

# Metabolic Bone Disease

Metabolic bone disease (MBD) is a horrible disease, but is totally preventable with a good diet. Malnutrition caused by a poor diet or an inappropriate diet, even in iguanas that are not underfed, will cause MBD. More captive iguanas die from metabolic bone disease (MBD) than any other single cause.

All of the following health problems are, or can be, directly related to MBD:

- Anorexia
- Bleeding
- Constipation
- Gingivitis
- Mouth rot
- Egg-binding
- Failure to thrive
- Curvature of the spine
- Seizures and tremors
- Swelling of the legs, jaws, eyes, and abdomen
- Broken bones or softening of the bones

So what is this dreadful disease? When the iguana is not metabolizing enough calcium, the body robs it from bones to supply what is needed elsewhere. Because calcium is so important to the blood, in heart functions, muscle function, and the metabolism of food, it must be present in sufficient quantities. Obviously, this theft of calcium from the bones can't continue and eventually the body begins to break down and all of the problems I've just listed begin to show up.

Treatment begins with correcting the diet—adding more vegetables that are high in calcium, such as collard greens, turnip greens, mustard, and kale). UVB lighting must be used as well, and when possible, time outside under the sun. Some veterinarians also treat MBD with injections of calcium, vitamin $D_3$, and calcitonin. Oral neocalglucon may also be prescribed.

The sad thing about MBD is that it is so deadly to iguanas but is so easily prevented.

It is important to always have an appropriate place to lay eggs in the cage of female iguanas. This could be a plastic box with a lid and a hole in the side large enough for her to crawl through. It should be filled half full of damp potting soil.

If there is no box available, your female may hold the eggs in, and this could severely threaten her health—sometimes to the point where surgical intervention might be needed.

Very young female iguanas sometimes begin to produce eggs before their bodies are fully mature. They may not have enough calcium in their system to place shells around the eggs, or have enough calcium to lay them. These females usually need veterinary assistance.

## Failure to Thrive

Most young iguanas will triple in size their first year. Any iguana that doesn't grow rapidly may be suffering from MBD, or there may be something incorrect in the environment. The appropriate heat, light (UVB), and correct photoperiods are needed for this rapid growth. A good diet, too, is essential.

> Most young iguanas will triple in size their first year. The appropriate heat, light (UVB), and correct photoperiods are needed for this rapid growth.

## Gout

This problem is characterized by swollen joints, especially in the feet and toes. It happens because there is too much meat in the diet, producing too much uric acid in the iguana's bloodstream and the uric acid begins depositing crystals in body tissues, especially the joints, lungs, and kidneys.

Gout is usually caused by the iguana eating animal protein. These herbivores cannot metabolize animal protein properly, and gout is the result. Changing the diet usually corrects the problem, although bad cases need veterinary help.

# Common Iguana Health Problems, and What to Do

| Problem | Possible Causes | Treatment Options |
|---|---|---|
| Bloating | Intestinal blockage | See vet |
|  | Internal parasites | See vet |
|  | Spinal injury | See vet |
|  | Metabolic bone disease | See vet |
|  | Kidney failure | See vet |
| Bumps and Lumps | Burns | Check lights, lamps, and sources of heat; see vet |
|  | Wounds | Clean; medicate; find cause |
|  | Tumor on old beardie | See vet |
|  | Abscesses | See vet |
|  | Blisters, blister disease | See vet; clean and dry cage |
|  | Eggs (for females) | See vet |
| Constipation | Not enough fiber | Change diet |
|  | Overfeeding | Change diet |
|  | Obesity | Change diet and increase exercise |
|  | Anorexia | See vet |
|  | Kidney disease | See vet |
|  | Imminent egg laying | Make sure female has an egg-laying box |
|  | Internal parasites | See vet |
|  | Metabolic bone disease | See vet |
| Diarrhea | Internal parasites | See vet |
|  | Too many fruits | Change diet |
|  | Bacterial infection | See vet |
|  | Salmonella infection | See vet |
| Egg-Bound | Failure to lay eggs | Provide a box with potting soil |
|  | Not pregnant | No problem |
|  | Unable to lay eggs | See vet |
|  | Eggs resorbed | See vet; improve diet; check for parasites |
| Loss of appetite | Gravid female | Provide egg-laying box |
|  | Breeding season male | Will go away |

| Problem | Possible Causes | Treatment Options |
|---|---|---|
| Loss of appetite (continued) | Environmental stress | Maintain a stable environment |
| | Environment too cool | Raise temperature |
| | Stress from other beardies | Keep alone |
| | Infection | See vet; clean cage; improve husbandry |
| | Metabolic bone disease | See vet; improve diet and husbandry |
| | Intestinal blockage | See vet |
| | Parasites | See vet; improve husbandry |
| Mouth Breathing, Sneezing, Runny Nose | Infection | See vet |
| | Allergic reaction | See vet |
| Mouth Rot, Drooling, Deformed Jaw | Trauma to mouth | See vet |
| | Too much soft food, fruits | Change diet; see vet |
| | Gums exposed | Metabolic bone disease; see vet |
| Poor Shedding (Dysecdysis) | Malnourishment | Change diet |
| | Injuries | Help the shed with baby or mineral oil |
| | Mites | See vet; eliminate mites |
| | Skin infections | See vet |
| | Air too dry | Soak in tepid water |
| Protrusions | Prolapsed intestine | Diarrhea; see vet |
| | Prolapsed hemipenis | Many possible reasons; see vet |
| | Prolapsed vagina (females) | Many possible reasons; see vet |
| | Tongue | Many possible reasons; see vet |
| Twitching, tremors or seizures | Lack of vitamin $D_3$ and calcium | Supplement vitamin $D_3$ and calcium. Increase exposure to fluorescent reptile light and/or sunshine |
| Partial paralysis/ hind leg extension | Prey too large | No treatment options |
| Vomiting | Intestinal blockage | See vet |
| | Poisoning | See vet |
| | Kidney failure | See vet |

## Respiratory Infections

Iguanas commonly sneeze, but these sneezes do not mean the iguana has a respiratory infection. Instead, iguanas sneeze to excrete salt. White, flaky material around the nostrils is salt; this is the body's way of getting rid of it.

However, iguanas can get respiratory infections. Upper respiratory infections involve the head and nose. Symptoms include a runny nose. Lower or chest infections are usually more serious and can turn into pneumonia. Symptoms include wheezing, gasping for air, and breathing through the mouth. Other symptoms may include a frothy discharge at the nose or mouth, reduced appetite, and reduced activity levels. Antibiotic treatment is usually recommended, but changes in husbandry may also be required because respiratory infections can be caused by an environment that is too humid, too cold, or too dry.

# When Your Iguana Changes Color

Iguanas do not change colors as completely as some chameleons can, but your iguana's color changes can give you clues to his physical health and emotional well-being.

Most hatchlings are bright green, sometimes almost fluorescent green. As they mature, most turn greenish-gray to gray, depending upon where they came from. Suriname Iguanas, for example, usually remain quite bright, often with blue overtones. Many Peruvian Iguanas are very gray. It's important that you know the normal color of your iguana.

During breeding season the males brighten. Some,

## The Most Common Drugs for Iguanas

I am not providing this information so that you can diagnose or treat your own pet. I am providing it as a resource for you and your veterinarian to better care for your pet. Your veterinarian may decide on another treatment option, and I encourage you to follow his or her advice.

External Parasites:

- Ivermectin 10 mg/ml = .01 ml/lb body weight by mouth, subcutaneous, or intramuscular

Internal Parasites:

- Panacur (fenbendazole) 100 mg/ml = 25 mg/kg by mouth, once every two weeks for two to three treatments
- Albon (sulfadimethoxine) 50 mg/kg, for three days, stopping for three days and then repeating the treatment for three more days

Bacterial Infection:

- Baytril (enrofloxacin) 23 mg/ml = 5 mg/kg every 24 hours; intramuscular initially, then by mouth
- Amikacin sulfate 50 mg/ml = 2.5 mg/kg every 72 hours; intramuscular

especially the populations from Mexico south into Central America, have bright orange coloring on the legs and sides. Some from Venezuela have bright pink overtones on the face, spines, and legs.

An iguana that is cold will be very dark. In the wild, this would help the iguana warm up, since darker colors absorb heat faster. However, an iguana that turns very dark, almost black, is usually hurt and should be checked out immediately. If you can't find what's wrong, take him to your vet.

A muddy color—grayish-greenish-brown—means something's wrong. The iguana may have an infection, is constipated, or has a bellyache. You need to check it out and see what's wrong. A muddy color is not as much of an emergency as is the very dark color.

If your iguana is lying motionless in his cage and has turned a yellow-mustard color, get him to the vet immediately! This color usually means shock and imminent death.

## Behaviors That Signal Health Problems

Your iguana cannot tell you, verbally, that he has a bellyache or an earache. He must rely on your observation skills to notice that something is wrong. However, he can sometimes show you with his actions or behaviors that there is a problem. You just need to watch him!

Agitation or irritability can occur just before your iguana sheds, or just before breeding season. Females often get irritable just before they lay their eggs or if they are egg-bound. Iguanas suffering from pain may become very irritable, may change color and darken, and may flip their tail from side to side.

Head bobbing is usually a territorial behavior, telling the world (especially other iguanas), "Hey, this is my area!" However, agitated, rapid head bobbing may be followed by a bite, so watch carefully as you approach an iguana rapidly bobbing his head, especially if the head is also twisting or turning sideways as it bobs.

Excessive hiding suggests a severe problem. The iguana is severely stressed, ill, injured, or is reflecting his reaction to his environment.

## Nursing Your Iguana Back to Health

Although iguanas can be somewhat delicate

and can easily die when ill or injured, injuries and sickness do not have to be a death threat. Many, many iguanas have recuperated from injuries or illness and lived long, healthy lives. However, your iguana will need your help to do so.

First of all, follow your veterinarian's instructions regarding medications. If antibiotics are to be given for 10 days, give them for 10 days even if your iguana is looking better after six days. The full course of treatment is important for any medication.

Keep your veterinarian posted regarding any changes in your iguana's condition. Those changes may or may not be important, so give your vet the information and let him (or her) decide how important they are.

Cold-blooded reptiles—including iguanas—cannot run a fever when they are sick, so they require hot environmental conditions to heal. The basking spot should be heated to 95°F—100°F is better—and let the rest of the cage cool to room temperature. Make sure the rest of the cage is cooler so that your iguana can regulate his own temperature—moving from the heat to the cool and back to the heat—as his body needs.

Don't allow your iguana to dehydrate. Make sure clean water is always available plus Gatorade or Pedialyte can be given to your iguana by eyedropper or syringe several times a day.

Offer your iguana a good, balanced diet, complete with vitamin and mineral supplements as needed, but also provide special foods your iguana always likes to eat. These special foods can be used to tempt a reluctant eater.

Keep stress levels to a minimum. Don't take your iguana outside now, or fit him with a new harness. Don't let the

**Did You Know?**
Ticks cannot penetrate a lizard's scales but will work their way between scales, penetrating the softer skin underneath.

dog or cat harass him, and see to it that the kids in the family to leave him alone.

## Don't Procrastinate!

Iguanas can live long and healthy lives in captivity. Good food, a proper environment, and your observation skills can all help your iguana achieve that long life. However, if you notice a problem developing, don't procrastinate. Begin working on solving that problem right away, because by the time your iguana shows you there is a problem, it has probably been developing over time. Quick action is often necessary.

# 6

# Iguana Body Language and Behavior

**In This Chapter**
- Reading Iguana Body Language
- Understanding Iguana Behaviors
- Each Iguana Is an Individual

We humans are used to seeing the body language that other people use to communicate. We may or may not respond to it consciously, but we do respond to it. For example, when you are talking to someone and that person crosses his arms across his chest and steps back from you, you subconsciously understand that he is reacting negatively to what you are saying.

Iguanas use body language, too. In the wild or in association with other iguanas or even other animals (such as predators), they use it to communicate. In captivity, an iguana uses it to communicate with you, even if you don't always understand or respond appropriately. The more you know about your iguana's body language and the more you understand about his behavior, the easier it will be to interact with him.

## Reading Iguana Body Language

Body language is used to convey a message. The message may be subtle, such as a tongue flick at a flower that says, "I'm going to eat this flower." Or it may be very drastic, such as a full-body display to another male that says, "I'm bigger and more masculine than you!" The body language of iguanas is relatively crude, especially when compared to the body language of humans. Iguanas lack the many facial muscles that allow mammals to twitch a nose, wiggle a whisker, curl a lip, or sneer. Lacking these facial expressions, iguanas use larger, wider, bigger movements to express themselves.

This isn't to say that iguana body language is lacking in any way; it certainly seems to work for them! However, when we look at body language, we're used to looking for facial expressions, so iguana body language is a whole new game. But the more you recognize the various phrases of your iguana's body language, the better your understanding of his behavior will be.

### Head Bobs

Head bobs are the first bit of body language that most iguana owners recognize. When an iguana bobs his head, it looks as if his head has been disconnected from the bones in his neck, because the head moves so freely. It bobs up and down quickly, fluidly and without the muscular restrictions we might have with such a movement.

Both sexes bob their heads, although males do so more than females and the most dominant male iguanas bob even more frequently. Head bobbing is also more prevalent during breeding season, although it does occur all year-round.

When an iguana bobs his head, he might be conveying ownership of food, a perch, a basking spot, or a territory. The head bob is also a greeting; sort of a greeting with a warning: "Ah ha! I see you!"

A male greeting a female will bob his head to show her the size of his head, his dewlap, and his jowls—a display of his masculinity. The head bobbing will be combined with the rich coloring of breeding season and may or may not be combined with other body language displays, depending, of course, on her answer to his head bobs.

A male with a female will bob his head to claim ownership of both the female and the territory. This head bob will probably be combined with brighter coloration (especially during breeding season) and may or may not be combined with other body displays.

Iguana owners often see one or two gentle head bobs when they greet their lizard, or when they enter the lizard's room or space. This is a greeting: "I see you."

Rapid, jerky head bobs signal that the iguana is in a bad mood: "Leave me alone!" or, when it's breeding season, "I'm a man!" These rapid bobs often signal an aggressive mood and you should be very watchful. Although the presence of a female may make this response stronger, a female is not necessary—the male iguana still knows it's breeding season!

**Did You Know?**
Iguanas are, in the wild, prey species. Other species catch and eat them. That's why your iguana (especially while young) will try to escape from you.

## Still the King

Each evening we try to make time to bring Conan out of his room and cage so that he can spend time with us. We usually place him on a large towel on the back of the sofa. Here he can relax, watch what's going on around us, and yet feel safe.

One day while he was out, Conan noticed our new baby iguana, Draco, and jumped down from the sofa back to walk over to Draco's cage. They looked at each other—the three-month-old baby and the then eleven-year-old veteran. Draco dashed behind a log in his cage and hid, just his eyes showing. Conan bobbed his head and inflated his dewlap—as if saying, "I'm still the king here, kid!" Draco wasn't about to argue!

A strong series of head bobs where the head also moves side to side, almost a twisting type of bob, signals definite aggression. You should always pay attention to these head bobs. The iguana is upset, aggressive, and is in no mood to put up with anything. This is not the time to trim his nails!

## Dewlap

The dewlap is the flap of skin under the iguana's lower jaw. Babies and juveniles have a very small dewlap that is hardly noticeable. Females have a small dewlap, too, but it's bigger in proportion than those of juveniles. Adult males develop a large dewlap, and very dominant males use their dewlap to communicate their dominance to the world.

The extent of the extension of the dewlap is a good indicator of the iguana's mood or level of excitement. The more extended the dewlap, the more excited the iguana is. The dewlap is extended from the jaw, neck, and chest when the iguana is using head bobs to convey messages. A "Good morning" head bob from iguana to his owner may be accompanied by a partially extended dewlap. A breeding season head bob from a male to a female iguana will be accompanied by a fully extended dewlap.

During breeding season, when the dominant male iguana will have brighter colors—perhaps orange, red, or pink—on his legs and shoulders, the dewlap, too, will show brighter coloration than the normal gray or green shown during the rest of the year.

## Tongue Flicking

An iguana usually flicks his tongue when he is curious about something or is exploring. If the iguana wants to explore a new piece of furniture, for example, as he climbs on the piece of furniture he will flick his tongue out very quickly, and then just as quickly pull it back into his mouth. It looks as if he is tasting the piece of furniture. The tongue may not be extended far; just enough to touch the item being investigated, and sometimes just enough that the tip of the tongue clears the mouth.

When the tongue flicks out and back in, it is picking up molecules from what is being investigated. These molecules are then passed to the Jacobson's organ in the roof of the iguana's mouth, which then analyzes the molecules. The information from the Jacobson's organ is part taste and part smell, and gives the iguana some additional sensory information about what is being investigated.

> An iguana usually flicks his tongue when he is curious about something or is exploring.

Iguanas will use tongue flicks to gain information as they are exploring new places and things. The tongue flicks seem to give the iguana information regarding the place—who has been here, what has been here and when—as well as whether the iguana himself has been there before.

The iguana will also use tongue flicks when offered food. If the food is familiar, there may be one tongue flick and then the food is eaten. If the food is unfamiliar, the iguana may do three or four tongue flicks before trying (or deciding not to try) the food.

During breeding season, the tongue flicks will come fast and furious if a member of the opposite sex is around. A female will tongue flick the air, while a male will tongue flick the air and every surface where the female has been, and will even tongue flick the female when he approaches her. A male will also tongue flick the air and surfaces if a rival male is nearby.

## Eyes

Because the iguana's face is made up of scales instead of skin, and because iguanas lack the many facial muscles that mammals have, the face is not as expressive as that of people, dogs, cats, or even horses. However, the iguana can use his eyes to convey messages and iguana owners quickly learn how to read those messages.

> The iguana can use his eyes to convey messages and iguana owners quickly learn how to read those messages.

When he's interested in something, the iguana will look at it. If it is a few feet away, the iguana will look at it straight on. If the object is close, the iguana will turn his head slightly, since there is a gap in his field of vision directly in front of his nose. Sometimes the iguana will turn his head slightly, look at the object with one eye, and then turn his head and look at it with the other eye. This usually signifies extreme interest, and the iguana usually follows up this type of staring by approaching the object and tongue flicking.

## Hissing

A hiss is not really body language, but it is a means of communication that many iguanas use. Iguanas hiss by filling their lungs with air and then rapidly expelling it. A hiss is usually a sign of unhappiness, and you may hear your pet hiss when you pick him up off his basking perch when he's relaxed and doesn't want to be disturbed. When he hisses, if you continue what you're doing with him, it can also be a signal that more aggressive behavior will follow, such a tail whip or a bite.

Hissing doesn't seem to happen between two iguanas or between an iguana and a predator. Instead, it seems to be a means of communication that iguanas have developed to use with their humans.

If the iguana is watching something that could be dangerous, such as the family dog or cat, he will usually position himself broadside to the predator and watch carefully out of one eye.

When faced with stress that he can't do anything about, an iguana will close both eyes as if to say, "If I don't see it, it isn't there." When we take Conan to reptile seminars or talks, when he's had enough of the people staring at him, he simply closes his eyes. He isn't asleep, he's just making the crowd go away by not looking at it. He will do the same thing when we trim his toenails.

## Spines and Enlarged Scales

The iguana's spines and enlarged scales are not an active part of his body language—he can't actually *do* anything with them—but they do serve as a means of communication. Scales and spines are both made of keratin and skin, with the stiffer, harder scales and spines containing more keratin than the smaller, softer scales.

Essentially, they are made of the same thing that fingernails, horns, hooves, and feathers are made of—they're just a different shape.

Large, dominant male iguanas develop large jowls with large scales. When the iguana bobs his head and inflates his dewlap, these large jowls with those oversized scales make him look even bigger, emphasizing his size and masculinity. This just places that much more emphasis on any body language he displays!

The spines on any iguana can help make the iguana look larger (especially when he's puffed up) and more dangerous to attack. After all, those spines could get stuck in your throat! In addition, when the iguana is trying to freeze or hide, the spines help conceal him by breaking up the lizard's outline.

## Tail Movements

An iguana's tail, which is important in his daily life for balance, is also an active part of his body language and a very potent weapon. When the iguana is relaxed, the tail will be relaxed also, usually lying directly behind him in a straight line from the spine. (Iguana tails are relatively stiff and most iguanas do not like to bend them or keep them bent.) As the iguana gets more excited, the tail will respond by showing tenseness or by moving.

> Iguana tails are relatively stiff and most iguanas do not like to bend them or keep them bent.

Much longer than the iguana's body, the tail gives him a weapon that can deter a predator before the predator is close enough to grab his body. When threatened, the iguana will turn sideways to the threat and the tail usually begins moving side to side, sometimes very slowly, as if the iguana is just warming up. Just before using the tail as a weapon—just before whipping it—

the iguana will twitch his tail. The whip will follow so quickly that you can't actually see it. You will just see the dog or cat move back quickly, startled and hurt, yelping or yowling!

If your iguana whips you with his tail, it can leave large welts on your skin. A big iguana's tail could even break the skin.

## Puffing Up

Size is important to iguanas. The largest iguana will be better able to hold on to prime territory and to impress females during breeding season. Larger iguanas are also more likely to scare off predators. Therefore, one of the iguana's best means of defense (and offense) is to appear larger.

Iguanas puff up by turning sideways to the threat, standing tall, inflating the lungs, and compressing the body laterally so that they appear twice as large. The spines along the spine make the iguana look even taller and larger. This puffing up is accompanied by head bobbing, an extended dewlap, a twitching tail, and often an open mouth that threatens a potential bite.

Puffing up should always be taken seriously. An iguana who is puffed up is ready for action and could easily bite you (probably more than once) and whip you with his tail.

## Learning to Look

As you can see, many of these single bits of body language are used together. A head bob might be accompanied by an extended dewlap and a tongue flick. A tail whip is probably part of a puffed up display. All of these pieces of body language go together to give us a way of understanding what our iguana is trying to convey—both to other iguanas and to us.

It's important to learn to watch our iguanas. Each iguana will use his own body language in a slightly different way. In addition, a long-term captive pet iguana will learn what works with his owner and what doesn't. Many have actually learned to change some of their responses. For example, Conan has learned that if he closes his eyes, Paul will leave him alone. Therefore, if Paul is petting Conan when he wants to be left alone, the iguana just has to close his eyes and Paul will stop. Because both Conan and Paul understand this; it works for them.

> Each iguana will use his own body language in a slightly different way.

## Understanding Iguana Behaviors

Iguanas have a tendency to respond in specific ways to specific situations. Some behaviors are the same with all iguanas, while others are particular to a certain group, such as breeding males or juveniles. Behaviors happen for a reason, usually because they provoke a response—either from other iguanas, from predators, or from you.

Behaviors are an extension of body language, which is why I've put them both in this chapter. It is very difficult to discuss one without the other.

### Biting

An iguana can give a dangerous bite. Luckily, bites are usually the iguana's last means of defense and long-term captive iguanas don't

## Olfactory Messages

Body language is dependant upon visual clues; we (and other iguanas) see the body language and react to it. But iguanas also use scents to communicate with one another.

Under the thighs of male iguanas are a row of large pores. These pores excrete a waxy substance that is full of clues to that particular iguana's individuality, state of health, pheromones, breeding readiness, and more.

As the iguana moves around his territory, this waxy substance rubs off on logs, rocks, perches or grass, and other iguanas can smell it, deciphering the messages it contains.

---

bite very often. When scared, cornered, or threatened, an iguana usually tries all of his other means of defense before he bites. He will puff up, hiss, whip his tail, and probably even try to run away. If none of those things work, then he may try to bite, but even an attempted bite may be just that—an open-mouth warning. If even that doesn't work, the iguana may then actually bite you.

Baby iguanas cannot do too much damage when they bite—they are too small and not yet strong enough to give you more than pinch. An adult iguana, however, can bite hard. Some bites require stitches! However, not every iguana bite will be such a hard bite. Sometimes the bite is a warning: "Hey! Back off!" If you respond correctly to the warning by stopping whatever it is you're doing, there will probably be no more bites. However, if you continue, the next bite might be harder.

## Anger

An angry iguana is a big iguana. Even a baby can make himself look much bigger than he really is, especially when he's angry. An

## Dropping the Tail

Iguanas, especially young iguanas, can drop or release part of their tail if they are attacked. If the predator grabs the lizard by the tail, the tail has several fracture planes where the vertebrae can actually separate fairly easily, releasing the end of the tail. That section of tail will continue to twitch for quite awhile, distracting the predator so that the iguana can escape.

Meanwhile, the blood vessels in the remaining tail close off, keeping blood loss to a minimum. The tail will re-grow—more quickly in young iguanas than in older ones—but the new tail is never quite as complete or pretty as the original tail.

angry iguana will inflate himself, perhaps puffing himself up, and will gape his mouth wide open while bobbing his head. His tail will probably be twitching and may even whip.

If he's being held, an angry iguana will also try to escape, and may shred you with his claws as he tries to do so. Those small, seemingly inconsequential toes have very sharp claws and can easily scratch, making you bleed.

It is rarely worth your time to try and reason with an angry iguana. So whenever possible, put him away and let him get over his anger.

## Defensive Fighting

An iguana who is cornered with no means of escape and feels that he is being attacked will fight in self-defense. In this situation, the iguana will most likely turn sideways and use his tail as a defensive weapon, whipping you or the predator. The iguana may also try to bite, and in cases of self-defense, the bite could be quite severe.

If you want to gain your iguana's trust, it's best to never put him in a situation where he feels he's cornered and must fight you. Once he's fought you and learned to think of you as the predator, it will take awhile for him to forgive and forget.

## Bluffing

When threatened, either by a predator or another iguana, some iguanas may try to bluff their way out of trouble. Bluffing usually occurs when the iguana is large and confident, or when the predator (or trespassing iguana) is small, or when the iguana is cornered and cannot escape.

The iguana will first inflate his lungs, puff up his body, and stand on tip toes so that he looks larger. He will turn sideways to the threat, again, to look bigger than he is. The spines along the backbone will help finish the larger-than-life picture. If the bluff continues, the iguana will open his mouth wide to look more intimidating.

Most bluffs don't have to go any further than this, but if they do, tail action will follow. The tail will twitch first, as if being aimed, and a tail whip will follow.

## Flight

Iguanas are herbivores, not carnivores, and although they do have some ways to defend themselves, their best defense is often running away. In the wild, iguanas are hunted and eaten by many predators, so hiding is also an important survival skill. However, being able to escape from danger is just as important.

> **Did You Know?**
> Although lizards can make noise, especially when threatened, they are not verbal creatures. Body language is much more important.

Taking flight from danger might mean jumping down from a tree and dashing to another one, running along the ground to find cover under some bushes, or even jumping from a tree into water and swimming away. Some iguana researchers have seen iguanas in Central and South America jump from very tall trees, some estimated to be 100 feet tall, into water. Those iguanas swam away without any sign of injury or distress from such a long leap.

> Iguanas are herbivores, not carnivores, and although they do have some ways to defend themselves, their best defense is often running away.

Although taking flight from danger is successful only when the iguana escapes that danger, running away usually doesn't mean running a long distance; iguanas are not track and field stars! However, iguanas are capable of moving very quickly for short distances.

## Freeze

When reptiles freeze in place, they are using natural coloration, a lack of movement, and their body outline to try to blend into the background. The iguana's natural gray, green, or brown coloration can disappear quite easily in the foliage of a tree. The stripes on the tail look much like the shadow of twigs in the tree, and the blotches of color on the iguana's sides look like shadows from leaves. The iguana's spines along the backbone help break up the lizard's outline even more, making him harder to see.

Many predators are also keyed to movement, so when a prey species freezes, it often seems to disappear into the background. The success of this behavior depends upon whether the predator knew the reptile was there in the first place and how well the iguana can hold the position without moving. For example, your

## Flight or Freeze?

What determines when an iguana will run from danger and when he will try to freeze and hide from it? Often the iguana's body temperature is the key.

When reptiles are cold, their body is less able to move quickly. Muscle movement, respiration, and blood flow are diminished, and fast movements are not as likely. A cold reptile is more likely to try and freeze in place, trying to appear invisible.

When reptiles are warm, however, the blood flow to their muscles and their rate of respiration are faster. Quick action is much easier, and many reptiles will then try to escape from danger rather than hide from it.

iguana may try to freeze in place when you approach him in the morning. You know he's there on his perch, so he isn't invisible at all, but he doesn't realize that. However, once you touch him, he knows his cover is blown, and at that point he may move, perhaps even running away.

## Defending Territory

Iguanas rarely try and defend their territory against other animals, especially those that could be predators, but they will defend their territory against other iguanas and sometimes against other lizards. Usually the largest and most dominant males show the most vigorous territorial defense, although large females may defend their territory against trespass by other females.

Defense usually begins with puffing up, turning sideways to the other iguana, gaping the mouth wide open, and sometimes whipping with the tail. Sometimes, if the two iguanas are evenly matched, there may be a fight but it rarely escalates to that point.

If two males live in close proximity to each other, however, such as sharing a cage, fights could erupt. The dominant male may eventually severely injure, maim, or even kill the less dominant male. Some dominant males cannot even share territory with a female except during breeding season. Iguanas can be very solitary creatures.

## Eating

Eating behaviors are usually fairly relaxed and often begin with tongue flicking. Once the food has been tested with a few flicks, eating begins.

Some pet iguanas will bob their head when they see their owner approach with their food dish. This is a greeting and shows the iguana's excitement for the food.

If you try to get your iguana to try a new food or to eat when he isn't hungry, he may refuse to do a tongue flick and may close his eyes. The closed eyes give the message, "If I don't see it, it isn't there!"

## Dominance

Dominant males are usually the biggest iguanas (or the ones who think they're the biggest!), and they emphasize their size by puffing up, standing tall, and inflating themselves. Dominance stand-offs usually begin with both males posturing straight on at one another or sideways toward one another. After some posturing, the smaller and usually less dominant male will lower himself, often to his belly, and will move away. Dominance stand-offs rarely turn into fights unless the males are in a small area and cannot get away from each other.

## Courtship

Courtship behaviors can be quite elaborate. The male's colors are usually bright, and he begins with head bobbing. Head bobbing will continue—often at a very rapid pace—throughout the courtship. The female may or may not bob her head in return, depending upon her mood and whether or not she is receptive to him. Other male courtship displays may include puffing up so that he looks larger, standing tall (again, so he looks larger), and tongue flicks up and down her body.

After breeding, the male may continue to stay close to the female, and will continue his head bobbing and courtship displays as long as she is receptive to breeding.

## Breeding Season Aggression

One of the few times your iguana can actually be a danger to you is during the breeding season. At this time (usually December through March in North America), large, adult, sexually mature males can be quite aggressive. They have been known to gape their mouth wide open at their owners, bob their head, puff up sideways, and charge at their owner. Charges may end with posturing or a single bite to the leg. Unfortunately, some males will charge and then actually attack their owner, climbing up the owner, biting multiple times, whipping their tail, and scratching with their claws. A large iguana can cause significant harm.

I will discuss breeding season aggression in more depth in chapter 9. Your best defense is to watch your iguana during breeding season, observing his body

> **Did You Know?**
> The spines on the iguana's back are made of keratin, just like your fingernails.

language for cues that signal aggression. When he starts bobbing his head at you quite vigorously and puffs up at you, leave him alone!

## Each Iguana Is an Individual

To understand your iguana's body language and his related behaviors, you must watch your iguana and pay attention to what he does.
What does he do when:

- You greet him in the morning. Does he bob his head at you very gently one or two times? Does he open one eye to acknowledge you and then go back to sleep?
- You feed him. Does he bob his head in greeting? Does he tongue flick the food? When you give him something new, does he investigate it with tongue flicks or does he close his eyes and wish it away?
- You trim his toe nails. Does he try to escape from you? Does he try to whip you with his tail? Or does he close his eyes and ignore you?
- You take him outside for some sunshine. Does he revert to being a wild animal and try to escape? Does he scratch you, trying to escape? Or does he hide in your arms knowing you will protect him?
- You rub gently under his jowls. Does he relax, taking a deep breath and sighing? Does he close his eyes?

The more you watch your iguana, the more you will see of his own unique body language. And of course, the more you see, the more you will understand!

# 7

# Can You Train Your Iguana?

### In This Chapter
- How an Iguana Thinks
- The Fundamentals of Training
- Housetraining

Anyone watching an iguana sleep on his basking log, opening one eye to acknowledge the arrival of his owner and then closing that eye again, might think iguanas are incapable of training—or even learning. After all, iguanas really don't look very intelligent.

However, iguanas are capable of learning if—and only if—they understand the advantages to them. That means there has to be some motivation for the iguana to learn. If you keep motivation in mind, you will be able to see how your iguana learns and you will find your iguana is much smarter than you ever suspected!

## How an Iguana Thinks

Keep in mind when you think about training your iguana that in the wild, the iguana is prey. He eats plants and everyone else eats him. Therefore, his mental processes are geared around self-defense and escape, finding and eating food, and reproduction. If he can successfully do these things, he is more likely to survive.

As a pet, he will still fight you if he feels threatened (more so before you tame him), but escape (especially in a cage or a small room) is severely restricted. You provide his food, so he doesn't have to search for that, and reproduction may or may not happen. In addition, captivity provides things like television, other pets, additional people, and a variety of other strange things a wild iguana never sees. In captivity, the iguana has the same instincts he had in the wild, but things around him have changed. You need to keep this in mind when you're training him.

Iguanas do have several mental characteristics that affect their ability to be trained and to accept training. Let's take a look at them.

### Awareness

Iguanas are very aware of what is going on around them. Again, as a prey species, they must be watchful, alert, and ready to escape. In fact, many owners say that owning an iguana is like having one of those pictures on the wall where the eyes seem to follow you all the time. The iguana may not move much and may appear to be a green bump on the log, but he is very much aware of you.

> Iguanas are very aware of what is going on around them.

This awareness can help you train him, since it's much easier to work with an animal who is aware of you rather than one who ignores you.

## Memory

You will find that your iguana has quite a good memory. Many iguanas, once hurt by a veterinarian, will remember that and will try to fight or escape if they see that vet again—or that vet's office. Iguanas will react differently to friends, acquaintances, and strangers.

Iguanas also remember places and things. If they are frightened or hurt in a particular place, that will be remembered and associated with that place. Iguanas don't forget. Good things are remembered, too, but those memories don't seem to be as strong. Perhaps fear and hurt make stronger memories because things that cause fear and hurt can threaten the iguana's survival.

This memory can aid you in training your iguana, if you take the training slow and keep it positive. You iguana is capable of learning words and their meanings. However, if you lose your temper and get angry or frustrated, your iguana will remember that, too.

## Reasoning Ability

The ability to think through problems is one measure of intelligence. Iguanas, of course, have no use for algebra or chemistry, but they do have some reasoning ability. The ability to think and reason is very important to training and learning. The iguana that thinks can put together the concept of a moving lure, the sounds you make in association with it, and the end result of getting to eat the lure. Sort of, "Ah ha! If I follow the stick with the strawberry on it and get down when I hear the sound 'down,' then I get to eat the good fruit." Obviously your iguana is not thinking in words, but that could well be his line of reasoning.

This ability to reason also comes into play when the iguana is moving around on his own. When an iguana is getting ready to jump, especially a long jump, you can see him thinking. Jumps are not made without thinking—the iguana isn't that athletic. Instead, jumps must be carefully thought out and planned. He will pose his body, adjust his feet, and twitch his tail as he looks toward his target, and sometimes, after thinking, the iguana will decide not to jump. You can see him relax and turn away. Obviously, he felt it was too far, he couldn't make it, or perhaps it just wasn't worth it after all.

## Stubbornness

Iguanas can have amazingly one-track minds. If an iguana is focused on something, it is very difficult to change his mind. For example, if your iguana is roaming the living room and decides to go to the kitchen, you can tell him "no!" a hundred times and it probably won't change his mind. The best thing to do when you're trying to change an iguana's mind is to change the situation or location. If he wants to go in the kitchen, take him to the bathroom instead. By changing the circumstances, you are more likely to change his mind or make him forget what he was thinking about in the first place.

> If an iguana is focused on something, it is very difficult to change his mind.

## Iguanas Like the Familiar

Your iguana will quickly come to recognize the people around him, especially the people (or person) who pay attention to him, pet him, and feed him. You will notice that he will be aware of strangers in your home and will react differently to them than he does to you.

This stubbornness can affect your iguana's training for the better or for the worse. If he wants to understand you, wants to do what you wish and is stubbornly trying to do it, then of course this trait is for the better. However, if your iguana puts on his stubborn hat and decides to ignore you, there isn't a whole lot you can do.

# Taming Your Iguana

If your iguana is still half wild or tries to escape from you whenever you try to handle him, you will need to tame him before you do any training. Training is really only effective with an iguana that is tame and trusts you.

Taming your iguana consists of frequent, brief handling sessions that are completely non-threatening to the iguana. You want your iguana to learn that you will not cause him harm; that you provide good food and comfortable petting.

Your goal when taming your iguana is to create a sense of calm in him so that you can handle him, pick him up, and carry him without the iguana feeling fear. A calm, trusting, non-fearful iguana is the result of frequent calm, gentle handling.

## Out of the Cage Calmly

One of the biggest mistakes iguana owners make is chasing their pet around the cage trying to catch him. If, every time your hand goes into the cage, the iguana is chased by this hand, your hand will become an incredibly scary thing. Pick up your baby iguana the first time you reach in—every time you reach in. Pick him up firmly around the ribcage with a finger or two or three (depending upon how big he is) under his chest between his front legs—holding him tightly so that he can't escape, but not so tightly that you cut off his breath or hurt him. As you pull him from the cage, place the rest of his body on your forearm and tuck his tail between your arm and side. His head should be above your hand, which is under his chest and between his front legs. His body is on your forearm with his hind legs hanging down on either side of your arm. His tail is behind you, between your arm and your body. In this position he is secure, held close to you, and he can't whip you with his tail.

If an iguana doesn't feel secure—if he feels like he might fall—he will dig in with his claws. Those claws on the fragile-looking toes may not look like weapons, but they are and they can easily draw blood. A baby iguana might not hurt you too badly, but a large adult iguana can claw chunks of flesh from you if he tries. It's not a bad idea to wear a heavy, long-sleeve shirt when handling and taming an adult iguana.

Once you have your iguana in hand and out of the cage, sit down and make yourself comfortable. You want to handle him slowly and gently, so take your time. Most iguanas like to have their forehead rubbed gently with one finger. Many also like to have their neck rubbed, especially under the chin and behind the jowls. You can also gently rub the body, especially along the spines and down the tail. Many iguanas are touchy about their feet, so don't handle the feet too much right now. The key is slow, gentle, calm handling so that you teach the iguana to trust you—that you aren't something to be afraid of.

## Hand-Feeding

Hand-feeding your iguana some treats is a sure way to teach him that you are not a predator but rather, are the source of good things. Instead of looking at you with fear, your iguana will look to you for snacks. Hand-feeding is also an important part of the training process, since you will be using treats as both lures and rewards.

Teaching your iguana to eat from your hand is not difficult. Offer your iguana a variety of different foods during mealtimes and watch to see what he likes. If you offer a selection of foods, what does he always eat first? Does he really like strawberries? Grapes? Cherry tomatoes? When you know about two or three different foods that your iguana always seems to enjoy, set these aside for hand-feeding.

Slice up his favorite food into bite-size pieces. Before you feed your iguana—when he's hungry—take a piece of the favorite food and offer it to him, moving your hand slowly into the cage. Let him sniff it and then hold it in front of him but slightly to one side. Remember, iguanas have a gap in their vision directly in front of their nose.

As your iguana takes the food from your hand, gently rub under his jowls or along his back next to the spines. When

**Did You Know?**
Many cultures believe that strong windstorms are the result of a legendary dragon flapping its wings.

he finishes that piece, offer him another and then rub him again. When your iguana will eat from your hand in his cage, try feeding him when he's out of his cage.

## When He Thrashes

If your iguana tries to escape from you and begins to thrash around, clawing with the feet and whipping with the tail, try not to let go. If your iguana learns that thrashing works, he will continue to do it. Instead, simply hold on to your iguana and try to protect yourself from harm until he tires out. He will tire out relatively quickly—iguanas don't have a lot of stamina. In addition, when he tires and finds himself in the same position, it will dawn on him that he didn't get away, all that energy was wasted, and perhaps thrashing wasn't such a good idea.

If you are holding your iguana properly, hand under the body, fingers between the front legs and the iguana's body along your forearm with the tail between your arm and body, you can control a lot of the thrashing. Try to keep the tail between your arm and body so that he can't whip you. Keep your fingers between the front legs under the chest. He may try to wiggle away, but if you keep hold there, the front claws can't do much damage.

The back claws, however, on either side of your forearm, can reach up and claw you as he thrashes. If your iguana is prone to thrashing, especially in certain situations, wear a heavy, long-sleeve shirt when handling your iguana. With a heavy shirt, at least you have some protection from those back claws.

Make sure you don't get angry when your iguana thrashes. This is an offshoot of the fight-flight instinct that protects your iguana in the wild from predators. As your iguana becomes more tame, the need to thrash will disappear. But right now, it is instinct that causes him to do this. He isn't hurting you on purpose, so don't get angry. If you just can't help getting angry, don't take your anger out on him. If you scare him, you will make the problem that much worse.

## An Ongoing Process

Taming your iguana is an ongoing process. If you leave your iguana in his cage for several weeks and then try to take him out for handling, he will be wild and you will have to tame him all over again. It's best to set up a regular handling routine and bring the iguana out for handling and attention each and every day.

# The Fundamentals of Training

When you think of training your iguana, don't expect to train him to jump through a hoop, count to 10, or ride a tiny bicycle. Those are not realistic expectations. However, you can teach your iguana to housetrain himself, to recognize his name and several other words, and even to respond to a few of them. Many iguanas learn to recognize a word that means they've made a mistake or should stop what they're doing. Of course, recognizing the word and actually stopping the action are two different things. Setting reasonable goals is important when you're training your iguana!

> You can teach your iguana to housetrain himself, to recognize his name and several other words, and even to respond to a few of them.

# A Target Stick

Using a lure is an easy and effective way to train your iguana, but only when your arm is long enough to put the lure where you want your iguana to go. What can you do when your arm just isn't long enough?

A target stick works like an extension of your arm. Go to the hardware store and buy a dowel. Three feet long is usually long enough. Then fasten a clothespin to one end (duct tape works well for this) so that the clip part faces outward. Now you can put the piece of fruit (or whatever you use as a lure) in the clothespin. Using the longer reach of the dowel, you can teach your iguana to move places where you can't reach—such as into his large cage or up on a high perch. If your iguana is already out of reach, you can use the lure to have him come down.

## Lures and Rewards

If you would like your iguana to do something—something that requires him to move—you need a lure. A lure can be a piece of strawberry, a cherry tomato, or a grape; something brightly colored, easily seen, that your iguana likes to eat. You can use the lure to encourage him to move.

For example, if you want to scrub down his basking perch or log, you can teach him the command "climb down." Choose a time when he is warm and ready to move. Hold the lure in front of his nose and tell him in a nice tone of voice, "Iggy, climb down." As he takes a step or two toward the lure, praise him, and let him have the treat. Then, with another piece of treat, lure him forward another step or two, moving him toward where you wish him to be. When he's off the basking perch, give him a final treat, rub his jowls or forehead, and in a happy tone of voice, tell him what a wonderful iguana he is.

The piece of fruit acted as a lure to encourage the iguana to move—to follow it—and also acted as a reward. When he took a couple of steps forward, you gave him the piece of fruit—that's the reward. When he finished what you asked him to do (even though he simply followed the lure), you gave him another piece of fruit plus you rubbed his forehead and praised him in a happy tone of voice. The rubbing and praise are also rewards.

The key to using lures and rewards is that these must be things your iguana likes. It doesn't do any good to try to train him using a strawberry as a lure and reward if he doesn't like strawberries. So do some experimenting when he's hungry and try a few things. See what food or foods your iguana really likes, and use one or more of those as lures and rewards.

## When Your Iguana Makes a Mistake

If you share your house with a dog, you know that dogs are very sensitive to your voice. A sharp "Bad dog!" will devastate some dogs—the dog may even slink off and hide. Many iguanas, however, seem to be immune to verbal corrections. In fact, there isn't much that makes an iguana feel bad, and this adds a whole new dimension to training.

Some iguana owners use a spray bottle with water in it to stop or interrupt bad behavior. Many times a spray in the face will stop an iguana in his tracks. However, many iguanas like to have water sprayed or misted on them, so make sure your iguana doesn't learn to do something you dislike because you spray him. The spray could end up being a reward instead of a correction!

**Did You Know?**
Reptiles have been feared and respected, and have been used as food, but were rarely ever domesticated.

Some iguanas will react to a harsh verbal correction, and it's certainly worth your while to try to teach your iguana that "No!" means "You've done something I'd rather you didn't do again." But keep in mind that your ideas of right or wrong have no meaning to an iguana. Your iguana has no idea why you get angry when he climbs the curtains, shredding them as he goes. Because he has no idea that is wrong, he also has no idea why you are so angry—nor does he care. Therefore, it's important to control your anger and temper. Teach your iguana the "no" correction as best you can, but also think about how to use alternative actions to curb unwanted behaviors.

## Alternative Actions

One of the worst things you can do with an iguana is argue with him. If he wants to do something, don't try to change his mind. Simply change his location or situation so that he forgets what he wanted in the first place.

In addition, if you know that your iguana likes to do certain things that you'd prefer he not do, plan ahead and offer him alternatives. If your iguana likes to climb—and most do—provide him with something to climb on so that he doesn't end up climbing up your curtains. The larger cat trees with a heavy base, carpeted poles, and large beds at the top are perfect for big iguanas. Most iguanas can climb the carpet fairly easily, and with a little practice, learn to maneuver over and through the holes and play areas on the cat tree. A heat lamp mounted above the cat tree can be turned on when the iguana is perched there. In addition, many of these cat trees are attractive and can be left in the living

> One of the worst things you can do with an iguana is argue with him.

## Time Out

A time out is a good training tool for when your iguana gets over-stimulated or excited. When he's thrashing, trying to escape from you, trying to bite or whip you, or otherwise acting in an undesirable manner, simply put him back in his cage.

Since most iguanas enjoy their time out of the cage, this does serve as a time out. However, don't put the iguana in his cage and then yell at him—he won't understand—nor should you deprive him of food and water. Just put him away and leave him alone for awhile. Later, when he's calmed down, you can bring him back out.

room or family room. When you want to take your iguana out of his cage so that he can spend time with you and the rest of the family, he can be perfectly comfortable yet out of trouble on the cat tree.

## What Can You Teach an Iguana?

What you decide to teach your iguana will depend on you, your iguana, and how much patience you have. Many iguana owners are satisfied if their iguana just relaxes when he's held. Other iguana owners like to see how much their iguana can learn.

Here are some ideas:

- Recognize his name. Use a happy, higher-than-normal tone of voice when you say his name, and follow it with petting or a treat.
- Come when called. Use a lure to lead the iguana in to you.
- Follow the target stick and lure.
- Go back to your cage. Use a treat or the target stick and lure.
- Come out of your cage. Use a treat to lead him out.

## Can You Teach "No Bite?"

Biting is one of an iguana's few means of self-defense, so trying to train an iguana not to bite when he's afraid will be very difficult. Some iguana owners have tried to teach the concept of "no bite" by verbally correcting the iguana each time he tries to bite. Whether this is entirely successful is debatable; it may stop an occasional casual bite, but a truly fearful bite will not be stopped by any words you speak.

What is much more successful is the taming process itself. If your iguana is tame, calm, and trusting of you, then he has no need to bite.

You can also teach him tricks if you want to. Some iguana owners have taught their iguanas to stand up (lifting the front half of their body up) for a treat. I have seen iguanas who will bob their head in response to a hand signal mimicking a head bob. It's up to you; how talented a trainer are you?

## Housetraining

People who don't have an iguana are flabbergasted to know that iguanas can be housetrained. It's simply expected from dogs and cats, but most people do not expect that kind of self-control from a reptile. Iguanas, however, are for the most part, very clean and usually choose one place to relieve themselves. You can use this tendency to go in one spot to housetrain your iguana.

Most iguanas go to the floor of their cage, so if your iguana likes to go in one specific spot, place a cat litter box in that spot. Use a cat litter made from recycled paper products—not a clay or

clumping litter. Your iguana may decide to taste the litter, and the paper products will not hurt him should he swallow some, while the clay or clumping litter could cause severe intestinal damage.

If your iguana doesn't recognize the box as a place to relieve himself, take the box out of his cage for a few days. Put newspaper in the spot where the iguana relieves himself, and keep clean paper there. When the iguana is regularly relieving himself on the paper, cut the paper so that it matches the size and shape of the litter box and keep placing it in that spot. After a few more days, place the paper there and sprinkle some of the clean litter on top of the paper. Not a lot—not enough to cover the paper—just enough to introduce the litter to your iguana. Do this for a few days. If your iguana is OK with this, pick up the paper, place the litter box in its place, and put the newspaper in the box with a little litter sprinkled on top of the paper. Again, do this for a few days. When the iguana is using the box with the paper, sprinkle more litter on the paper, and then a few days later, even more litter. When the paper is covered with litter and the iguana is using the box reliably, stop using the newspaper.

> People who don't have an iguana are flabbergasted to know that iguanas can be house-trained.

When your iguana uses the litter box, clean up after him right away. Many iguanas will not go back to the box if it is already soiled.

If you want to change the location of the box after the iguana is already using it, move it gradually (inches at a time) toward the new spot. Do not move it abruptly! Your iguana doesn't like change, and may refuse to use it in the new spot if you change the location too quickly.

## The Magic of Water

Many iguanas prefer to relieve themselves in water. This can be a very dirty habit, especially if the iguana relieves himself in his drinking water. (Of course, in the wild he would be in running water, which would quickly carry his wastes away.) For health and cleanliness, try to housetrain your iguana to use a litter box with litter in it.

However, if your iguana insists on going in water, you will have to be on top of things and make sure the water container is emptied right away, cleaned thoroughly with bleach, and rinsed before you refill it with water.

You can use this tendency to your advantage, though. If you will be taking your iguana outside, to the vet's office, or to a reptile event, place him in some warm water before you leave. After a few minutes he will probably relieve himself. Then, when you take him out with you, you know he's already done what needed to be done!

## Relax!

Most iguanas have a spot that, when rubbed, totally relaxes them. When we rub Conan on his forehead and behind his jowls, he acts as if he is hypnotized. He closes his eyes, goes limp, and is totally relaxed. You can use this to teach your iguana to relax in your arms.

When holding your iguana on one arm, in the correct position, begin rubbing him with the other hand. Rub the spot or spots he likes as you gently and quietly talk to him. When he is relaxed and not fighting you, either let him sleep (if he's fallen asleep) or offer him a special treat. Then put him back in his cage or on his cat tree. The trick is to stop before he begins thrashing.

Although you don't want to teach your iguana that when he thrashes you will release him, you also don't want him to hurt you when he claws your arms. So by teaching him to be calm and relaxed when you hold him, you can avoid the whole situation. Begin slowly, encouraging him to be calm for just a minute or two at a time. As he trusts you more, you can try to keep him calm for longer periods of time.

Ultimately, you will want to be able to keep him calm when you take him outside or go to the veterinarian's office. If you think that's asking too much of him, it isn't. In fact, it's very realistic. But it requires training and trust.

## Taking Your Iguana Outside

Be very cautious about taking your iguana outside, away from his outside cage or your securely fenced yard. Many iguanas feel threatened and vulnerable outside, and many otherwise tame iguanas have freaked out and escaped from their owners. If you decide to take him outside, use an iguana harness and leash.

There are a variety of harnesses and leashes available to iguana owners. Choose a harness that will fit snugly around your iguana's front legs and up the sides without crushing his spines. The leash should attach to the harness above the spines. Do not use a harness that constricts or puts pressure on the neck or chest—these can cause harm and even break an iguana's bones.

### Introducing the Harness

Don't introduce the harness and take your iguana outside all at the same time. That's how iguanas learn to hate their harness. Instead, put the harness on your iguana just before you

## Making a Harness

You will need a piece of newspaper to make a pattern for the harness. The harness will have a roughly rectangular shape, so cut a rectangular piece of paper from the newspaper that is long enough to reach from one inch above your iguana's spines, under the iguana's chest and back up to one inch above the spines.

Now mark the newspaper pattern where you need to cut holes for your iguana's front legs. Figure out how big a circle you need and how far apart the two circles should be. Cut the leg holes out of the newspaper. Try the paper harness on your iguana to make sure the leg holes are correct.

While the paper harness is on your iguana, check the width. It should be wide enough to have a little excess material in front and back of the leg holes but not so wide that it's bulky or inhibits your iguana's movement. If you need to trim some width, mark the paper harness now.

Bring the two ends of the paper harness up above the spines. You will need to cut a hole in each side for the leash to attach, so with the two ends held up, note where the spines end and mark a hole slightly above the spines. Mark, too, where you need to trim excess length.

Take the pattern off and lay it on a small piece of soft, cured leather. Cut the leather to match your pattern, making sure to place the leg and leash holes correctly.

Place the softest side of the leather next to your iguana's body.

feed him and let him wear it for half an hour or so as he's eating. Then take it off. Do this two or three times over the first week.

Then put the harness on him when you have him out of his cage with you. Pet him and hand-feed him while he's wearing his harness. You want to teach him that positive things happen when he's wearing the harness.

When he is comfortable with the harness and doesn't fight it, then you can take him outside.

## The Great Outdoors

Make sure the harness and leash fit him and are secure—not constricting tight, but tight enough that he can't escape. Have on a long-sleeve shirt to protect yourself, and take your iguana outside by carrying him in the correct position.

Once outside, place him somewhere other than on the ground. A retaining wall is good, as is a hedgerow of bushes or someplace else that is off the ground. Your iguana will feel very vulnerable on the ground and much more secure raised up a little. However, don't put him in a tree unless you are a very, very good tree climber!

Hold on to your iguana's leash (he may try to dash), but otherwise just let him relax and look around. If he starts to panic, take him back inside. Five to 10 minutes is good for the first excursion. Later, as your iguana gets more relaxed outside, you can extend the time you take him out.

Don't leave him alone outside on his leash. It's too easy for him to get it tangled and hurt himself, or to thrash around and hurt himself. Worse yet, he could thrash around and get loose. Outside on the leash, your iguana is also extra vulnerable to attack by birds of prey or passing dogs. So to protect him, stay outside with him.

## Walking on the Leash

Teaching your iguana to walk on a leash really means you will learn to walk with your iguana as he decides to walk. You

> **Did You Know?**
> Your lizard, if fed and watered daily, can go for a few days without handling should you get busy. However, if alone too long, you will have to re-tame him all over again.

will go where he wants to go—not the other way around. You can encourage your iguana to walk with you by using the target stick and a really good treat, but even the tamest, most intelligent, nicest iguana is going to have his own agenda, and it's usually not the same as yours!

If you want your iguana to go somewhere specific, pick him up and carry him there—don't drag him on the end of the leash. That will build negative connotations about the leash and your iguana will soon fight you every time you try to take him out. Dragging him certainly won't make him walk!

## Training Requires Patience

Training an iguana requires a great deal of patience on your part. Your iguana can learn, and if you are patient enough, he will learn. But you can't force him and you can't shame him. You must simply help him and make it worth his while.

> Training an iguana requires a great deal of patience on your part.

You also need to set realistic goals. Your iguana will never walk as nicely on a leash as will a well-trained dog. That's just not important to an iguana. So instead, concentrate on the things that are realistic. Teach your iguana his name, to follow the target stick, and to rest comfortably in your arms without thrashing. Those are realistic iguana training goals.

# 8

# Routine Care

### In This Chapter

- Buy Your Iguana a Calendar
- A Clean Iguana
- Setting Up a Routine

One of the most important things you can do as a reptile owner is keep track of what's happened with your iguana. Having a journal or calendar is one way of remembering when your iguana last shed, when he broke a toenail, and how he reacted during the last breeding season. All of this information can be very important to his long-term health and care.

Your iguana will also need some ongoing, regular care to maintain his good health. Just as you need to brush your teeth and wash your hair regularly, your iguana will need to be bathed and have his nails trimmed. It's all part of keeping your iguana happy and healthy.

You will also have to spend time keeping your iguana's environment clean. A clean cage is much healthier for your iguana that a dirty one, of course (and smells much better!), and a clean cage is also nicer to have in your own house.

## Buy Your Iguana a Calendar

No, your iguana won't make notes on his calendar. He's smart, but not that smart! However, a calendar will help you keep track of things that have happened. You should note, first of all, the date you brought home your iguana and how old he was at that time. So many pet owners look back after a year or two and can't remember how old their pet is. "Did we get him after we bought the new car? No, we brought him home in the old one, but was it before we took Charlie to summer camp or after?" If you write it down and keep a calendar, there is no question about it!

Make note of things that happen with your iguana—even routine things. Jot down when he first shed after you brought him home, and then every time he's shed after that. This way you can see how long he goes between shedding and you can establish a pattern. Then, if he doesn't shed when it's time, you can decide whether or not there is a problem.

Make notes every day, such as, "Conan ate normally, enjoyed his strawberries, and defecated after his bath. I cleaned his cage and bleached it." Then, should there be a problem, first of all you can recognize it, and second, when you take your iguana to the veterinarian you can flip through the calendar and tell your vet what has happened and why you feel there is a problem.

When you first set up your calendar, include the following information:

- The iguana's name.
- Where did you get the iguana?
- How old is he?
- What do you know about him? Is he wild-caught? Captive-bred? Did you buy him or adopt him? Do you know if he is an <u>Iguana iguana</u> or another type of iguana?
- Is your iguana a male or female?
- How big is he? Include both length and weight.
- Include a photograph or two of your iguana when you brought him home.

Daily calendar entries can include information about such things as:

- Eating habits: what was eaten and what wasn't? Did your iguana eat well or did he refuse his food?
- Defecation habits
- Activity, including activity levels in the cage and time out of the cage with you.
- Bathing: did you soak the iguana in the tub today?
- Shedding

Routine (but not daily) entries can include information about your iguana's care. When was he allowed out to bask in the sun? How did he behave last winter, during the breeding season? How did he react to your houseguests during the holidays? When did you trim his toenails? Not only will these notes help you track your iguana's health and behavior, but they can remind you to do things,

**Did You Know?**
Introduce your lizard to a lukewarm water bath gradually. Once he's used to it, he'll enjoy it.

Routine Care

## Old Times

It's fun to look back at your reptile calendar and see what you've written. For example, some of my old notes for Conan look like this:

9-10-94 Conan ate everything today—everything—what a pig! Feces normal, activity normal, spent a couple of hours out in the sun.

12-1-94 Conan is still shedding; had trouble with his spines—used baby oil and worked them off. Trimmed his nails today. Appetite normal, defecation normal.

6-25-95 Conan spent the day at the fair for a reptile educational event. Probably 20,000 people came by and saw him. The two most common comments were, "Is it real?" and "Who said dinosaurs were extinct!" Conan was calm, well-behaved, and patient! He didn't eat while away from home but ate normally at home.

11-7-96 Soaked Conan in the tub while I cleaned the cage; took it apart and bleached it. Gave him a new basking log. Replaced fluorescent tube over his cage. Appetite, feces normal.

12-29-97 Conan is in full breeding season; his colors are up—very orange on his legs, sides, and chest. He's bobbing his head at everything but isn't showing any aggression to us.

2-15-98 Conan weighs 20 pounds even! He's a bit chubby, though, wish he would walk on a leash. Ha! An iguana on a treadmill! He does appear to be over his breeding season for this year.

As you can see, entries like this paint a picture of Conan. I can look back and see what he did, how he reacted, and how he was feeling.

too. If you haven't had him out to bask in the sun for a week or so, a quick look at the calendar will remind you of that.

You can also keep track of other things. When did you replace that fluorescent UVB reptile light over his cage? They should be replaced every six months, so is it time to buy a new one? How long did that ceramic heat element last? If you noted when you bought it, that will tell you whether it lasted a reasonable length of time.

Once a quarter or so you should measure and weigh your iguana. Note his length and weight on your calendar. You can also note anything different or unusual at that time. Perhaps he has a small lump that you should watch or a crooked toenail. These notes can be important later.

I have a small, inexpensive calendar for each of my reptile pets. I keep each one in a plastic document protector and keep it with the reptile's cage. Then, as I care for my pets, the calendar is handy and it's easy to make notes about my pet and his care. Please don't shrug and say to yourself, "That's a lot of work." It really isn't! It only takes a second or two to make some quick notes and slide the calendar back into the document protector. It will all pay off when you need to double-check on something relating to your pet's care or health.

## A Clean Iguana

Iguanas don't groom themselves the way cats do, but their scales do seem to shed most dirt. Their ability to shed their skin every so often helps, too, but neither of these are enough to keep your iguana clean. He's going to need your help.

> Iguanas don't groom themselves the way cats do, but their scales do seem to shed most dirt.

### A Regular Bath

Most iguanas enjoy water. They swim quite well naturally, using their tail as a rudder, and take willingly to water. That's good, because a weekly bath is one of the easiest ways to keep your iguana clean.

Put enough water in the bathtub (or a plastic swimming pool, if it's warm enough outside) so that your iguana can stand on the bottom and breathe comfortably. You don't want it so deep that he has to swim; even though he can, he can easily tire and drown. A rubber mat on the floor of the tub will help give your iguana traction as he relaxes there. Before putting the iguana in the tub, move your shampoo, razor, soap, and anything else your iguana might knock over or pull into the tub.

The water should be lukewarm—80°F is fine. If your iguana usually likes his bath, but begins to thrash as soon as you put him in the water, test the temperature again. If the water is too warm, your iguana can be burned or overheat. If the water is too cool, he can chill and become too torpid to keep himself out of the water.

Let your iguana soak in the tub for awhile. He may swim for a little bit, but he will probably just relax and enjoy it. You can splash some water on his head and shoulders, just to wet him down completely.

Some iguanas defecate in the water, especially in a warm bath. If your iguana does this, immediately drain the water, rinse out the tub with a little bleach, and then refill it.

After your iguana has soaked for awhile, drain the water out. With your iguana still in the tub, take a little liquid soap (not one with additives and moisturizers—one with only soap) and a soft-bristled brush (like one for cleaning your feet) or a soft toothbrush and begin scrubbing your iguana. Use the brush very softly and gently, but scrub his sides, his spines, down his tail, around his vent, under his jowls, and all over. Make sure you get all the dried food from around his jaws. Most iguanas really enjoy this scrubbing; it should feel good to them. If your iguana protests, you may be scrubbing too hard. Remember, even though he has scales, there is skin between each scale and some of the scales are harder or softer than others.

Rinse him off, making sure you get all of the soap off him. Now you can towel-dry him—being careful not to break his spines—and put him on his basking log under the heat light. Make sure he doesn't chill after the bath.

## After Your Iguana's Bath

After your iguana's bath, once he's dried off and back in his cage, scrub your bathtub using a bleach-and-water solution or a bleach cleaner. Make sure the tub, the tub walls, the shower curtain, and all the things in the tub are well scrubbed and clean. The chances of you or a family member contacting salmonella or anything else from the tub are small, but with good cleaning the chances become negligible.

# Cleaning the Cage

Your iguana's cage needs to be cleaned at least as often as he is. While your iguana is soaking in the bathtub, you can be cleaning his cage. Then, when you put him back in his cage, both are equally clean. It doesn't make any sense to clean him and then put him back in a filthy cage!

Don't use the kitchen sink to clean any of your iguana's stuff, nor should you use the kitchen sponge or scraper. Instead, use the outside hose or a deep sink in the garage, and have a set of sponges and scrubbers just for cleaning reptile equipment and cages. Liberally use soap and water to clean and bleach

> **Did You Know?**
> Nail trimming can be difficult; sometimes it helps to have one person hold the lizard while a second person wields the nail trimmers.

to kill bacteria and salmonella on anything to do with your iguana.

Your iguana's perch or basking logs should be scrubbed with soap and water, rinsed with a bleach-and-water solution, and then allowed to air-dry. If you can't air-dry them, rinse the bleach solution off before you dry them. Don't put them back in the cage until the rest of the cage has been scrubbed and dried.

> Your iguana's cage needs to be cleaned at least as often as he is.

When scrubbing, make sure you get all the food, feces, and shed skin from all of the cracks and crevasses of the logs or perches. All of these things can harbor bacteria (including salmonella) and mites. A good bleach rinse in the cracks and crevasses can help keep them free from bacteria and mites.

The floor of the cage should be scrubbed after the substrate is removed. If you're using newspapers or paper towels for substrate, just fold them up and throw them away. If you're using alfalfa pellets or bark, these substrates need to be removed and replaced. With the substrate out, scrub the floor of the cage with a bleach-and-water solution, then before you mop it up, scrub the sides of the cage, too. When all of the cage has been scrubbed, towel it off, dry it thoroughly, then put clean substrate in, then the perches or basking logs.

Once a month or so you should completely take apart the cage—taking it outside when you can—and completely scrub it. By taking it apart, you can get to all the cracks and crevasses where bits of food, shedded skin, and other things can lodge and harbor bacteria. When possible, after scrubbing and rinsing with bleach and water, let the pieces of the cage dry in the sun. The sun is great for disinfecting, too!

Don't forget to clean around the cage, as well. The walls and floor around the cage should be cleaned just as thoroughly as the cage itself.

## Clean the Potty Area

Where does your iguana relieve himself? If he has a litter box on the floor of his cage or in a spot outside his cage, that needs to be cleaned daily. Many iguanas will not use the box once it has been soiled. If you leave it dirty, your iguana may decide not to honor housetraining, and that would be a shame. However, even if your iguana will go back to a dirty box, he will then step in his old feces and spread it all over. Icckkk! Keep that box clean!

Clean the area around the box, too. Sweep up scattered litter, feces that missed the box, and anything else that ended up on the cage floor. If you clean it up regularly, it won't be spread all over.

## Clean the Feeding Spot

Food and water dishes should be removed and scrubbed daily. Many iguana owners keep two sets of dishes so that one can be cleaned while the other is being used.

Many iguana owners feed their iguana outside of the cage because, to be truthful, iguanas are not known to be tidy eaters. Food is often pushed aside for something better and ends up on the floor, or food gets pushed off the plate as it's eaten. Iguanas are active eaters, too,

> **Did You Know?**
> If your lizard doesn't care for his body care and grooming routine, feed him a special treat as you work on him.

and the food often ends up *on* the iguana as much as *in* the iguana!

By feeding your iguana somewhere other than in his cage, you can interact with him as you feed him and you can keep the mess to a minimum.

Obviously the feeding area—whether in the cage or somewhere else—will need to be cleaned up after each feeding. Spoiled food can easily lead to salmonella poisoning.

### Cleaning Other Iguana Places

If you have a cat tree for your iguana, or if your iguana likes to perch in other areas around the house, don't forget those places when you're cleaning. Vacuum the cat tree, clean up any spots, and spray it with a bleach disinfectant. Use a bleach-and-water solution to wipe down the shelf in front of the window where your iguana likes to lie in the sun.

Cleanliness cannot be emphasized enough. When you keep your iguana clean, you are better able to keep him healthy. When you keep the iguana's cage, dishes, and other equipment clean, you cut down the risk of salmonella and other health threats, both to him and to you and your family.

## Regular Care

In the wild an iguana takes care of himself, and if all goes well, he will live to a ripe old age. However, if things don't go well, he may suffer or even die much younger. In the wild there is no one to trim his nails should they get overgrown, and if he doesn't shed completely, there is no one to peel off the dead skin.

Luckily, in captivity iguanas have some help. Your care can help your iguana stay healthy and live longer.

## Shedding Skin

Iguanas shed their skin regularly. This process, which scientists call *ecdysis,* gets rid of the old skin and bares the new skin underneath. Very young, rapidly growing babies shed more often than full-grown adults. Babies may shed every six weeks or so, while full-grown adults may shed once, twice, or three times a year.

Before shedding, your iguana's appetite may increase (sometimes a week or two before shedding begins), and then it will drop off while he sheds. Many iguanas also get a little grouchy while they're shedding—perhaps the itching of the old skin is annoying. Some iguanas maintain their composure during shedding but get a little grouchy when just the head is shedding. As with all things concerning iguanas, it's important to learn what is normal for your iguana, so you know when something is happening that is not normal.

> Many iguanas get a little grouchy while they're shedding–perhaps the itching of the old skin is annoying.

Snakes often shed their skin in one complete piece, beginning at the head and ending with the tip of the tail. Iguanas are not nearly as neat! Iguanas shed in patches and pieces, and there doesn't seem to be any order to it. Some iguanas shed the skin on their head first, then the sides, the tail, the belly, and finally the legs. Others will lose the skin on the body first and then progress to other parts.

Since there is no uniform way iguanas shed, it's important to watch your iguana and discover his pattern of shedding. This is

# The Spines

The spines along your iguana's back are made of keratin—the same stuff that makes up your fingernails—and the outer covering sheds each time your iguana sheds his skin.

Young iguanas usually shed their spines just fine, but as iguanas get older they may damage a spine here or there or the spines may grow crooked or twisted. These damaged spines are less likely to shed completely (or at all), and the retained covering can inhibit the new growth underneath.

You can help your pet shed by massaging some baby oil or mineral oil up and down the spines. After a day or two of massaging in the oil, the spines should be soft enough to come right off.

particularly important because sometimes old skin is not completely shed, sticking to the new skin underneath, and this can cause problems. If old skin remains stuck to the toes, for example, it can become tight, cutting off the circulation and eventually causing the loss of the toes. However, if you watch your iguana, you can see the shedding begin and watch its progress.

If you are giving your iguana a weekly bath, you will notice that the bath will seem to loosen the old skin. If your iguana starts shedding but the skin seems to be sticking, you can give him another bath or you can use a spray bottle to mist him with some warm water. Just make sure he doesn't chill after you mist him.

When they are shedding, most iguanas appreciate something rough to rub up against. The process must itch, because an iguana with a large rough stone or a bark-covered log will go back and forth, and rub and rub and rub against the rough surface.

If your iguana has large pieces of skin hanging off him, you can help him and pick the skin off. Be careful, though; just as human sunburned skin should peel off easily, so should shedded iguana skin. If the skin sticks, leave it alone—it's not quite ready to come off and if you pull it, you could damage the new skin underneath.

If your iguana appears to have shedded completely except for an attached piece of skin here or there, you can help those last pieces finish shedding. A drop or two of either baby oil or mineral oil on those spots will soften them. If you then massage gently with a couple of fingers, the skin should detach.

Some problem areas that often don't shed well include the spines, the tip of the tail, the toes, and any part of the skin that has previously been injured, such as scars. During and after every shed, check those places and make sure the old skin is completely gone.

## Trimming Toenails

An iguana's toes are long, slender, and quite fragile looking, so the strength of the toenails often takes new iguana owners by surprise. However, the toes and toenails are made for climbing trees and are flexible and incredibly strong—strong enough to draw blood when an iguana uses them on bare skin!

> An iguana's toes are long, slender, and quite fragile looking, so the strength of the toenails often takes new iguana owners by surprise.

In captivity, an iguana isn't as active as he is in the wild. As a result, the nails aren't worn down. When combined with the fact that iguana nails grow very quickly, weekly nail trimming becomes a necessity.

There are nail trimmers made specifically for trimming reptile nails. If you can find one of these, they work very well. If you can't find them, cat nail trimmers work well for smaller iguanas and dog nail trimmers work okay for larger iguanas. You also need to have some styptic powder on hand in case you accidentally hit the quick and cause a nail to bleed.

After your iguana has had his bath, he will be relaxed and his nails will be softened by soaking in the water. While he is relaxed and lying on his log or on his cat tree, simply trim one nail at a time by reaching over with the clippers, touching only that nail. Don't try to pin down his foot or hold on to one toe; that will cause him to react and fight, possibly pulling his foot away. If you're holding onto one toe when he jerks away, you risk damaging that toe. Instead, just look at his foot carefully, decide what you're going to do, and then reach over quickly with the clippers and do it!

When you trim, just take off the tip of each nail. Don't take off as much as you would for a dog or cat—the quick is longer in iguana nails—and your iguana needs his nails for climbing in his cage, on his basking log, and on his cat tree.

If your iguana gets anxious, stop trimming and let him relax. Come back in 10 minutes and trim a few more nails. Don't try to physically restrain him; that only makes most iguanas fight and struggle even harder. This is routine care and needs to be well tolerated by your iguana, so do it when he is relaxed and will allow you to do it without fighting.

The quick is a bundle of blood vessels and nerves that runs down the center of each nail—just as it does in dog and cat nails—and is just as sensitive as the quick is in your nails. If you accidentally hit the quick, your iguana will probably jerk his leg away. Don't try to hold it—just let go. If you hold it, you risk damaging the nail, the toes you are holding or his foot. Instead, let him jerk his foot away, wait a few minutes and while you're waiting,

## Your Iguana Needs Sleep

You know you are happier and healthier when you get enough sleep, and your iguana is the same way. Although you may not realize it, your activities greatly affect how much sleep your iguana gets.

Your iguana is diurnal, which means he's active during the day and sleeps at night. People are the same way, except that the invention of electric lights has allowed us to be more active later into the night, instead of going to sleep when the sun goes down as most real diurnal creatures do.

If the iguana's cage is in the family room, he will never sleep soundly as long as lights are on and people are in and out of the room. Look at your routine and that of other family members and make sure you can arrange for your iguana to have eight to 10 uninterrupted hours of sleep each night.

watch to see if the quick is bleeding. If it is, dip that nail into the styptic powder, getting a big lump of powder on the nail. Let that sit for a few minutes before you try to trim any more nails.

## What Else Does Your Iguana Need?

Once your iguana is bathed, his cage is clean, his nails are trimmed, and his skin is shed, what else does he need? Not much, and that's one reason why people enjoy iguanas as pets. They are relatively undemanding.

Your iguana will enjoy some attention from you, of course, and time out of his cage. Although iguanas don't need aerobic exercise, some activity every day is good for them. A walk around the house and a climb up the cat tree is good. Let him set the pace—just give him the opportunity to do what he wants and needs.

Your iguana will also appreciate some sunshine if the weather permits. Half an hour basking in the sun is good for your iguana's physical and mental well-being. Just make sure when you put him outside that he is in a secure, well-locked cage and has some shade. Never leave him in the sun without shade. If he overheats, he will quickly die.

## Setting Up a Routine

It's much easier to make sure things get done as they should be done when you set up a routine. This way, rather than just doing them when you remember (and don't procrastinate!), chores are done regularly.

Daily:

- Feed the iguana.
- After feeding, pick up, remove, and clean his dishes.
- After feeding, clean up the feeding area.
- Clean potty area.
- Check your iguana all over, looking for skin that hasn't shed or other problems.
- Give him attention from you.
- Give him time out of the cage and a chance to be active.

Weekly:

- Bathe the iguana.
- Trim his toenails.
- Clean the cage thoroughly, removing all perches and basking logs and cleaning them, too.
- Clean underneath, behind, and around the cage.

- Check the heat elements, heat lights, cords, and other electrical devices to make sure everything is working properly.
- Give him a chance to bask in the sunshine, weather permitting.

Monthly:

- Take the cage completely apart, take it outside when you can, and scrub and bleach all the pieces and parts.

Annually:

- Set up an appointment with veterinarian for a general exam. Bring in a feces sample to check for parasites.

# 9

# Breeding Your Iguana

### In This Chapter

o Should You Breed Your Iguana?
o Courtship and Breeding
o Taking Care of the Babies

**B**reeding captive reptiles is a labor-intensive, sometimes expensive, and often frustrating endeavor, but when it succeeds, the excitement is wonderful. My husband and I started with our turtles and tortoises, and I still have the first turtle that hatched in our incubator. As our first born, he will have a home with us forever.

But reptile breeding isn't easy. After all, a captive life may be better for our iguanas in some ways (freedom from hunger and a lack of predators, for example), but it still isn't a natural life. We can't duplicate the conditions the wild iguana lives in, nor can we duplicate the wild diet. The behaviors that happen in the wild—for example, male iguanas battling for territory and the right to breed a female—don't happen in captivity. Nor can we give a female iguana the room to roam so that she can choose her own place to lays eggs. However, if you want to do it and can do what is needed, you can breed your iguanas and it can be wonderfully rewarding.

## Should You Breed Your Iguana?

First of all, let's look at this from another direction. Should you breed your iguana? Your iguana will not do all the work as far as incubating and rearing the babies. In fact, she will lay the eggs and then it's up to you. Can you spend the money for an incubator and spare the time to incubate the eggs and raise the babies? In addition, although a female iguana may only lay 20 eggs in her first clutch, subsequent clutches may have 30 to 40 eggs! You could conceivably be producing a lot of iguana babies!

What would you do with all these babies? Where would you keep them after they hatch? Do you have the room and equipment to house them and to keep them warm and fed? You will need to keep them at least a month or two to make sure they are eating well and thriving before you send them to new homes.

> Breeding your reptiles can be very rewarding, but it can also be expensive, time-consuming, and labor-intensive.

Speaking of new homes, where will you find homes for 30 or more iguanas? Don't count on friends buying or adopting any of the babies—even if they said yes before you bred your pets, when it comes down to actually taking one home, some will back out. So what can you do with them? You could put an ad in the newspaper and try to sell them that way. Or is there a pet store or two near you that would buy

## Iguanas Are Threatened in the Wild

In many parts of their native territory, iguana survival is threatened. Habitat destruction and the habit of eating iguanas for food—as well as past collections for the pet trade—has reduced some populations significantly.

Some pet owners think that by breeding their pets, the populations of wild iguanas can be saved. Although their heart is in the right place, the survival of wild iguanas is a complicated subject and is not so easily solved.

First of all, most iguanas imported for the pet trade today are raised on iguana farms. Very few wild-caught iguanas are shipped into the United States for the pet trade, since these iguanas simply do not adapt to captivity well. Therefore, other than the iguanas used as breeding stock for these farms, the pet trade is not depleting wild populations. In addition, many of the farms are required to release a certain percentage of each year's hatchlings back into the wild to boost the wild populations. Increased farming can also supply iguanas to the people who look upon the iguana as a valuable food source, thus, reducing the pressure on wild iguanas.

But survival of the wild populations depends upon saving their habitat as well as increased iguana farming. And breeding your iguana in the United States will not relieve that problem.

the babies from you? Would you feel comfortable selling your babies to a pet store? Take my word for it, you're going to become attached to these little green babies!

Don't go into breeding with the hope of retiring on the proceeds. Although there is a demand for captive-bred (rather than wild-caught or farm-raised) iguana babies, they are not in enough demand to enable you to charge a significant price for them. So don't think you will make a lot of money breeding iguanas. You won't, and in fact, you will probably lose money after you figure out all the costs involved.

Before you decide to breed your iguana, read this chapter thoroughly and make an educated decision. Breeding your reptiles can be very rewarding, but it can also be expensive, time-consuming, and labor-intensive.

## Spaying and Neutering

If you decide that breeding your iguana is not for you, have your iguana spayed or neutered. This reduces the breeding urges, especially in a male, and will stop the female from producing eggs. A healthy female iguana will produce eggs even when she is not kept with a male, and this is a continual drain on her system. Proteins and calcium are used in great quantities to produce eggs. If she's not producing eggs, her body can use those nutrients to keep her healthy. In addition, she runs the risk of becoming egg-bound (retaining her eggs rather than laying them). By having her spayed—a hysterectomy—she will no longer produce eggs.

A neutered (castrated) male will no longer go into breeding season each winter. Some males become quite aggressive during breeding season—so much so that they have been known to attack their owners or even their prospective mates. Neutering reduces this male aggression.

## Before You Breed

Successfully breeding your reptiles—including your iguanas—requires some planning. This isn't a project to undertake at the last minute. There are a few things you will need to do before you allow your iguana and his/her significant other to breed.

## Male or Female?

Obviously, you will need a male and a female iguana to successfully produce fertile eggs. Although a female will lay eggs without access to a male, those eggs are unfertilized. Do you know for sure that you have both a male and a female?

It is very difficult to accurately sex a baby or juvenile iguana, since all of the iguana's sexual equipment is internal. However, iguanas are sexually dimorphic, which means there are differences between the sexes that are visually apparent. Unfortunately, those differences are not apparent until the iguana reaches sexual maturity. That means when you buy two baby iguanas, hoping for a male and a female, you might as well flip a coin to determine which is which!

There are, however, two sexual characteristics that can help you accurately tell males from females once the iguanas have reached sexual maturity—at least two years of age with good care and feeding. Males develop enlarged femoral glands on the underside of each thigh. This row of glands appears as small bumps on young males and gets more pronounced as the males get larger, older, and more mature. During breeding season, older dominant males will have secretions from these pores that appear as waxy, chalky residue. This residue contains pheromones of the male.

> It is very difficult to accurately sex a baby or juvenile iguana, since all of the iguana's sexual equipment is internal.

In addition, males develop broad, heavy jowls. These jowls, along with the large dewlap and brighter colors, help differentiate males from females.

You can also look for a few other characteristics. Males are usually larger than females of the same age, although some

## Male Physical Anatomy

Male iguanas have two penises, called hemipenes. The hemipenes are located internally in two little pouches under the tail, just behind the rear legs and immediately inside and to the back of the vent. (The vent in reptiles is called the anus in mammals.)

During copulation, increased blood pressure inflates the hemipenes and they come out of their pouch. In mammals the sperm moves through a tube from the testicles—which are located close to the penis—through the penis and are ejected. In iguanas, the testicles are also located internally and are found in relatively the same position as the ovaries in female iguanas. The hemipenes themselves do not have an internal tube for the sperm, but instead have an external groove and the sperm moves along this groove to the female.

females, especially mature females, may have a larger, heavier body than some males. Males usually have larger dorsal crests and spines than do females.

Males also have a few behaviors that give away their sexual orientation. Although males and females both bob their heads in certain situations, males bob their head more frequently and for more reasons. Males also show more mounting behaviors than do females, who may mount other animals to express dominance.

## Physical Condition

About six to eight months before breeding season, take both the male and female iguana to the veterinarian for a complete examination. Both iguanas should be in good health before they begin breeding.

Bring in fecal samples for your vet to check for parasites. An iguana infested with parasites may appear to be healthy, and you may not realize your iguana even has parasites. But parasites can make enough of an impact on your iguana's health to affect reproduction.

If the male isn't in good health, he may simply have a low sperm count and you will likely end up with fewer fertile eggs. However, he may also have damaged sperm, which can cause birth defects as well as low fertility.

It is even more important that the female be in tip-top form. Since she has to create and nourish the eggs until they are laid, and since she can lay from 20 to 40 eggs per clutch, this takes a considerable amount of her reserves. She should be free from parasites, well-nourished, and in excellent health.

## The Environment

If you haven't already done so, this is the time to make sure your iguanas' environment is the best you can provide. Make sure the iguanas have plenty of space. Keep the cage very clean to reduce the possibility of salmonella and mites.

Replace the fluorescent UVB light above your iguanas' cage with a new bulb. Most manufacturers recommend replacing these bulbs every six months anyway, and this is the time to make sure you have a new one above the cage.

Whenever the weather makes it possible, give both the male and the

> **Did You Know?**
> Iguanas have colonized areas of Florida, especially southern Florida. A breeding colony has been found in the wooded areas around Miami's International Airport.

## Female Physical Anatomy

A female iguana longer than 10 to 11 inches from nose to vent is usually large enough to lay eggs. Age doesn't seem to have as much to do with maturity as does size.

Like mammals, female iguanas have ovaries. The egg moves to the oviduct, where fertilization takes place if the female has been bred. The egg will then move down the oviduct, where the eggs rest until they are ready to be laid.

Prior to laying, a special shell gland coats the eggs with a leathery shell that is primarily calcium—hence, the breeding female's need for plenty of calcium.

---

female time outside to bask in the sun. An outside cage is a good investment.

Set a timer so that your iguanas get 14 hours of light each day and 10 hours of darkness. This photoperiod is important for breeding.

### Pre-Breeding Nutrition

If you are already feeding your iguanas a healthy diet, neither the male nor female need anything special before breeding. However, if you have been kind of haphazard about feeding, this is the time to concentrate on diet. Both the male and the female need a good balanced diet made up of a variety of foods for months prior to breeding.

Make sure the female is getting plenty of dark greens and other foods rich in calcium. Don't supplement her diet with a lot of calcium—although she will need that later. Right now just make sure she is well fed and does not lack calcium.

# Courtship and Breeding

So, your iguanas have been declared healthy and free of parasites, are well-nourished, live in a good environment with correct light and photoperiods, and are sexually mature. Now what?

## Breeding Season

In most parts of the wild iguana's natural range, the breeding season is usually during the drier times of the year so that the babies hatch during the rainy season when food is plentiful. In captivity, the breeding season varies. Some iguana owners living in northern North America say they see their male's behavior begin to change in October to November, with that behavior continuing through December. My husband and I live in Southern California and we see Conan's breeding behavior begin in late November, early December, and continue through February or March.

> You will be able to tell that the male is coming into breeding season by his attitude and appearance.

You will be able to tell that the male is coming into breeding season by his attitude and appearance. He gets very macho, will hold himself higher on his feet or toes, and will try to make himself look bigger. You will see more head bobbing, often for little or no reason. He may begin to challenge you, threatening to bite even when he would normally be gentle.

His color will get richer or brighter, depending upon where his ancestors were from. Conan gets very orange on his legs, sides and chest, with a touch of color on his dewlap and jowls. Males from other regions may show pink or red coloring, brown, black, or even blue. A male iguana is his most handsome during breeding season.

## Male Aggression

As breeding season gets closer, many males get quite aggressive. In the wild this aggression would serve to defend their territory, to chase away any other males, and to defend their chosen mate. In captivity, if your male lives with a female (at least during breeding season), the same reasons apply. However, if your male lives alone, the aggression may still surface, especially in older, larger, more dominant males.

Aggressive males will bob their head more, will posture more, puffing up to look larger, and may threaten to whip with their tail. They may gape their mouth wide open, as if daring anyone to come closer!

In some cases, males have been known to jump off their perch and charge their owners, with eyes glazed over like a drug addict and mouth wide open, ready to bite. Although the idea of a 20-pound lizard attacking a 150-pound adult human may seem humorous—and in some ways it is!—it is also scary because a large iguana can inflict a serious bite.

Unfortunately, some male iguanas seem to target their female owners. Male iguanas seem to sense (perhaps pick up the pheromones) menstruating women and will charge those women.

It's usually a good idea to limit any handling of the male iguana during breeding season. Plan ahead of time and trim his nails before breeding season begins, and then during breeding season do only what is necessary for his good health.

## A Bachelor Forever

We picked up an adult female Green Iguana as a rescue and decided that since she was very pretty, we would allow her and Conan to mate, if they so decided! What a mistake! Conan was more than willing; in fact, too willing. To make her hold still, he would bite her. This by itself isn't too unusual; however, Conan didn't just grab her, he ripped her skin all the way through to underlying muscle tissue. We called our vet on a Sunday morning to get her stitched up and at that point, we decided Conan was going to remain a bachelor! We found the female a new home!

If your iguana attacks you, don't run away. Running away reinforces his dominance—after all, when he attacks other male iguanas, they run away from him! Instead, stand your ground and when he comes at you, step to the side as he charges and pick him up, holding him so that his gaping mouth is away from you. You have just shown him that you are more powerful than he is—like a huge bird of prey that might eat him for dinner—and have ended his attack. You can then put him back in his cage for awhile.

Whenever you handle him during this period, have a heavy towel with you and keep that between you and him so that if he charges you, you can toss the towel over his head. When you need to handle him or pick him up, wrap him in the towel, keeping his legs back flat along his sides.

## Boy Meets Girl

It's usually a good idea to put the male and female iguanas in separate cages close to each other for awhile. Since iguanas can be very territorial, let them get used to one another before they are able to do anything about it. Then, when the male's body language is telling you that breeding season has arrived, let them both out of the cage.

Don't put one in the other's cage—that's asking for a fight, because they are territorial. Instead, let them have the run of a room. Expect a lot of head bobbing and posturing. The female may even try to run away and hide from the male. Let her do so—she may not be ready to breed yet. Don't try to interfere, just let them get to know one another.

After awhile, put them away in their respective cages and do the same thing the next day. As you get closer to breeding season, the behavior will change from interest to courtship.

## Courtship

When the female is close to being ready to breed, she will stop running from the male and will begin to stand still when the male approaches her. He will flick his tongue at her, touching her up and down her body, especially around the head and neck. He will be doing a lot of head bobbing—so much so you would expect him to have a headache!

> Courtship can last for two to three weeks before the actual breeding, and during this time, both iguanas—but especially the male—may show a decreased appetite.

The male will also be doing a lot of posturing right now, standing tall, puffing up, and showing the female exactly what a large, handsome iguana he is.

Courtship can last for two to three weeks before the actual breeding, and during this time, both iguanas—but especially the male—may show a decreased appetite. He is so focused on the female that he won't eat. So he doesn't get dehydrated, make sure water is always available. In addition, you can offer him some Pedialyte or Gatorade by eyedropper or syringe, if you can get close enough to do so without provoking him to attack you. Continue to offer him food even if he's not eating much.

## Breeding

Although the male does the courting, breeding cannot proceed without the female's cooperation. She chooses her mate, and for the survival of the species, she wants the largest, healthiest, most fit male. It is possible that if you have one male and one female, she may not accept him no matter how much he courts her. Usually, in captivity the female will accept the available male, but it is not unheard of for the female to find the male unacceptable—for whatever reason!

When the female is ready to be bred, she will stand still (or at least stop running away quite as much) and the male will try to grab her by the back of the neck. Sometimes the males can be quite rough—even breaking the skin—especially if the female isn't very cooperative. Conan will be celibate for the rest of his life because he was very rough with his female companions—to the point where we had to take one female to our veterinarian early one Sunday morning for stitches. Conan bit her severely on the sides and neck, tearing deep wounds through the skin down to the muscles underneath.

Luckily, most males aren't quite as rough and will just try to grab the back of the female's neck enough to hold her

> **Did You Know?**
> When looking for your new pet, don't forget to call the local shelter. Today it's not unusual to find reptiles waiting for homes at the local shelter or animal control.

still. Once the male has a hold on her, he will try to tip her hips slightly as she lifts her tail. When she lifts her tail and he has tipped her hips slightly to one side, he can insert one of his hemipenes into her vent.

When breeding is completed, he will let go of the back of her neck and she will run away from him—usually very quickly! It's a good idea to check the female at this time to make sure his bites haven't broken the skin.

If you allow it to continue, breeding will take place two to three times a day for a week or two. It's usually a good idea to continue to cage the iguanas separately during the night and for a few hours during the day to give the female time to relax, eat, and sleep. The males can be very, very persistent during this time and, if given their choice, will not take a break at all!

## Gestation

Gestation is the time when the eggs have been fertilized and are developing within the female. During this time the female needs a good quality, varied diet that includes plenty of dark green vegetables containing lots of calcium. A calcium supplement should be added to her food three times a week.

As the female gets larger she will eat less. About three to four weeks before laying her eggs she will almost totally stop eating. It's as if there is no room inside her for any food! Continue to offer her some favorite foods anyway, and make sure water is always available. You can also offer her Pedialyte or Gatorade by eyedropper or syringe to make sure she doesn't get dehydrated.

Make sure the female has a basking spot where she

## Iguana Eggs

The iguana's eggs are leathery, not hard like a chicken's egg. They also differ from bird eggs in another very important way: The yolk in bird eggs is suspended in the middle of the egg with the albumin (egg white) surrounding it. The chick develops in the middle of the egg and the parent birds move it regularly. In reptile eggs, however, the yolk is fixed—usually at the bottom of the egg—and if the egg is turned, small blood vessels can rip and tear, killing the developing reptile.

Once an iguana egg is laid, you can usually safely move it for about 24 hours. This gives you time to get it set up in an incubator. However, after the first 24 hours, the egg should not be rotated at all and handling should be kept to an absolute minimum.

has easy access to the heat (up to 95°F is fine). She needs more heat now while her eggs are developing, so allow her to bask as much as she wants. The thermal gradient is still important, of course, so don't heat her entire cage. You don't want to cook her! Just make sure she has access to the heat.

You don't want her to jump very much as she gets larger and heavy with eggs, so make her cage as easy for her as possible. Make ramps for her to get to heights, and when she's out of her cage, control her movements somewhat so that she doesn't hurt herself or her eggs.

Be very careful when you pick her up and handle her during this time. The eggs make up a large portion of her internal mass and they are very fragile. Pick her up under her hips and shoulders, rather than under her abdomen. As gestation progresses, her abdomen will expand and she will appear lumpy. You will be able to see the shape of the eggs developing in her abdomen.

# Keeping Records

Now that you are fairly certain the breeding has been successful, you will have to begin keeping records. Breeding records are an important contribution to reptile keepers' knowledge all over the world. Your observations, when combined with other iguana breeders' observations, can be an incredible wealth of information. When reptile keepers share information and knowledge, books such as this one can be written, sharing even more knowledge.

The clutch record should contain the male iguana's name or identification, the female's name or identification, and your name as breeder. The species is <u>Iguana iguana</u>—Green Iguana. Of course, you made notations on each iguana's individual record or calendar exactly when each act of copulation took place. Enter these dates on the clutch record.

When the eggs are laid and you place them in the incubator, draw a diagram of the eggs in their incubation boxes, numbering each one on the diagram so that each egg is identified. Weigh each egg as you place it in the vermiculite (more about that in a moment) and note the egg's weight in grams.

When the eggs hatch, you can make note which eggs hatched in what order and which eggs were infertile. You can also note anything unusual that happened during breeding, egg laying, incubation, or hatching.

For example:

Male: Big Guy, 10 years old, 15 pounds

Female: Little Girl, 6 years old, 8 pounds

Eggs laid on May 31, 2000

Egg 1: 13.6 grams; hatched 90 days/healthy

Egg 2: 13.0g; 90/healthy

Egg 3: 9.0g; infertile/pulled at 45 days

Egg 4: 12.9g; 90/healthy

Egg 5: 12.4g; 91/weak, small, died

Egg 6: 13.9g; 90/healthy

## Preparing the Nest

When the female is refusing to eat at all—about three weeks after her appetite began to decrease—you will need to provide her with a nesting box where she can lay her eggs. This can be a large plastic storage container with a lid. This container must be large enough that she can move around and get comfortable inside. For a large adult female, the box should be at least three feet long on the long side. Cut a hole in one side large enough for the female to climb in. Edge the hole with several layers of duct tape so that the cut plastic edge doesn't scratch her abdomen as she climbs in and out.

Put a mixture of potting soil and sand in the box and moisten it just enough so that it holds together. When she digs her nest, the soil should hold together so that the dirt doesn't fall in and refill the hole as she digs. You should check the soil every day and dampen it when needed.

Place the box so that the female has access to it every day. Place it on the floor of her cage, or if it is too large, prop open the door to her cage so that she has access to the box. If the box is not available, she could drop her eggs anywhere—even on the floor of her cage—or she may retain them, which could cause her severe health problems.

## Egg-Binding

Egg-binding or retention (called dystocia) occurs when a female doesn't or can't lay her eggs. A female may not lay her eggs if there is no suitable location—if a nesting box hasn't been provided—or if she doesn't approve of the nesting box.

Since breeding is not necessary for the production of eggs, some owners of female iguanas do not provide a nesting box for the adult iguana and she may then retain her eggs too long. If she is scratching at the floor of her cage, looking distressed and quite large in the abdomen, she needs a nest box.

Egg-binding may also occur when there are some misshapen eggs that cannot be passed, or if there is an oversized egg that is too large to be laid. Occasionally a female will produce too many eggs and will become so full of eggs that she simply can't lay the eggs and she will become egg-bound.

If a nesting box is provided and the female still doesn't lay her eggs, veterinary care is needed. A female retaining her eggs can die. If the vet is able to save her, often spaying is recommended for females prone to becoming egg-bound.

# Eggs and Incubation

Once the breeding is completed and both the male and female seem to have survived in good shape, it's time for you to get busy. There is more for you to do during this phase of reproduction. Although the female will lay the eggs, she doesn't have anything to do with incubating them. Nor does she want anything to do with the babies. So guess who's baby-sitting?

## Laying Eggs

The female will lay her eggs (called oviposition) when she is ready and is comfortable with her surroundings and the nesting box. Try to keep the household quiet around her when it's about her time. If things are too disruptive, she may not relax enough to lay the eggs.

To lay the eggs, the female will dig a tunnel or a hole. What she digs or how much seems to depend upon the individual iguana. Some dig quite an elaborate tunnel so that the entire female iguana can fit into the tunnel. These females lay their eggs at the deepest part of the tunnel. Other females dig a much simpler hole, digging straight down with their back feet.

Many females, if disturbed during digging, will desert that partially dug hole and begin another one when the disruption ends. Therefore, be very careful about disturbing her right now.

Each female iguana will lay her eggs according to her body's timetable. Some can produce a large number of eggs relatively quickly, while others are very slow and methodical. As long as eggs are being produced and she doesn't appear to be blocked or have any distress, just leave her alone and let things go along naturally. Unless she's laying in an inappropriate spot where the eggs might be damaged, just leave her alone and plan on coming back to get the eggs when she's done. If she's laid the eggs in a hole or tunnel in the nesting box, there is no problem getting the eggs later; you know where they are!

Young iguanas laying their first clutch may lay as few as six to 10 eggs, although 20 seems to be the average for well-nourished, healthy females. A large, healthy, mature adult female may lay as many as 70 eggs!

If your iguana suddenly stops laying but she still appears to be carrying eggs, call your veterinarian immediately. She may have an egg she can't pass or she may be too weak to continue. Your vet may take an X-ray to see if any eggs are retained, and if there are, what condition they are in. He may also recommend intravenous fluids to prevent shock, and either surgery to remove a blocked egg, or, if he feels she can pass it, oxytocin to stimulate the uterine muscles.

When she's done, the female will cover up the eggs, using her back feet to scoop dirt over them. When she leaves the nest, you can offer her food and water and make sure she's comfortable under her basking light. Then you can go back and carefully dig up the eggs.

After she has laid her eggs, the female's abdomen will appear deflated, like an empty balloon. She will be hungry and tired. Make sure she is offered plenty of water and several small meals each day. She should recuperate relatively quickly.

## Removing the Eggs

Scoop the dirt away from the nest with your hands, being very careful as you go deeper. The eggs are leathery and actually quite fragile. I can tell you from experience that you will feel horrible if you break one—even unintentionally—as you dig them up!

The eggs can be moved safely for about 24 hours after laying, but most people recommend leaving them the same side up (without rotating them) even right after laying. Once the eggs are dug up, fill in the hole again, and take the eggs to the incubator.

## Incubating the Eggs

You should set up the incubator before the eggs are laid so that the temperature inside is already stable. The last thing you want to do is let the eggs get too hot or too cold where you're trying to get the incubator temperature just right. Eggs that get too hot or too cold will die.

I prefer to use a commercial reptile incubator. I use a Lyons Electric. I started with a tabletop model that had two pull-out trays, but within two years had to upgrade to the floorstanding model with eight pull-out drawers. The benefit to the commercial incubator is that everything is already set up. All I have to do is plug it in and adjust the temperature. Commercial incubators are not cheap, however, and the larger, better quality ones can cost a few thousand dollars.

You can make your own incubator, though, and in fact, the first reptile eggs we hatched were incubated in a homemade incubator. There are several different ways to make an incubator, and some are better and more reliable than others. Since I haven't tried all the various types available, I will explain one model that worked for us.

## Making Your Own Reptile Incubator

You will need:

- One medium to large picnic cooler
- One submersible aquarium heater (from a pet supply store)
- One waterproof thermometer
- Two bricks
- One metal rack that fits inside the cooler
- Depending upon how many eggs, one to three plastic shoeboxes
- Vermiculite

Take the lid off the cooler or prop it open. Cut or drill three or four holes in the lid, with each hole about a half an inch across. You don't want to lose too much heat through the holes, but you do want fresh air to be able to come through.

Fasten the submersible heater to the bottom of the cooler with suction cup-type holders (they usually come with the heater). Cover the heater with a couple of inches of water and turn the heater on. As the water heats, adjust the thermometer until the water reaches 86°F.

While it's heating, use the bricks and metal rack to make a shelf above the water level. The eggs in their plastic shoeboxes will rest on this shelf.

Dampen the vermiculite so that it balls together in your fist. (Vermiculite is used because it is clean, holds water well, is inexpensive, and poses no threat to either the eggs or the hatchlings.) This damp vermiculite gives the eggs something to sit on, plus it helps maintain the temperature and humidity in the shoebox. Put a couple of inches of damp vermiculite in each plastic shoebox and set the box on the metal shelf. Place the thermometer on the vermiculite in the shoebox. Cut or punch some holes in the lid of the plastic shoebox to create some ventilation, and place the lid on the shoebox.

Close the lid of the cooler and let the incubator warm up. Check it in a few hours. You are going to want the temperature on the vermiculite inside the shoebox to be 86°F. Adjust the heater as needed. Once it reaches 86°F, close the incubator and keep it closed. Just check routinely to make sure there is water in the bottom covering the heater and the vermiculite remains damp in the shoebox.

When it comes time to move the eggs, prop open the cooler and take the lid off the shoebox. Pick the eggs up *very* gently. Don't rotate them; keep the same side up. Place them in the vermiculite so that they are half buried—scoop a small hole with one finger and set them gently in that hole. Don't push the eggs into the vermiculite, just place them. Half of the egg should be in the vermi-

## Setting Up a Commercial Incubator

A commercial incubator will come with its own instructions about how to turn it on and heat it up. As with the homemade incubator, have it set up and at the right temperature before the eggs are laid. Even with a commercial incubator you will need a plastic box and damp vermiculite to house the eggs. Some commercial incubators have shelves placed too close together to fit a shoebox, so you may have to use food storage boxes that are not quite as tall as shoeboxes. Cut holes in the lids for air circulation, and put the boxes containing the damp vermiculite, with the lids on, into the incubator and allow it to come to temperature. You want the temperature in the shoebox to be 86°F.

culite and half exposed to the air. Once all the eggs are in the box, close the lid to the shoebox and close the lid to the cooler.

Check the cooler every day to make sure the heater is working properly and there is water in the bottom of the cooler. Two or three times a week, open the shoebox and mist the eggs lightly with warm water so that the vermiculite remains damp.

Fertile eggs are good sized and usually weigh about 12 to 14 grams (one ounce is about 28 grams). They are slightly oval, and are white with a chalky appearance. They feel firm to the touch. Fertile eggs also get larger for the first two months, absorbing water from the vermiculite and humidity from the air.

Infertile eggs are usually smaller than fertile eggs and are not as white or chalky looking. Sometimes they are off-color, yellow, brownish, or just look bad, and may get moldy. They are often soft to the touch. The bad eggs should be removed and discarded as soon as you know they are infertile.

Other than checking on the eggs, misting them, and adding water to the vermiculite, the eggs should be disturbed as little as possible. The developing blood vessels are very fragile and even gentle handling could cause blood vessels to rupture.

# When the Eggs Hatch

Eggs incubated at 86°F usually hatch in about 90 days. A couple of weeks before they hatch, the eggs may get slightly smaller. At this point, start checking them daily. Make sure the vermiculite remains damp but not wet.

At about 80 days, make up another shoebox with damp vermiculite and put it in the incubator so that it can warm up. Cut or punch some air holes in the lid, put the lid on the box, and just leave the box in the incubator.

Just before hatching, the eggs may dimple, or may even appear to collapse inward. That's normal, so don't panic. The hatchling will open the egg first to begin breathing. Once he's taken a breath or two, he may appear to rest from his exertions. Don't force him out of the egg—he's absorbing the rest of the yolk sac—and he'll come out when he's ready. His lungs are also finishing their development and getting used to breathing air. Some hatchlings take 12 hours to come out of their shell.

If the hatchling is taking awhile and appears to be drying out, when you mist the eggs and vermiculite you can gently mist him, especially around the edges of the slit egg. Make sure you don't drown him with the mister, though.

Some hatchlings, when they first come out of their shell, will still have a piece of the yolk sac attached to their bellies. If any of your hatchlings do, gently pick them up and transfer them to the new shoebox that you just set up. It should still have damp, warm vermiculite in it and should already be up to temperature. Let your new hatchling rest here for a day or two while the yolk is absorbed.

Breeding Your Iguana 197

## If the Eggs Don't Hatch

There are, unfortunately, many reasons why eggs won't hatch successfully. Some of those reasons are:

- The male is infertile, for a variety of reasons.
- The female's health was not good enough to produce viable eggs. That includes poor nutrition and/or parasite infestation.
- The incubating temperature was not correct.
- The incubating medium was too dry.
- The eggs were disturbed and/or turned during incubation.

Never try to remove the yolk sac; in fact, just leave it alone. It will be absorbed and the excess will dry up and fall off. Sometimes when a hatchling leaves the egg, the yolk sac is slightly torn by the edges of the egg. In this case you can apply some antibiotic ointment to the torn sac and should reapply it twice a day until the yolk is absorbed.

Eggs from the same clutch may hatch over several days. If they don't all hatch at the same time, don't panic. As long as the egg appears to be okay, just leave it alone. The baby will hatch when he's ready. If you open the egg—hoping to help—and the baby isn't ready, he will die.

## Taking Care of the Babies

As the hatchling iguanas absorb their yolk, they should be moved to the nursery. A nursery cage can be a large, tall-sided plastic storage container. The heavy, opaque, plastic containers that are about three feet long by 18 inches wide and about the same height work well. I prefer to use these rather than glass aquarium tanks because most baby iguanas will beat themselves against the side of a glass cage—not understanding the concept of glass—and often hurt themselves. In a solid-sided cage—such as these plastic containers—the baby iguana is a little calmer.

Depending upon how many eggs you had successfully hatch, you may need to set up several nursery cages. Separate the iguanas into the larger, medium sized, and smaller hatchlings. This way the smaller, weaker hatchlings won't feel as intimidated by the larger ones.

Use layers of newspaper or paper towels as a substrate. With these, you can just pick up layers of paper as needed to keep the cages clean. Cleanliness is very important, and the babies won't help you. As they move around, they will step in anything and everything.

> The things that are most important to successfully raising baby iguanas, besides food, are eliminating stress, and providing a secure environment with proper lighting and heat.

An incandescent light above each cage container should heat one spot to 95°F. There should be several basking spots and branches within the heat circle produced by this light so that all of the hatchlings can warm themselves. Babies need this high temperature, so make sure you check it with a thermometer. Don't guess at this!

A fluorescent light producing UVA and UVB rays can be shared amongst the cages. Set it on one cage for a few hours, then move it to another. By rotating it, each of the hatchlings will get adequate light.

The things that are most important to successfully raising baby iguanas, besides food (which I'll discuss next), are eliminating stress, and providing a secure environment with proper lighting and heat. With these things, the iguanas should grow up without problems.

## Feeding the Babies

Water should be supplied in a bowl with shallow sides. Make sure this is shallow enough so the smallest, weakest baby can get out of the water easily. Change the water often, as the babies will walk through it and defecate in it.

Hatchling iguanas often don't eat for a few days after hatching, so be prepared for this and don't panic when they don't eat. However, when they are ready to eat, they can eat the same thing that larger iguanas eat, except that it should be chopped up into smaller pieces. Remember these are babies and the food must be small enough so they can swallow it without choking.

I talked about diets for baby iguanas in chapter 3, but just as a reminder, a sample diet for a hatchling iguana could look like this:

- 40 percent calcium-rich green vegetables: alfalfa, collard greens, mustard greens, dandelions, spinach greens, cabbage, bok choy, Swiss chard, kale, beet greens, green beans, broccoli
- 40 percent other vegetables: grated squash, zucchini, bell peppers, sprouts, grated carrots, canned or frozen mixed vegetables, tomatoes, okra, sweet potatoes, clean rose blossoms, clean hibiscus blossoms
- 20 percent other foods: whole-grain cereals, whole-grain bread, commercial iguana food, tofu

A varied diet is important. The best ingredients will make no difference at all if only a few good ingredients are offered. Instead, feed a varied diet that gives the hatchling iguana a variety of foods.

Supplement the foods with a vitamin-mineral and calcium supplement three to four times a week. Although a good diet should supply everything your iguana babies need, this is extra protection.

## Finding Homes for the Hatchlings

Be prepared to keep the hatchlings for at least a month or two. You want to make sure they are healthy, eating well, and growing before you send them away.

When you decided to breed, you came up with some ideas about what you wanted to do with these babies, and now is the time to implement them. Do you have some people lined up who seriously want a captive-bred, home-raised iguana? Are you going to sell your babies to a pet store? Can you deal with the fact that you won't know where these babies will end up?

You can also try putting a classified ad in the local newspaper, and then screening the callers very well. Have they owned iguanas before? What happened to that (or those) iguanas? Are they prepared to do what is needed to give this hatchling a good, long life?

You helped bring these babies into the world, so it's your responsibility to make sure they have the best life they can. Be careful!

# 10

# An Iguana in the Family

### In This Chapter
- Time Together
- Your Iguana and Your Family
- Keeping Your Iguana Safe at Home

Having an iguana in the family is certainly not like having a dog in the family. Perhaps because domesticated dogs have been living with us for thousands of years, they just kind of fit right into our family. Iguanas, however, take a little more adjustment to make them fit in. However, given time, a little effort, and a lot of patience, an iguana can become a vital, integral part of your family.

## Time Together

One of the most important things you can give your iguana (other than good care, of course) is your time. Your iguana is not going to come begging to you for attention. He's not going to drop the tennis ball in your lap like your dog will, nor will he sit in the hallway meowing for petting like your cat will. Your iguana, if left alone, will sit in his cage very quietly day after day.

> One of the most important things you can give your iguana (other than good care, of course) is your time.

However, the more he's left alone, the less socialized he will be and the wilder he will become. All the taming you did will disappear! You can keep your iguana tame only by spending time with him. Part of that time can be spent cleaning his cage, caring for him, and trimming his toenails. Other time can be spent doing things with him. This time can be, as the saying goes, "quality time."

## Time for Care

As I've already mentioned, caring for your iguana does require some time and effort on your part. How much time depends on many things, including how organized you are, how big your iguana is, how big his cage is, and how it's set up. However, you can estimate some time that might be required.

### Every Day

- Feeding your iguana: If you get your iguana's greens and groceries while you're shopping for yourself and your family, then shopping won't take any additional time. However, if you need to make a special trip to the pet store to pick up some commercial iguana food and some vitamins, that takes some time.
- Actually preparing your iguana's food won't take more than 10 minutes, tops, even if you have to soak some dry iguana food in warm water. Washing his food and water bowls will take a few minutes, as well.

- Cleaning his feeding area: Iguanas are not the neatest eaters! Food ends up pushed out of the bowl and dribbled here and there. This mess will be repeated every day, and the feeding area should be cleaned every day. However, it should only take you a couple of minutes to pick up spilled food and wipe down the surface where the food bowls sits.
- Cleaning his potty area: This could take a few minutes, depending on how you have the area set up. If your iguana has been trained to use a large kitty litter box, simply scoop the feces or dump the box, rinse it out and refill it with clean litter.

If he's had some accidents elsewhere in the cage, then of course you will need to spend a little more time cleaning up after him.

So far, doing these daily chores you've spent about 20 minutes caring for your iguana.

**Now and Then** Some of the other chores don't have to be done every day, but let's see how much time you'll need to set aside for them.

- Tidying up the cage: Every other day or so you will need to go through the cage, picking up or vacuuming up shedded skin and old food. You will need to clean up any feces that missed the litter box and scrub down any dirty surfaces. Depending upon the size of your iguana's cage and how active and how dirty he is, this should take 15 to 20 minutes.
- Completely cleaning the cage: Once a week you should thoroughly clean the cage. This means taking everything out of it, scrubbing everything, replacing cage substrates, and washing walls. If your iguana is young and is still in a 30- to 40-gallon tank aquarium, this might take a half an hour. If your iguana is full grown and is in a large iguana cage, this project could easily require a full hour's work.

- Cleaning the outside enclosure: Once a week you will need to clean your iguana's outside enclosure. This is easier than cleaning an inside cage because you should be able to use the hose to rinse it down, then scrub it, then rinse it again. Depending on how the cage is set up and how big it is, this should take a half an hour to 45 minutes.
- Cleaning other places: Where else does your iguana go? If he has a cat tree, once a week you will need to vacuum that. If he likes to lie on the back of the couch, you may want to vacuum up any shedded skin. Of course, you will clean up any accidents as they happen. These chores could take five minutes to 15 minutes.
- Cleaning your iguana: Your iguana should be clean, too, and will need a weekly bath. If you put him in the bathtub while you're cleaning his cage, you can do two things at the same time. Leave him in the tub as long as it takes to clean his cage. Just check on him often to make sure he doesn't get chilled and keep the water shallow so he doesn't drown.
- Your iguana also needs some personal care, as I discussed in chapter 8, and all of these little things take some time.
- Trimming toenails: If your iguana is calm and relaxed, this little chore might just take two or three minutes. However, if he's excited, or excitable, it could take 10 times as long! In other words, do it quickly, safely, and when your iguana is relaxed.
- Other body care: You may have to help your iguana shed some dead skin off his spines, or you may have to rub some mineral or baby oil into the dead skin on his toes so that he can shed it better. You may have to trim a toenail that caught on something and tore. Depending upon what your iguana needs, this could take five minutes or 15.

## Time for Taming

Taming and training your iguana also requires time, and this time is well spent. Unlike cage cleaning, when you're taming and training your iguana you're spending time touching and bonding with him. This is the proverbial "quality time."

Usually you'll spend the most time taming your iguana in the first months after you bring him home. Once the iguana is tame, you shouldn't have to repeat the process. However, if the iguana has been left alone for several months without much handling or interaction, you may have to repeat the entire process again.

Taming an iguana usually requires several things, each of which takes time.

- Hand-feeding your iguana: When you've prepared your iguana's food, offer him a few pieces by hand. This isn't time-consuming at all and only takes a few minutes.
- In and out of the cage: Teaching your iguana to go in and out of the cage (as I discussed in chapter 7) will take a little bit of time—probably 10 to 15 minutes each time—especially when your iguana is still wild. Once he is tame and calms down, it will be much easier, of course.
- Gentle handling: During the taming process, you should take the time to handle him at least once a day—and two or three times is even better. Ideally, you should sit on the sofa with the iguana in your hands or on your lap for five minutes each session.
- Training: Once your iguana is tame, you can begin training him. The time spent doing this will vary tremendously, depending upon many different factors. If you are a very good animal trainer and your iguana is calm and attentive, each training session might be five minutes and very productive. If you are new to iguana training and your iguana is distracted, a single training session might be 15 minutes long.

> During the taming process, you should take the time to handle him at least once a day—and two or three times is even better.

## Hand-Taming a Baby

Draco, our baby iguana, is still not quite hand-tamed. He will try to escape from our hands when we reach in for him so we plan our movements ahead of time. We don't want him to think our hands are monsters that chase him! So we reach in with a piece of strawberry, tofu, or other good food. When he takes it, we then we gently pick him up.

Your iguana also needs exercise. Exercise is good for the body—the iguana's as well as our own—and unfortunately, many captive iguanas become couch potatoes. Therefore, you need to take the time to make sure your iguana gets some exercise. You can combine this with a handling and training session if you want.

# How Do You Exercise an Iguana?

Exercise has as many benefits for iguanas as it does for us. With regular exercise, the iguana's body maintains muscle tone and keeps blood flowing throughout the body, and everything functions as it should. With exercise and stimulation, your iguana's brain remains alert and attentive. There is no downside to exercise.

There are several ways to make sure your iguana gets some exercise.

○ Environmental enrichment: Many zoos use environmental enrichment to keep their captive animals active and mentally alert. Favorite foods are hidden throughout the animal's enclosure, which means he must move around, sniff, and explore to find all the hidden treats. You can do the same thing in your iguana's cage, outside enclosure, or even in your family room. Hide some bits of food in easy-to-find places at first, and help your iguana find them. As he gets better at searching for the bits of food, you can make the hiding spots more difficult—but do this gradually so he doesn't get discouraged and quit.

Once your iguana gets the hang of this, it can be great fun. You can hide different foods in a variety of places: a piece of corn under the edge of the sofa, a piece of squash on the cat tree, and a green pea under the coffee table. Just remember where you hid everything so you can go back later and pick up what your iguana missed!

Some dog toys also make great iguana toys. The Kong is a hard rubber toy that looks like a colorful snowman. It has three balls of different sizes squished together and it's hollow. You can put some favorite foods in the Kong and then let your iguana figure out how to get them out. Some small grapes work well, or some small chunks of squash.

The idea of the environmental enrichment is not just that your iguana gets some extra treats, but that the treats are rewards for moving around. With treats in hiding places or treats in dog toys, your iguana will be off his basking log and moving around, getting some exercise.

○ Using the target stick: Use the training target stick to have your iguana follow you around the house, climb up on the sofa, climb up his cat tree, and do other activities. Remember, iguanas don't run marathons, so even a walk around the house is exercise.

# Your Iguana and Your Family

Iguanas usually tend to be one-person pets. Maybe one person is more active in their care or perhaps one person is more

patient with the taming process. Although this is quite common, it doesn't have to be this way. In fact, the iguana will be more successful as a pet when the whole family can interact with him.

## Your Iguana and Your Kids

It's important to supervise young children when they are interacting with the iguana. If you're supervising, you can quickly halt any inappropriate behavior on the kids' and the iguana's parts. Make sure the children don't tease the iguana, scream, and run from him, or handle him inappropriately. Make sure the iguana remains calm with the kids, takes food nicely from them without biting, and doesn't whip the kids with his tail.

> It's important to supervise young children when they are interacting with the iguana.

Children will get bored quickly if all they are allowed to do is watch the iguana perched on his basking log. However, if you allow the kids to do some things—even small things—with the iguana, they will be much more interested in him. What can your kids do with the iguana?

- Hand-feed him special treats.
- Pick some rose blossoms for him in the backyard.
- Watch him when you put him in the bathtub.
- Help you rub baby or mineral oil into his skin where old skin hasn't shed yet.
- Supervise his actions when he's allowed out of his cage in the house.
- Use the target stick to exercise him.

Before you consider leaving your kids alone with an uncaged iguana, make sure they can handle him safely. They should know

## Should a Child Own an Iguana?

It's hard to recommend a lizard that could grow to six feet long and 20-plus pounds as a good child's pet! However, some of the best, most knowledgeable, and most committed iguana owners I've talked to have been teenagers. Therefore, I will say that an iguana can be a child's pet, but I will add quite a few reservations.

- To show the dedication and perseverance needed to be an iguana owner, the child should earn all or most of the money needed to buy the iguana and the cage.
- The child should be required to do some research and reading on iguanas, their care, and needs before being allowed to get the iguana.
- After doing the research, the child should be able to tell his/her parent(s) exactly what an iguana will need as far as caging, care, and diet.
- The child's parent(s) must be involved in the decision to get an iguana.
- The child's parent(s) must be involved in the iguana's care and should supervise day-to-day care and activities.

how to pick him up, how to control him if he thrashes or whips his tail, and when to let him go (rather than try to hold him).

You should also have some rules established regarding the iguana. Are children allowed to take him out of the cage if you are not home? Can they take him out of the cage when friends are over? Who is allowed to take him out of his cage? Who is allowed to handle him? Where are they allowed to take him? Is the iguana allowed in the family room, the kids' bedrooms, or outside?

Make sure, too, that the kids understand that they are to thoroughly wash their hands after handling the iguana. If friends are over, they are to wash their hands, too.

If you have an adult male iguana, do not let the kids have unsupervised access to the iguana during breeding season or any other time. An aggressive adult male could hurt the kids.

## Your Iguana and Your Spouse or Roommate

Having an iguana as a pet can sometimes cause trouble in a relationship, and when there's trouble, the iguana's future can be threatened. A spouse or roommate may have said "yes" when first asked about acquiring an iguana, but then found that actually having an iguana was more complicated than they thought. More than one spouse or roommate has said, "It's either the iguana or me! Choose!"

Because iguanas are so large and require a very large cage, and cages rarely fit into a home's décor, this can cause trouble. If your spouse really enjoys an attractive house with matching furniture, colors, and styles, the iguana cage could be an eyesore. However, cages do not have to be unattractive. There are several manufacturers that build really attractive iguana cages, or you can hire someone to build a cage that will satisfy your spouse's requirements.

> It's important to supervise young children when they are interacting with the iguana.

Iguanas can also make a mess. The area around the cage could get messy with spilled food, shedded skin, and feces that missed the litter box. To keep your spouse or roommate happy, keep this area clean. You may also want to keep a throw rug or two on the floor under the cage. This could make housecleaning chores easier.

When your iguana is out of his cage, make sure he's supervised. It only takes a moment for an unsupervised iguana to climb up on the desk and knock everything off. If there are already some hard feelings about the lizard, having the bills, mail, and other paperwork knocked to the floor will certainly not endear the iguana to your spouse or roommate! Broken knick-knacks, vases, or other collectibles will also cause bad feelings, so make sure you supervise the iguana carefully.

Sometimes a spouse or roommate is jealous of the time spent with the iguana. Make sure your better half doesn't feel as if he or she has been replaced by a lizard. Although this may sound absurd, it happens, especially when you bring home an exciting new pet and are spending a lot of time with him.

The best way to make sure your spouse or roommate will accept your iguana is to try to incorporate them into activities involving the iguana. Have them hand-feed the iguana. Let them see what you're doing while you're taming and training the iguana. Ask for their opinion or input about what to do with the taming and training and let them try working with the target stick. You are more likely to have their backing and support for the iguana if they come to like him. If they don't like the lizard, or don't care, it's more likely there will be bad feelings.

## Your Iguana and Your Other Pets

My dogs respect Conan. They have each, at some time, been whacked with his tail and they know the strength behind that tail. However, all of my dogs now are younger than Conan and met him when they were puppies and he was already a full-grown adult. Because they know his strength, I doubt that any of the three

> **Did You Know?**
> Where are family members allowed to take the new pet? Do you want him in one room? Outside? Or restricted to a few rooms?

dogs would even think of attacking him, but we don't take this for granted. The dogs are never left alone with Conan.

Now, my dogs don't respect our other lizards at all, including the leopard geckos and bearded dragons, and especially not the baby rhinoceros iguana, Draco. All of these lizards are small, obviously weak (compared to the dogs), and look like prey to the dogs. Therefore, these lizards are always securely caged when the dogs are inside and taken out of their cage only when the dogs are outside.

The same rules apply to our cats. The small reptiles are securely caged when the cats are in the same room and are taken out only when the cats are nowhere around.

Keep in mind that cats and dogs are, by nature, predators. The instinct to chase and catch something that is moving, especially moving quickly, is more than some dogs and cats can control. If a juvenile iguana took off running across the room, even my well-trained dogs would have a hard time ignoring that invitation to chase! Most dogs and cats would immediately dash after the moving lizard, and if they were able to catch him, would kill him. Many iguana owners tell me their pets of different species get along just fine with no attempts to eat one another. My response? Wonderful, but don't trust them! It only takes one second for a dog or cat to grab a lizard and kill him. It's not worth the risk.

> Don't let a large bird out of its cage at the same time the iguana is out of his cage.

Your reptiles should also be protected from large birds. Macaws and parrots could easily take a chunk out of an iguana, hurting him terribly, and possibly even killing him. Don't let a large bird out of its cage at the same time the iguana is out of his cage.

## Train Your Dog!

Your dog is capable of quite sophisticated training. Depending upon your skills and desires, you can teach your dog to behave himself when the iguana is out of his cage. Have your dog lie down and stay on a small rug (which can become his target or spot) on the other side of the room from the iguana. But again, even with training, don't leave the dog and iguana alone together! Instincts easily override training.

Small birds, on the other hand, could become a meal for many reptiles, and although very few iguanas look upon a bird as prey, it has happened. One iguana owner told me her large female iguana ate the pet parakeet! Apparently the parakeet was out of its cage flying around the house and landed right next to the iguana, who was basking on the back of the sofa. The iguana looked at the bird, gave one tongue flick and swallowed the bird whole!

Although that could be considered very unusual, I wouldn't put it past an adult iguana to tongue flick or "taste" a small bird just to see what it was. A tongue flick obviously wouldn't hurt the bird, but a nibble might.

Iguanas shouldn't be housed with other reptiles, either. You can have several different cages with reptile residents in the same room, but don't put other reptiles in the same cage with your iguana. Unless the reptiles are from the same geographical area, the chances of the reptiles having different parasites or carrying diseases from which iguanas have no immunity is too great. In addition, roommates often don't get along. Who gets the basking spot? Who eats first? There are too many risks. Our female iguana, Cannibal, has that horrible name because as a baby iguana she ate all of her roommates!

In addition, iguanas are not social butterflies, are very territorial, and do much better alone. You can have other pets while keeping an iguana, just protect the various pets from one another.

## Keeping Your Iguana Safe at Home

We already know that most accidents happen in the home. People trip and fall, lose their balance on a ladder, or cut themselves with a kitchen knife. Home can be a dangerous place. It can be just as dangerous for your iguana, so take a few minutes and make sure your iguana is as safe as you can make him.

Your iguana's cage should already be a safe place for him with nothing in it that could injure him or allow him to injure himself. Make sure, too, that there is nothing close to the cage that your iguana could reach and damage or that could hurt him. For example, is there an electrical outlet right next to his cage? What would happen if he spilled his water and it splashed onto that outlet? Are there any collectibles or breakable knick-knacks within reach of his tail? Dangers are not always obvious.

Taking nothing for granted, look at the cage from an iguana's viewpoint. What is in the cage that is dangerous, uncomfortable, or unusable? What should be changed or rearranged?

Then look at the immediate vicinity of the cage. Look for lights or lamps, electrical outlets, extension cords, knick-knacks, and other breakables. Look, too, for valuables that could be damaged. What about books that shouldn't be splashed by water?

Next, look at the places where you allow your iguana time out of his cage. Does he perch on the back of the couch? Do you have a favorite afghan that would catch his toenails? You ought to put that away when you bring out your iguana. Is your sofa brand new? Don't let him climb on it—have him perch on the old chair instead.

Does he have a cat tree? Is it firmly anchored so that his weight won't cause it to fall? Where is it? What is within reach of it? Move any valuables or dangerous items.

Do you allow your iguana to roam around the house? Make sure you keep him in sight at all times and pay attention to him. Not only could he break or harm lots of stuff—especially if he tries to climb—but he could also harm himself. Bookshelves, curtains, entertainment centers, plants (real and fake), and anything tall is of particular interest to your arboreal lizard.

Once when Conan was out, my husband got distracted and forgot to watch him. Conan tried to climb every potted plant in our living room, and at that time we had several. As he tried to climb them, he broke a few (he is a big, heavy lizard), knocked over the rest, and proceeded to spread leaves and potting soil all over the living room. The next time Conan was out of his cage, my husband watched him more carefully!

## Changes in the Normal Routine

Iguanas are creatures of habit and love a regular routine. Although most iguanas become quite confidant and blasé as they get older, anything that upsets the normal routine is frightening to many young iguanas. Therefore, holidays (especially the winter holidays) can be times of uncertainty for your iguana. Houseguests can also be upsetting. However, you can help your iguana cope with changes.

> Although most iguanas become quite confidant and blasé as they get older, anything that upsets the normal routine is frightening to many young iguanas.

## Holidays

If you like holidays and like to decorate the house, make sure you take your iguana into consideration when you do so. If you can, make the changes a few at a time so that your iguana can get used to them. Plus, don't hang decorations on his cage; it won't be appreciated! In addition, they might be eaten, or at least tasted.

If the Easter bunny visits your house, leave him a note and ask him to leave the eggs and candy somewhere away from the iguana's cage. This is not only to protect the iguana (he might try to taste the eggs or candy) but to protect the kids (to reduce the risk of salmonella, they should not eat any eggs or candy the iguana has touched).

Flag Day and the Fourth of July present a few different problems. Don't hang flags on your iguana's cage, and don't carry him with you to the city parade. Brightly colored flags blowing and snapping in the breeze could be quite disturbing to your iguana. Make sure he's at home, on his basking log, with the cage door firmly latched before the fireworks begin. Most iguanas are not overly sound sensitive, but many have been known to panic at fireworks going off nearby. If your iguana seems upset, cover his cage with a heavy blanket, close all of the doors and windows to the house, and make it as quiet as you can.

Halloween can also be a problem. If you wish to make your iguana a part of your act, that's fine as long as you're careful. If you make him a costume, make sure it fits him very well, without any pinching or binding. Don't squash his dorsal spines and make sure he can move. Teach him to wear the costume a small piece at a time. Put it on him, hand-feed him a choice bit of food, and then take it off. When you are wearing your costume, especially a mask, let him see you put it on and then take it off. Don't try to scare him—you will only damage the trust he has in your relationship.

Thanksgiving usually doesn't pose any problems to iguanas unless guests come over, and I'll talk about that shortly. Don't feed your iguana turkey and gravy or cranberry sauce. Instead, keep him on his normal diet. Too many new or different foods could cause gastrointestinal upsets.

Christmas and iguanas don't always go well together. Picture in your mind a Christmas tree falling over because a heavy iguana tried to climb it! It has happened many times and will happen again in the future. To an iguana, a tree is something to climb. Keep a close watch on your iguana when he's anywhere near the Christmas tree, or better yet, exercise him in a different room so that he's nowhere near the Christmas tree. If you can't watch him every minute, put him back in his cage and close the door. It only takes a second for him to make a dash for the tree and start to climb.

If your house is decorated for Christmas, again, watch your iguana. Holly, poinsettia, and mistletoe can all be dangerous if your iguana eats them. Tinsel off the tree, glass balls, and candles may attract your iguana with their bright colors and sparkling reflections, but all can be dangerous. Your iguana can also be incredibly destructive to decorations. An iguana doesn't belong in the middle of your mother's (or spouse's) favorite and fragile Nativity scene!

You may have to restrict your iguana to a few safe places during the holidays. Keep him in your arms when he's in the

**Did You Know?**
President Theodore Roosevelt kept a number of pets while he was in the White House and among those was a lizard named Josiah (species unknown) and a garter snake named Emily.

room where the decorations are, and let him down to exercise in another room away from the attractive but dangerous holiday decorations.

## Guests Can Be Upsetting

Like new decorations, guests can be upsetting to your iguana. Strange people in the house are threats as far as your iguana is concerned. Your iguana knows who lives in the house with him. He knows their smell, their appearance, and how they move. He knows what to expect from each one—who feeds him, who scratches his spines, and who rubs his forehead. Strange people are exactly that, and many iguanas, especially sexually mature males, do not like trespassers.

> Strange people in the house are threats as far as your iguana is concerned.

When your guests first arrive, ask them to simply ignore your iguana. Tell them to walk on past him without acknowledging him at all. This will relieve his stress. After all, if they don't see him, they won't prey upon him.

In a day or two they can hand-feed him, offering him something special so that he'll take it from someone different. If he closes his eyes, ignores the treat, and pretends they don't exist, have them go back to ignoring him.

Make sure your guests understand that staring is a threat. If your guests have never lived with an iguana, they will want to stare—after all, he is different! However, staring will make your iguana feel very uncomfortable.

Don't let your guests take your iguana out of his cage, handle him, or pick him up. Remember, no matter how tame he is with you, that tameness is with you specifically. *You* have tamed him. *You* have taught him to trust you. You didn't teach him to trust all people; just you. He may not (and probably won't) accept handling from strangers and he may hurt them by using his claws or his tail while trying to get away from them. In addition, you may damage your relationship with him; if your guests frighten him, it may take awhile for him to relax again with you.

Make sure, too, that your guests don't treat your iguana roughly. Some people seem to think that iguanas are rough and tough—like dinosaurs used to be—and want to wrestle with them or treat them roughly. Iguanas are surprisingly fragile, though, and cannot tolerate rough handling. Not only could rough handling break some toes, legs, or the tail, but this rough handling could ruin all of the taming you have done with your iguana.

## It's Vacation Time

We all look forward to that week or two each year when we can get away from the daily grind. You may go camping in the mountains, relaxing on a cruise ship, or shopping in Paris. The whole idea of a vacation is to get away from the daily stress of life and do something relaxing. So what happens to your iguana when you go on vacation?

Most iguanas don't travel well. Not only does the change in routine upset most iguanas, but they also lose their sense of security. At home your iguana is comfortable. He knows the sights, smells, and sounds of home. When traveling, everything is new and potentially threatening. If you are doing a lot of traveling, staying in a different place each night, your iguana will never get comfortable in his surroundings. That's a lot of stress.

In addition, it is very difficult to provide the correct temperatures for your iguana while traveling. Your iguana is most comfortable at 85°F. I doubt you will want your car heated to 85° (with the windows closed) for your entire trip!

> When stressed, many iguanas will stop eating and drinking—a dangerous reaction to traveling.

When stressed, many iguanas will stop eating and drinking—a dangerous reaction to traveling. If chilled or overheated, this could combine with the lack of appetite and create a very, very sick iguana. It is much easier to leave your iguana at home while you're on vacation.

## Leaving Your Iguana at Home

When my husband and I travel, we leave our reptile pets at home and have a trusted pet sitter come in to care for them. This way, our pets remain in their respective cages where they are comfortable and secure, and where they are kept in the correct humidity levels, temperature and so on. Not only does this enable them to remain stress-free, but then I don't worry about them either and can enjoy my vacation.

Our pet sitter is a professional who does this for a living and is a member of Pet Sitters International (www.petsit.com). I prefer to hire someone to watch my pets—rather than have a neighbor baby-sit them—because the pet sitter is a licensed and bonded professional and is reliable. If I ask her to come over twice a day, I know she will, whereas if I ask a neighbor or a neighbor's teenager, I feel I may be intruding or asking them to spend too much time with my pets when they might prefer to be doing something else.

Years ago, my husband and I had a bad experience with a neighbor pet-sitting for our menagerie. Apparently, one day the

## If You Must Travel with Your Iguana

If you absolutely must travel with your iguana, such as for a job transfer, make some arrangements ahead of time. Find a plastic crate (such as a dog crate) large enough so that your iguana can hold his body and most of his tail straight. If part of his tail is curved, that's okay. Feed your iguana in the crate for a few days so he gets used to it.

Before you leave home, take your iguana to the veterinarian and get a health certificate stating that the animal is in good health. Some states require this when you cross the border into the state.

If you will be traveling during cool weather, go to a store that sells camping supplies and pick up a few chemical reaction heaters—the kind you tuck into a pocket to keep your hands warm. You can use one of these at a time wrapped in a towel to keep your iguana warm in his crate.

Carry some Gatorade or Pedialyte with you and a syringe with the needle removed. If your iguana doesn't want to eat during the trip, regularly give him several syringes full of either of these liquids several times a day, so that you can prevent dehydration.

neighbor's son left the lid to one of our snake cages open and the snake escaped. When we came home, we had to go down to the local shelter to identify, claim, and bail out our wayward snake. We got our snake back, but it wasn't the homecoming we would have preferred.

However, with a pet sitter, we leave instructions about how each animal is to be cared for and fed, and how the cage should be cleaned. When we get home, everything is as it should be. It's a wonderful way to come home from a vacation!

Don't wait until the last minute to look for a pet sitter. Most good ones book up early, especially around the holidays, and you may be out of luck. So start months ahead of time.

When you talk to the pet sitter the first time, tell him or her that you have reptile(s) and specifically, an iguana. Make sure this person likes iguanas and isn't afraid of them. If he or she is afraid, tell them "Thank you" and continue calling other pet sitters.

When you've found a reputable pet sitter who isn't afraid of reptiles, invite the pet sitter over to meet your iguana. Invite him or her to touch or pet your iguana and to hand-feed him. Show them where everything is kept, where feces should be disposed of, and where cleaning supplies are stored.

Before you leave on vacation, give your veterinarian a letter authorizing the pet sitter to get necessary care for your iguana should something happen while you're gone. If you have limits as to how much should be spent, put that in the letter. If there will be an emergency number for you—such as your cell phone number—put that in the letter as well.

> Don't wait until the last minute to look for a pet sitter. Most good ones book up early.

Leave detailed instructions for the pet sitter. Don't assume that he or she knows *any*thing (although she probably does!). Put it in writing anyway. What should your iguana be fed, how much, and how should it be served? Chopped? Diced? Whole? How often should the water be changed? What schedule are the lights on? Is there an automatic timer for the lights? Where are lightbulbs kept in case one burns out? Tell him where feces should be disposed of and leave out some garbage bags.

Just before you drive away, call your pet sitter to verify her assignment. Make sure she has the key to your house and ask her if she has any questions. This last call will make sure you don't have to worry, so you can have a good time on your vacation.

## Boarding Your Iguana

If you can't find a pet sitter in your area who will care for your iguana, or if you aren't comfortable having someone in your house when you aren't home, you can look into boarding your iguana. Most boarding kennels are not set up to care for reptiles, especially large iguanas, but some dog and cat boarding kennels will care for iguanas if you can bring in your cage.

In this situation, your iguana remains in his own cage, which is good, but the environment around him changes and this could cause some stress, depending upon where his cage is situated in the kennel. Don't allow his cage to be set up in the dog area where barking dogs are dashing back and forth all day long. Setting his cage in the cat area usually isn't a good idea either, unless you have cats at home that don't bother the iguana.

If it's possible, the best location for the iguana's cage is in the kennel kitchen area, where people will go back and forth but there are not too many other pets. If this isn't possible, then a wide hallway where there wouldn't be any draft is the next best thing. Make sure you talk to the kennel people and find out where his cage will be set up before you make arrangements to leave your pet.

When you bring in your iguana for a stay, bring in his own food and instructions as to how to feed him. Leave instructions about his other care, too, including how often you want his water changed and his cage cleaned. Make sure they will leave on his lights or heat emitter, even at night. Leave the number for your veterinarian and instructions about when he should be called. Make sure your vet knows that the iguana will be staying at the kennel, too.

## One of the Family

Having an iguana as a pet means the iguana should fit into your family without too much disruption. Obviously, some disruption is necessary, because your iguana does need some special care and has some requirements that cannot be compromised. However, having an iguana shouldn't mean that you can never again have guests in the house or never go on vacation again. That kind of a commitment is going too far!

# 11

# When Your Iguana Grows Old

### In This Chapter
- How Long Do Iguanas Live?
- What We Know About Aging
- When It's Time to Say Good-Bye

You can look at just about any book on reptiles and find information about most species' geographical origins, body conformation and coloration, information about keeping it as a pet, and breeding instructions. But very few books tell you anything about specific reptile species and old age. Why is this?

It's only been recently that we, as reptile keepers, have known enough about reptile environmental and nutritional needs to enable our pets to live long enough in captivity to grow old. Until we gained this knowledge, reptiles in captivity lived short and sometimes horrible lives.

Today, however, we are seeing many reptiles, including iguanas, reach older ages than we ever thought possible, and although it's wonderful in one sense, this longevity brings with it other problems. Veterinarians are scrambling to find out how to treat aging iguanas. Medications and treatment techniques that work well for dogs or cats may or many not be as effective with iguanas. Iguana owners must try different things to adapt a cage and living quarters for iguanas showing signs of arthritis, and then are struggling with the loss of a pet who has been a part of the family for 15 to 20 years.

No one said iguana ownership was easy, and iguana old age can be quite difficult. However, there is a special joy that comes with living with an old companion. You've known this iguana for years. You know his likes and dislikes, his moods and his reactions to different things. You know where he likes to be rubbed or scratched, and you know where he has trouble shedding his old skin. An old pet is a special treasure.

The fact that this animal has lived to old age is a pat on your back, as well. You've done things correctly if he has thrived in captivity and lived to a ripe, old age. Good for you!

## How Long Do Iguanas Live?

Frank Slavens maintains records on reptile longevity in captivity, and his records show individual iguanas reaching 13 to 19 years of age. The oldest known iguana belonged to Don Burnham of California. His iguana, Iggy, passed away at the age of 29 years. (This is according to James W. Hatfield, III, who wrote *Green Iguana: The Ultimate Owner's Manual.*) Twenty-nine years is a long time, and very few (if any) other iguanas will make it to that ancient age. However, as our knowledge of iguana care and nutrition increases, and as veterinary knowledge progresses, I think we will see more iguanas living to 15, 18, and perhaps even 20 years old.

## What We Know About Aging

Aging in all animals—mammals and reptiles—seems to have some common characteristics. For one thing, there does seem to be something of a set life span for all animals. For example, domestic shorthaired cats that are spayed or neutered and live inside usually live to the age of 15 to 17. That seems to be the average life span for these cats.

> As our knowledge of iguana care and nutrition increases, and as veterinary knowledge progresses, I think we will see more iguanas living to 15, 18, and perhaps even 20 years old.

There are quite a few things that can affect the life span of any animal, making it either longer or shorter. Obviously, good nutrition is a big part of a healthy life, as is protection from danger. Injury, illness, and stress can also affect longevity. Although we don't yet know what the life span of iguanas in captivity will turn out to be, we know that it will lengthen as their quality of life gets better.

In the wild, aging animals slow down. Older animals can't run as fast to escape predators or to capture their prey. However, the experiences of years of survival have also made older animals wiser. After all, they have survived to old age and in the wild, many do not! Aging animals also don't take the chances young animals do; they rely on their wits and their experience rather than on bravado and physical speed or strength.

We don't know a lot about old iguanas in the wild. Since it's impossible to watch a single iguana for years, and since iguana

## When Is an Iguana Old?

There is no set age where you can then consider your iguana to be old. Aging in iguanas is usually a very gradual process. In fact, you probably won't even notice much difference until one day you realize that your iguana has changed right before your eyes. The iguana owners I talked to said by the time their iguana was 12 or 13, they considered their pet old.

research in the wild is still basically in its infancy, we can only admit there is much we don't know.

### What to Expect

As animals age, certain things change, both in the animal's behavior and in bodily functions. Although there are individual differences, some changes seem to apply to many different animals. Most iguanas become even more sedentary than they were as younger animals. With our old man iguana, Conan, we have noticed that there are days when he doesn't move about much at all. When he was younger, he would make several trips in and out through his lizard door to his outside cage, as well as several trips to and from his basking log. Now, he will get off his basking log to go eat, to go to his litter box, and to bask in the sun. Then he will go back to his log and remain there for the rest of the day.

Acting like a bump on a log isn't necessarily good for your iguana, even an older one. He needs to move around a little to keep his joints free and moving, to keep his bodily functions working, and to wake up his mind. So take him out of his cage, give him some physical and mental stimulation and keep him moving—within reason, of course! Obviously, you won't take him

# When Your Iguana Grows Old

## Keep Your Iguana Comfortable

As your iguana grows older, he may be less comfortable resting on a log. If he's has arthritis, it may be harder for him to climb up on or rest on a hard branch. You can make him more comfortable by giving him a basking shelf instead. The shelf should be wider than his body. A folded towel on the shelf will provide some comfort and will help hold the heat. Secure the shelf under his basking light and install a ramp so that he can climb up to it easily.

jogging. However, a daily walk around the living room or the backyard will be good for him.

Also, if you notice your iguana spending a lot of time on his basking log without moving, you may want to check the temperature in the rest of his cage. It might be too chilly. His old bones and joints will appreciate the warmth.

Since your iguana is no longer growing at the speed of light—as he did when he was younger—he will also shed less often. Some large, old iguanas may only shed once or twice a year. Your iguana's appetite will also slow down. He may go for a day or two without eating. Don't be too worried about a day or two; just keep him warm and make sure he has clean water. You can even give him a few ounces of Gatorade or Pedialyte to keep him hydrated. (Use a needless syringe to put the fluid in his mouth.) However, if he goes for more than four days without eating, talk to your veterinarian.

You may also find that your iguana is getting heavier, even though his appetite is decreasing. Obesity is very common in older animals, even reptiles. As your iguana moves around less, he uses fewer calories and the weight begins to accumulate. A heavier body type is normal in older iguanas, especially males.

However, don't confuse a wider, stockier body (which is normal) with an obese body. Obesity is not healthy.

## Illnesses of Old Age

Arthritis is very common in older animals. This usually first shows up as stiffness. Perhaps your iguana is having trouble jumping and you notice that he misses his jumps. He may even stop jumping altogether. He may also have trouble climbing. He may refuse to climb his cat tree or he may have difficulty getting up to his basking log. You will have to make some changes to his environment to keep him comfortable. For example, a leading ramp up to his basking log (or shelf) will ensure that he can still get up there to stay warm. Make sure, too, that your iguana moves around a little each day. He will do better when he keeps those joints moving.

> Although diabetes is not yet considered common in older iguanas, many veterinarians believe we will be seeing more of it as more iguanas live to older ages.

Diabetes occurs when the body's cells are unable to metabolize sugar in the blood due to a deficiency of insulin. Although diabetes is not yet considered common in older iguanas, many veterinarians believe we will be seeing more of it as more iguanas live to older ages. The first symptoms usually include increased water consumption, dehydration, and weight loss. A blood test can confirm the condition.

It seems that just about every animal on the face of this Earth except sharks can suffer from cancer, and that includes iguanas. I have known several iguanas that lived to 12, 13, 14, and even 15 years old and then died of cancer shortly after being diagnosed. Unfortunately, treatments for cancer in iguanas don't often lead to a cure.

## A Warm Bath Can Warm the Bones

If your iguana seems chilled or stiff, let him soak in a warm bath. Fill the bathtub with enough water for your iguana to soak but shallow enough so that he can touch the bottom. A temperature of 85°F is fine, and use a thermometer to test it. Let your iguana soak and move around until he limbers up. Then towel him off and put him under his basking light. Don't let him get chilled!

Kidney and liver failure are also a common in old age. The symptoms may be similar to those of diabetes, including increased thirst and dehydration. As with diabetes, a blood test can diagnose the problem. Many iguanas have lived for a year or two after being diagnosed with kidney or liver problems. Medications and a change in diet can often help.

Although deafness is a problem in many aging animals, it's not known whether old iguanas suffer from age-related deafness. After all, sometimes it's hard to get an iguana's attention even when he's young! You can try to test you iguana's hearing by making sounds. Drop a book to the floor, tap a spoon to a crystal glass, or pop a balloon and watch what his responses are.

Some veterinarians believe that as we see more iguanas getting older, we may see more with age-related eye problems. However, at this point we can only guess what those problems might be. Cataracts are a common eye problem in many species as they age, including humans and dogs. Some reptiles, including turtles, may get cataracts, but so far no one is willing to take a guess about whether cataracts plague older iguanas.

As you can see, there is a lot we don't know about aging in iguanas. So few iguanas have lived to what can realistically be called old age that we don't have enough knowledge upon which to base generalizations. We can look at aging in other animals and make comparisons, but there is just too much we don't know for sure.

## Working with Your Veterinarian

As your iguana grows older, you will be happy you took the time to keep his calendar journal up to date. Make note of when your iguana shed last, what his appetite has been like, and anything out of the ordinary as far as his bodily functions, activities, and behavior. Pay attention to details. Then, when you see something out of the ordinary, talk to your veterinarian. Use your skills as a knowledgeable, observant owner and your vet's medical skills to keep your iguana healthy, longer.

Work with your veterinarian. He may want to see your iguana a couple of times a year, even when there are no obvious problems. He may even want to run a few blood tests so that he can establish a normal range for your iguana. If you can afford the tests, do them, because when there are problems, your vet will have a normal reading to compare to.

Open and honest communication with your veterinarian will not only help you care for your aging iguana, but will also help you decide what course of care and treatment to follow, or decide when enough is enough. Keep in mind, too, as you talk to your vet, that aging is normal. If birth and growing up are the beginning of the circle, old age and death are the final connections.

Working with your veterinarian will also help other iguanas. Each iguana that lives to a ripe old age and is seen regularly by a veterinarian can increase the pool of veterinary knowledge about the species.

## When It's Time to Say Good-Bye

The human-animal bond is a special thing. When you look at it scientifically, the fact that two individuals from two totally different species can learn to trust one another and develop an affection for each other is absolutely amazing. I mean, really, iguanas and people are so drastically different! But in reality, the human-animal bond is anything but scientific; it's emotional.

No one gets a pet thinking, "Well, I'll keep this pet for 15 years and then suffer horribly when it dies of old age." If we thought that way, no one would have pets! But unfortunately, part of having pets and bonding with them means at some point we do have to deal with losing those pets. And if you care about your pets, it's never easy.

If you're lucky, you may wake up one morning, go in to check on your iguana, and find that he passed away peacefully in his sleep. Granted, this would be a shock for you, but it would be easy for him and would relieve you of the decision to have him put to sleep. Unfortunately, it's rarely this easy.

> **Did You Know?**
> We have no idea what the optimum life span is for reptile pets. As we learn more about their needs (and we continue to do so) they live longer.

### Euthanasia

Euthanasia means administering an overdose of a drug that stops the bodily functions. Some pet owners are firmly against any type of euthanasia. An acquaintance of mine says that whenever there is any spark of life, there is hope for the future—even if it's one day or even one hour at a time. However, the majority of pet owners would rather spare their pet any suffering, and opt for euthanasia when the time comes.

Deciding whether or not the time has come is the hardest part. Most pet owners use the phrase "quality of life." When the pet is still enjoying life, even the quiet life of old age, then life is still good. However, when that spark is gone, when life is a burden, then it's time to say good-bye.

So how can you tell when life is a burden?

- Your iguana stops eating.
- Your iguana stops drinking.
- Your iguana has an untreatable disease.
- Your iguana cannot move without pain.
- Your iguana is panting and in obvious discomfort.
- Your iguana's bowels are no longer working.
- Your iguana is no longer conscious.

Don't hesitate to talk to your veterinarian about euthanasia, but don't expect him to make the decision for you. He may be able to tell you that your iguana is in kidney failure or that he is in pain, but the vet cannot tell you to put your iguana to sleep. Only you can make that decision.

Each veterinarian has his or her own procedures for euthanasia. Some will come out to your home, while others ask you to bring your pet in to the office. If your vet asks you to bring your pet to his clinic, don't go alone. Ask your spouse, significant other, a friend, or a neighbor to go with you. You will need help driving home afterward. And I don't care how much you say you will be

## Saying Good-Bye to the Green Boy

Tom Sizeman, of Escondido, California, inherited Green Boy from his son. "I knew my son couldn't take the iguana to college with him, so I don't know why I was surprised when he asked me to keep Green Boy. I guess I had assumed he would find a new home for the iguana, maybe with one of his friends." At first, Sizeman kept the iguana for his son's sake, but later he found himself becoming attached to the iguana.

"I had no idea how much personality these big lizards have," he said. "I shouldn't have been surprised, I guess. I've had dogs before and I know that the more you do with a dog, the better the relationship. I just didn't realize the same thing applies to iguanas."

Sizeman learned as much as he could about iguanas, spent time with Green Boy, and even taught him a few tricks using the target stick. However, Green Boy grew older, as we all do, and eventually began having some age-related health problems.

"My son is now married and has a child, so I felt kind of strange calling him to tell him I was going to have to have Green Boy—his childhood pet—put to sleep. It was a tough phone call to make. I was even less ready for the grief I felt when Green Boy was gone." Sizeman continued, "I actually thought I might feel a sense of relief because I would no longer have the responsibility of caring for the iguana. I had no idea I would end up grieving for him!"

all right, you *will* need help! You cannot drive safely while you're crying, and you will cry.

You will have to sign a legal release form before your vet performs the euthanasia. This gives the vet permission to end your pet's life, and releases the vet from liability for doing so. The actual act of signing this form hits many pet owners very hard. It's as if the signing of the form symbolizes the pet's death. Be prepared for the form.

Some veterinarians will administer a tranquilizer to the pet first, to keep the pet calm, while others don't. Don't hesitate to ask your vet beforehand what the process is so you know what to expect. It can also be difficult sometimes to find an adequate vein in an old iguana. Ask your vet how he will handle that situation, should it occur.

If you can, stay with your iguana during the process. He will be calmer with you holding him than he would be with a stranger, and you will want his last few moments to be calm and peaceful. Rub his forehead in that special place or scratch behind his jowls. Tell him what a good friend he's been and then say good-bye. It will be very quick and peaceful.

If you need a few moments alone with your pet afterward, that's fine. This is when tears are perfectly acceptable and even expected.

## Accidental Death

Unfortunately, young iguanas can die, too. I've talked in previous chapters about caring for your iguana so that he will live to an old age, but sometimes accidents happen. For example, a friend used to bring her four-year-old iguana, Bitty, into her home office with her. The iguana would roam around, perch on the windowsill, and keep my friend company as she worked. One day, Bitty climbed up on some shelves holding craft supplies and books. The shelves came loose from the wall and fell, toppling their contents on top of the iguana, who was crushed and died instantly.

My friend was obviously shocked; her pet was healthy and strong one minute and dead the next. My friend thought the shelves were securely anchored to the wall and safe for holding heavy books, never mind the light weight of a half-grown iguana. But even though people told her it was an accident in every sense of the word, she blamed herself for her pet's death.

Iguanas can be surprisingly fragile creatures. Some of the deadly dangers that could threaten them include:

- Poisoning from craft, household, or automotive substances
- Poisoning from garden substances
- Household trauma, including crushing injuries
- Falls
- Eating inappropriate things, causing poisoning or obstructions
- Being stepped on or sat on by humans in the household
- Being attacked by other pets

A pet's accidental death can be just as traumatic as the death of an old pet, and sometimes even more traumatic. After all, when you have an old pet, you know—somewhere deep in your mind—that eventually your pet will die. You may not consciously admit it, but the thought is there somewhere. When you have a young pet, that thought is nowhere around. So when a young pet dies of a traumatic injury, the loss is compounded by the fact that you're emotionally unprepared.

## Afterward

So what happens afterward? If you can handle it both emotionally and financially, you may want to have your vet do a necropsy (an animal autopsy). Although this may sound cold and unfeeling, the knowledge gained may help future iguanas. A necropsy can help in several ways:

- If the cause of death is unknown, it may help pinpoint a cause.
- If your iguana died from a known disease, this could help your vet plan treatments for other iguanas.
- Your iguana could be of educational value to your vet and possibly even future vets.

If you decide not to do a necropsy, or after the necropsy is completed, your vet can handle disposal of your pet or you can bury him in your yard if you live in a place where that is allowed. There are also places where pets can be cremated. Then you can sprinkle the ashes in a special place.

Having a ceremony of some kind is important. It gives you closure to the entire process. What kind of a ceremony you have is entirely up to you. You may decide to invite over one or two friends or family members who understand your grief, or you may decide to do this by yourself. Don't let people who don't have pets talk you out of this or laugh at you. Emotionally, you need closure, and a ceremony can give you that. In addition, it will give you a bright spot to remember at this dark time.

> Having a ceremony of some kind is important. It gives you closure to the entire process.

My husband and I have a large rose garden where we sprinkle the ashes of our departed pets. The process of sprinkling the ashes is our ceremony—our closure—and then the roses are named for the departed pet. In the spring I may tell him, "Care Bear's rose blossomed this morning," or "Ursa's rose bush is covered with blooms!" We think this is a wonderful, beautiful way of remembering our pets.

## The Stages of Grief

If you have bonded with your pet, you will grieve for him and that grief is perfectly natural. Although people who don't have (or love) pets may make a hard-hearted comment—"What? You're grieving for a lizard!?!"—don't let their lack of caring bother you. Obviously, they haven't shared that special bond with a pet.

There are several stages to the grieving process. While your pet is growing older, you may suffer from some anticipatory grief. You know your pet is growing older and you know the end is near. Even if you don't know precisely when the end will be, you know that there is a limit to your pet's life, and that it is approaching.

Immediately after your pet's death, there will be shock and numbness. You may not feel anything right away. However, denial follows very quickly. You may wake up in the morning, go to your pet's now-empty cage, and say, "Good morning," only to realize that your pet is gone.

Anger follows denial. You will ask "why," about the entire process. Why did your pet have to die? Why did he have to die at this time, or in the place, or in this situation? You may question yourself and your ability to care for a pet. You may question your veterinarian's skills. During this stage of grief, anger is normal but don't let it consume you.

Acceptance follows denial and anger. When you reach acceptance, you are in the healing process and close to letting the grieving process go.

During and after acceptance, you will find that the pain will begin to fade although certain things may continue to

> **Did You Know?**
> As your pet grows older, you will find that you are increasingly treasuring each day with him.

poke at you for awhile. I take a lot of photographs of my pets and when I look back at older photos, I still get a twinge in the heart when I see my long-departed pets.

Don't try to deny your grief or bury it with activities. Grief is a process and if you try to deny it, you may postpone the process but you won't stop it. At some point, perhaps when you don't feel good or when work is stressful, it will surface and you may find yourself overwhelmed. Let the grief happen and just work it through. Sure, it's painful, but it is natural.

If you find, however, that you are stuck in one stage of grief and can't seem to find closure or acceptance, don't hesitate to ask for help. Long-term grief can lead to depression, which can be serious. There are a number of grief counseling services for pet owners. You'll find them listed in Appendix A.

## Your Spiritual Beliefs

Many pet owners take comfort in their beliefs that death is just a temporary separation and not a permanent good-bye. You may find it's much easier to work your way through grief if you believe that you will see your pet again someday. This idea, though, is not without controversy.

Many organized religions today do not believe that animals have souls and so cannot go to heaven. However, if heaven is so wonderful and so special, how can it be heaven if our pets are not there? I, for one, would be very lonely in heaven without my pets!

Many ancient societies believed (and some modern ones still believe) that animals did have souls and those souls continued on after death to aid and guide their earthbound people. Other societies were convinced that animals and people lived multiple lives and would be reincarnated again on this Earth.

Let your beliefs, no matter what they are, comfort you. After all, that is why we have them.

## Another Iguana?

Should you get another iguana? The decision is totally up to you. Some pet owners prefer to wait a little while, to work through their grief, and to rest their heart a little before committing to another pet. Other people just have to have a pet in the house and get another one right away. There is no right or wrong in this situation.

Sometimes it's a good idea to get a pet that is different from your previous pet. For example, you might want to get a bearded dragon or a leopard gecko instead of an iguana. A different pet would make sure you don't expect the new pet to be exactly like your old one.

However, if you can't stand walking past your iguana's empty cage, and you just have to have another iguana, you can. Go ahead and get a new iguana. You can begin the whole process all over again. Just don't try to turn your new iguana into your old one. Let your new pet develop his own personality and cherish him for that.

# 12

# The Future of Iguanas and Other Reptiles

### In This Chapter
- Not a Proud Past
- Threats to Reptiles and Amphibians Today
- Making a Friendlier Future

Humans have not treated reptiles kindly in the past. Not only do legends and myths show that we usually regarded reptiles and amphibians as the bearers of bad news or bad fortune, or the symbols of bad luck, death, or destruction, but we have also treated them badly in other ways. They (and their body parts) have been used as food, as decorative items, as artwork, and as clothing. Entire populations have been wiped out to supply the pet trade.

But these widespread disasters don't have to continue. Some steps have already been taken to protect reptiles and amphibians, including iguanas. More can be done. To protect the future of iguanas and other reptiles, we have to look beyond today's needs and desires and look to tomorrow. What can we do to protect these wonderful creatures?

# Not a Proud Past

The folklore from our past tells us something of how we regarded reptiles and amphibians. In the Nyasaland region of southeastern Africa, ancient legends consider lizards and chameleons to be messengers from God. The chameleon's task was to tell the people they should not fear death because there would be life after death, while the lizard's job was to tell them they should fear death because there was nothing afterward. Because the lizard moved much faster than the chameleon, he arrived first and scared and angered the people with his depressing news. When the chameleon arrived later, he was treated with scorn because the people didn't believe his more positive news. Today, the chameleon is still scorned and is killed on sight. The people believe the lizard scurries away from them because it is still afraid of the reaction to its bad news.

> The snake, in many societies, is seen as a symbol of deceit, death, treachery, revenge, and lasciviousness.

Snakes have had a difficult time since the serpent's betrayal in the Garden with Adam and Eve. The snake, in many societies, is seen as a symbol of deceit, death, treachery, revenge, and lasciviousness. It was thought to forecast coming temptation that must be ignored. Even today snakes are still feared by many people. In fact, snakes are feared by more people than anything else except spiders.

These attitudes have been reflected in how we treat reptiles. For example, although most livestock destined for use as food was and is treated fairly well, fed, and caged relatively kindly, reptiles destined for use as food have not been. The travesty of the Galapagos tortoises is a reflection of this mistreatment. In 1535, Spanish explorers found the Galapagos Islands and the giant tortoises that lived on the islands. For the next 400 years, explorers, sailors, and hunters would stop at the islands, load up with live tortoises, and sail off. Turtles and tortoises were piled upon one and other, sometimes several layers high, and never offered food or water. They would be kept barely alive on board ship with no food or water until they were slaughtered to feed the sailors. This large-scale slaughter eventually sent the populations of several islands into extinction and severely threatened the others.

Now, granted, extinction is nothing new. Just look at the dinosaurs. However, humans have been instrumental in sending more species into extinction than any single event in the history of the world!

# Threats to Reptiles and Amphibians Today

Although we have learned from mistakes made years ago, reptiles and amphibians today are still threatened. Some of these threats are from the same mistakes we made years ago, while new ones are coming to the forefront every day. Let's take a look at the biggest problems reptiles and amphibians are facing now.

**Did You Know?**
As we learn more about the needs of our reptile pets, many are living to old ages we have never expected.

## The Continuing Pet Trade

As I mentioned in chapter 1, thousands and thousands of iguanas have been imported into the United States, and the vast majority of those animals die in their first year of captivity. This horrible practice isn't limited just to iguanas; many different species have suffered the same fate.

North American box turtles were gathered up by the hundreds of thousands for export to Europe for the pet trade. Crates intercepted by authorities during transport would be opened to find hundreds of turtles crammed into one crate, piled upon one another so closely that the turtles were unable to move. There would be no food and no water. Needless to say, the vast majority of these turtles died during transit or shortly thereafter. So many box turtles have been caught that in places where they were once common, it is now almost impossible to find even one. Box turtles are now protected in many regions, in hopes that the remaining turtles will reproduce and perhaps save the species from extinction.

> So many box turtles have been caught that in places where they were once common, it is now almost impossible to find even one.

This same thing has happened all over the world. Plowshare tortoises in Madagascar, rhinoceros iguanas in Haiti, and many other reptiles are now protected in part because of the devastating effects of over-collection for the pet trade.

## Habitat Destruction

On a recent visit to the San Diego Zoological Society's Wild Animal Park, a wonderful open area where many different species can live as freely as possible while still in captivity, my husband and I listened closely to our guide. As she described the various species we were seeing, one phrase kept popping up, over and over again: "Threatened (or endangered) in the wild because of habitat destruction."

Habitat destruction refers to people moving into an area, clearing the land, building homes, farms or businesses, and changing the original nature of the area. Some animals, such as deer or coyotes, can often simply move away or adapt to the changing habitat. They are able to thrive near population centers. Other animals, though, especially reptiles and amphibians, cannot do this. They die under the wheels of cars or under the blades of the bulldozers. They dehydrate when water sources are moved or buried. They starve when food sources disappear, and they cannot reproduce when others of their kind are gone.

Habitat destruction is happening all over the world, from the Arctic Circle through North America to South America; from Europe through Africa and Asia. As humanity spreads across the face of the planet, animal habitats are disappearing at an alarming rate every day.

## Declining Amphibians

In many places in North America and in the rest of the world, amphibians are disappearing at an alarming rate. In some places, entire populations of frogs, salamanders, or newts have disappeared without a trace. Places where frogs used to be found, calling, breeding, and living in vast numbers, now show no signs of any frogs at all.

The Declining Amphibian Populations Task Force (DAPTF) is establishing working groups in places where amphibians have been known to live. These groups will survey amphibian populations and pinpoint where populations are in decline. The goal is to target those places where species are disappearing and identify any triggers or reasons why the populations are declining. The groups will also pinpoint populations showing abnormalities, such as the treefrogs found in California (outside their normal habitat) and the frogs in the Midwest that have missing or extra legs.

So far, experts believe there may be several reasons why amphibian populations are declining.

- The depletion of the ozone layer may be leading to increased levels of UVB radiation.
- Pollution from pesticides, fertilizers, herbicides, and acid rain may be poisoning habitats.
- The introduction of non-native species may be threatening the native amphibians by competing for food, by using the amphibians as food, or by eating the amphibians' eggs.
- The introduction of additional pathogens, or non-native pathogens, may be threatening the ability of the amphibians to survive.
- Global warning and climate change.

The importance of knowing why amphibians are declining cannot be emphasized enough. These creatures are an important part of the ecological balance of many habitats. Amphibians prey upon insects and other amphibians and are, in turn, the prey species for other predators. In addition, because amphibians are so sensitive to their environment, they are considered by many researchers to be an early warning system showing us that something is very wrong.

## Anti-Reptile Legislation

More and more cities, counties and regions are restricting the public's right to own specific kinds of pets. Legislation restricting

## So How Does This Apply to Iguanas?

What do declining amphibian populations have to do with iguanas? After all, iguanas are reptiles, not amphibians! Biodiversity is the variety of animals and plants within a specific environment and researchers have found that all of the plants and animals are interrelated. The loss of one species—or the introduction of one non-native species—has severe impacts on all of the other parts of an environment. This means the loss of one or more sensitive amphibian species in the environment where iguanas are found in the wild can signal impending problems for all of the other species in that environment, including iguanas.

For example, people moving into the area might use pesticides or herbicides. These could leach into the water table or be washed into local streams or lakes. Amphibians living in or near this water would be the first to die. Although iguanas may not react as quickly as the amphibians, the poisoning of the water will eventually affect them, too, when they come down to drink or bathe. In addition, the loss of the insect-eating amphibians could cause a population explosion of plant-eating insects, threatening the iguanas' food sources. Predators that normally ate amphibians may begin looking at iguanas as replacement food sources, as well. And this cycle just continues. Although this is a very simple explanation, the reality is much more complex.

dog ownership to certain breeds, or preventing the ownership of certain breeds, has become so common that the American Kennel Club has become involved in several legal fights. Cats, once long thought to be above the law, now have to be leashed or kept inside in several communities. And other legislative organizations have outlawed, or tried to outlaw, reptiles and amphibians in general, and certain species specifically.

All it takes is one case of salmonella caused by a reptile, or one reptile bite, or one escaped reptile incident covered by the media for someone to introduce legislation to limit or outlaw reptile ownership. Unfortunately, many times this legislation becomes law.

As of June 29, 1999, reptile ownership in New York City is illegal. The law doesn't focus specifically on reptiles, but instead on "exotic" pets. Basically, it classifies everything other than dogs and cats as exotic pets. There is no "grandfather clause" to protect people who already own those pets, so snake, bearded dragon, iguana and frog owners immediately became law breakers! Needless to say, the legal battles continue.

## Reptiles in Fashion

When you think of fashion, you may think of bizarre styles and perhaps even fur coats, but did you ever think that reptiles could be adversely affected by fashion? They can, and have been!

The 1990s saw many reptile fashions. At one Paris fashion show, Givenchy showed off full-length coats made of snake skin—not fake snake skin, but the real thing. The Italian fashion firm Prada has an entire line of shoes, purses, belts, and jackets made from various reptile skins. Ralph Lauren has shoes made from crocodile skins and Louis Vitton sells an alligator purse and lizard-skin-covered diary.

Although many of these skins, including the alligator, come from commercial farms, the demand for reptile skins increases the chances that poachers and hunters will renew their assaults against wildlife. Documentary films taken in Asia show wild snakes and lizards hung from trees and skinned alive to provide skins for the fashion industry. More than 150,000 reticulated python skins are known to have been legally brought in to the United States each year during the late 1980s and early 1990s. We have no idea how many came into the United States illegally! When you take into account that those numbers reflect one individual species, imported to only one country, you can see that the total numbers of reptiles killed for fashion is absolutely astronomical.

Buyers need to be aware that products made from skins are not necessarily made from farm animals raised for that purpose. Although thousands of American alligators are raised on farms for their skins (and meat), this is the exception. Most other animals are wild-caught. If buyers demand faux or fake skins, just as they do fake furs, the demand for reptile skins would decrease.

# It's Not All Bad News

Many people have seen the damage done to reptiles and amphibians in the past and are taking great strides to overcome this damage. These efforts, combined with future endeavors, could very well save many species and many reptile environments.

> Many people have seen the damage done to reptiles and amphibians in the past and are taking great strides to overcome this damage.

## Captive-Breeding Programs

Captive-breeding programs have been very successful in several different ways. Some programs—private, commercial, and at zoological parks—have successfully bred endangered and threatened species, keeping those species alive. Unlike the now very popular captive-breeding program that has brought the California condor back from certain extinction, many of these breeding programs for reptiles receive very little acclaim or publicity, but are successful nonetheless.

## Dr. Wegman Werner's Dream

Iguanas in Central America have been threatened in several ways, but one of the most devastating has been the loss of habitat. Forests have been cut down to make way for farming crops and raising cattle. Although people agree that natural land should be preserved, it's still a fact of life that people need to be able to support and feed their families. The people who live in the rainforests of Central American have repeatedly told the wildlife conservation experts that it's hard to care about the survival or extinction of a big green lizard when your children are hungry!

Dr. Wegman Werner believes that sustainable conservation projects need to take into account that wildlife needs preserving and families need to make a living. She has looked for practical ways of protecting wildlife while creating jobs and making enough profit to make the whole thing worthwhile.

Werner's Green Iguana Foundation aims to increase the Green Iguana population while encouraging people to farm them—yes, farm iguanas instead of cattle. In the tropics, iguanas are much easier to farm than cattle and do much less harm to the environment. To raise iguanas, the farmers must grow trees instead of clear-cutting the land. Iguanas produce more meat per acre than cattle, need a minimal amount of attention while growing, and don't tend to wander off the way cattle do. In addition, iguanas cause much less pollution to the local land and water than cattle do.

Iguana farming provides baby iguanas for export for the pet trade, larger iguanas for sale as meat, and skins for sale as leather. Iguana ham, sausages, and smoked meat will soon be available. At the same time, more than 100,000 iguanas have already been raised and returned to their native wild lands.

Breeding programs also reduce the need for the collection of animals from the wild. With thousands of iguanas being bred and raised on iguana farms, very few wild-caught iguanas are now available for sale. The same applies to many other species, including bearded dragons, leopard geckos, sulcatta tortoises and many other popular pet species.

In addition to ecological concerns, reptiles bred in captivity are already adjusted to captivity, having known nothing else, and make much better pets. Wild-caught reptiles are often stressed which reduces their immunity to diseases, parasites, and other health threats. Plus, many wild-caught reptiles simply never adjust to the confinements of captivity.

## Making a Friendlier Future

Even though so much of the news regarding reptiles seems very disheartening, it doesn't have to be that way. We are making progress in the right direction. Iguana farms that produce iguanas for the pet trade, for sale as a commercial enterprise for the native people, and for release back in to the wild are wonderful, and are a giant leap in the right direction. Captive-breeding programs that supply healthy, well-adjusted reptiles for the pet trade are also a tremendous improvement over collecting animals in the wild. However, we still have a long way to go, and reptile keepers and owners are the ones who will have to make things happen.

### Public Education

Because so many people view reptiles (which of course, includes iguanas) and amphibians in a negative light, or in a less than positive light, public education is vital to making sure we protect those animals in the wild. Public education can also help ensure that we continue to enjoy our rights as reptile pet owners in the future. Most reptile education programs target

**Did You Know?** Although there are thousands of species of lizards found worldwide, only about 100 are available to pet owners.

children since they are the future voters and pet owners. Effective programs for kids must be appropriate to the child's age and development, and must make a positive impact.

Many educational researchers have found that videos and movies are not effective in developing a child's sympathy toward an animal because the film does not connect emotionally with the child. It isn't real enough. However, when live animals are used and the child is allowed to touch the animals, an emotional connection is made and the child is more receptive to actually learning and remembering information about the animal.

Educational programs can be quite varied. A short program could discuss a local reptile's native environment, where he lives, how he lives and his daily routine, including searching for food. Programs could target more specific subjects, such as hibernation or the reptile's ability to shed his skin. Captive breeding, incubation, and raising young are also popular subjects. Incorporated into each discussion should be safe reptile handling, which can include how to keep from being bitten by a particular reptile. Good hygiene should also be discussed, and children should have the opportunity to wash their hands after touching the reptile.

When live reptiles and amphibians are used in educational programs, all care must be taken to ensure (as much as reasonably possible) that the animals are safe for the children to touch. Behaviorally, the animals should be calm (for their species) and used to being handled. You should also have cultures done to make sure the animals are not carrying salmonella or any other contagious bacteria, virus, or disease.

My husband and I have shared our reptile and amphibian pets with hundreds, if not thousands, of people—adults as well as children.

Conan, our old man iguana, has had his forehead rubbed by one-year-old babies and 99-year-old seniors and all ages in between. We talk about what iguanas are, where they came from, the benefits of captive breeding, what iguanas require to be good pets, and how long they live. Some of the most common questions are:

- Is that real?
- Is that thing alive?
- What is it?
- How much does he weigh?
- How long is he?
- How old is he?
- How long will he live?
- Does he bite?

We have found that when we're visiting children between the ages of six and 10, we need to talk about emotional things. How animals feel, for example. Kids of this age want to feel something for the animal. Line drawings of an iguana that the kids can color in later are always welcome.

Kids between 10 and 12 want to know more facts. Where do these reptiles come from? What do they eat? How do they become pets? Line drawings are still welcome, but the page should contain more factual information and questions to encourage thought.

> High school kids are sponges ready to learn anything you want to share with them, including more complicated issues.

High school kids are sponges ready to learn anything you want to share with them, including more complicated issues. The issues of conservation, preservation, biodiversity, and natural ecosystems are not too much for these kids.

## When People Are Afraid

Many people are afraid of reptiles, especially snakes. If, during an educational presentation, you are approached by someone who is afraid, don't make fun of them or joke about the fear. It is very real to this person and certainly isn't funny.

Instead, invite the person to watch as other people touch the reptile. Talk about the reptile itself as an individual: "Conan is an old iguana and very calm." Talk, too, about what he feels like. After all, your goal is to get the person to touch the animal, and they cannot feel an iguana's rough scales or soft dewlap until they can touch the animal.

Many will overcome their fear and touch the iguana—even briefly—after they have seen other people touch him. Sometimes their curiosity simply gets too strong and they have to touch the reptile. If so, praise the person's bravery with enthusiastic and real praise. Overcoming fear is very difficult.

Never force someone to touch a reptile. The person must be ready to do it on his own; your forcefulness could make the fear much worse.

## Suggestions for Future Conservation

Reptile and amphibian keepers can help conservation efforts in several different ways.

- Put your money where your heart is and donate money to herpetological societies pursuing worthwhile projects, including legislative initiatives.
- Do not collect reptiles and amphibians in the wild. Collecting in the wild removes breeding animals from their natural environment and adds stress to the remaining population. In addition, wild-caught animals often have a difficult time adjusting to captivity.
- Buy only captive-bred reptiles and amphibians. Ask for documentation or a guarantee to this effect.

## The Difference Between Preservation and Conservation

The differences are subtle, but basically, preservation means keeping things the way they are. For example, a preservation project would fence in a wildlife area and keep everyone out of it. Human impact would be severely reduced or eliminated.

Conservation means protecting the wildlife and the area, while at the same time allowing people access to the area for limited recreation, research, and enjoyment. Many conservation projects also allow the native people to harvest or use the resources of the area.

- Encourage others to buy only captive-bred pets. First-time reptile or amphibian owners probably don't even think about where their pet came from and have no idea of the problems associated with wild-caught animals. As an experienced reptile keeper, you are in a position to tell them about the advantages of captive-bred pets.
- Know the laws of your area regarding the keeping of reptiles and amphibians. Working outside of the law only endangers all reptile and amphibian keepers and owners. When one person is caught with an illegal pet and the media covers it, it reflects badly on all reptile keepers.
- Work within the system to get unfair or overly restrictive laws changed. By working within the system, legally, we can accomplish much more than we can outside of the system.
- Remain aware of pending legislation regarding the keeping of reptiles, amphibians, and other exotic pets. Be prepared to lobby or fight (within the system!) to keep your pets.

## Herpetological Societies

These are groups of people who share an enthusiasm for reptiles and amphibians. Joining a group is a wonderful way to socialize with people with the same interests, but it's also a great way to learn more about reptiles and amphibians. Within any group there may be a few people who specialize in iguanas, or a few who are enthused about snakes, or lizards, or geckos, or frogs. Most groups have speakers come to the meetings and share their enthusiasm and knowledge with the members. Many herp societies are involved in research, too, and contribute knowledge to both pet owners and the scientific community. If you're lucky enough to have a group in your area, join it!

○ Do not release captive-bred animals into the wild. Diseases or parasites carried by either the captive-bred animals or the wild animals can severely threaten all the other animals in an area. California desert tortoises in the wild are dying by the thousands because pet tortoises released back to the wild were carrying a respiratory infection the wild tortoises had no resistance to.

## Careers in Herpetology

Herpetologists are people who study reptiles and amphibians. Most have majored in biology, have a strong background in all the sciences, and then have specialized in either reptiles and amphibians in general, or one specific family of reptiles or amphibians.

Many herpetologists have advanced college degrees, but some do not. Some herpetologists began as reptile pet owners who developed an interest in their pets and began studying them. Many quite knowledgeable herpetologists are pet owners who became reptile breeders specializing in one or two specific species of reptiles.

Most herpetologists share a love for these creatures and have the desire and persistence to learn more about them. Although herpetologists can sometimes earn a living in this field, it is also a hobby or part-time occupation for many. Let's look at some of the occupations there are for herpetologists.

- Wildlife Management: These managers are employed by the state or federal government, or by private conservation organizations. Some may do field work observing animals, protecting them from poaching and other dangers, and establishing safe havens. Other positions may be more administrative and may include writing regulations. Academic degrees in biology or wildlife management are usually required for these positions.
- Zoological Parks: Reptile and amphibian keepers and curators work directly with the animals, while supervisors—well, they supervise. Zoo educators work with the public, usually children, and researchers study the animals themselves. These positions usually require a college degree—at least a bachelor's degree in biology for a keeper and more advanced degrees for the other positions.
- Museums: Curators and scientists generally spend most of their time researching and studying reptiles and amphibians. These positions usually require an advanced college degree in biology or related fields. Collection managers care for the museum's collections of preserved animals. Most museums usually have other, lesser positions available for students or part-time workers.
- Colleges and Universities: Reptile enthusiasts with a Ph.D. in biology who are interested in teaching can often find a place at a

college or university, although they will have to teach other related courses, too, in addition to herpetology. Researchers, research assistants and laboratory assistant,s are also employed by most universities.
- Veterinarians: Although very few veterinarians can make a living specializing only in reptiles and amphibians, many can make a living treating a variety of exotic species. Other veterinarians treat all pet animals and specialize in reptiles.
- Other Possibilities: People with an interest in reptiles and amphibians can follow a variety of career paths. Perhaps you want to teach high school biology or you might want to become an environmental technician. Perhaps you want to breed reptiles or become a pet shop owner. Maybe photographing reptiles and amphibians in the wild interests you. You could even lead conservation tours for other herpetologists to remote areas where exotic species can be found in the wild. Use your imagination; there are a lot of alternatives!

No matter what your field of interest, a good education is a necessity. Plan to attend a college with a good reputation in the biological sciences and then take all the science courses offered. Courses in chemistry, statistics, writing, and computer sciences will also be helpful. Take a Latin course if you can, as well, since all of the species' scientific names are in Latin.

Informal education can help you specialize in the area of herpetology that interests you. Do research on your own and read as much as you can. Join a herpetological club or society so that you can work with people who share the same interests.

Whether it's a full-time vocation, a part-time job, or a treasured hobby, herpetology has something for everyone who shares our passion for reptiles and amphibians.

# Appendix A: Resources

## Where to Find a Reptile Veterinarian

Association of Reptile and Amphibian Veterinarians
Wilbur Amand, Executive Director
6 North Pennel Road, Media, PA 19063
(610) 358-9530

## Iguana Information

International Iguana Society, Inc.
P.O. Box 43061
Big Pine Key, FL 33043

## Professional Herpetological Societies

American Society of Ichthyologists and Herpetologists
P.O. Box 1897
Lawrence, KS 66044-8897

Herpetologists League
Dr. Rebecca Pyles, HL Treasurer
Dept. of Biological Sciences
Box 70726, East Tennessee State University
Johnson City, TN 37614-0726

## On the Internet

www.sonic.net/~melissk/ig_care
Melissa Kaplan's Giant Green Iguana Information Collection

www.niad.org
National Iguana Awareness Day

www.members.home.net/iis/WelcomePage
International Iguana Society

www.theiguana.com
The Iguana Club

www.wcmc.org.uk/CITES
Convention on International Trade in Endangered Species

## Grief Hotlines

University of California, Davis
(916) 752-4200
6:30–9:30 P.M., Pacific Standard Time, Monday through Friday

Colorado State University, Fort Collins
(970) 491-1242
9:00 A.M.–5:00 P.M., Mountain Time, Monday through Friday

University of Florida, Gainesville
(352) 392-4700, ext. 4080
Leave a message and someone will return your call.

Michigan State University, East Lansing
(517) 432-2696
6:30–9:30 P.M., Eastern Standard Time, Tuesday, Wednesday, and Thursday

Ohio State University, Columbus
(614) 292-1823
Leave a message and someone will return your call.

University of Pennsylvania, Philadelphia
(215) 898-4529

Tufts University, North Grafton, Massachusetts
(508) 839-7966
6:00–9:00 P.M. Eastern Standard Time, Monday through Friday

Washington State University, Pullman
(509) 335-4569
Evenings, Monday through Thursday

## Magazines

*Reptiles,* Fancy Publications, P.O. Box 58700, Boulder, CO 80323-8700

*Reptile & Amphibian Hobbyist,* TFH Publications, 1 TFH Plaza, Neptune City, NJ 07753

*Exotic Veterinary Magazine,* P.O. Box 541749, Lake Worth, FL 33454-1749

## Bibliography and More Reading

Cloudsley-Thompson, John L. *Predation and Defence Amongst Reptiles,* R & A Publishing, Somerset, England, 1994.

Coborn, John. *Snakes & Lizards: Their Care and Breeding in Captivity*, Tetra Press, Morris Plains, NJ, 1991.

De Vosjoli, Phillipe. *The Green Iguana Manual*, Advanced Vivarium Systems, Escondido, CA, 1992.

Flank, Lenny, Jr. *Herp Help*, Howell Book House, NY, 1998.

Frye, Fredric L. B.S., D.V.M., M.S. *A Practical Guide for Feeding Captive Reptiles*, Krieger Publishing Company, Malabar, FL, 1991.

Hatfield, James W., III. *Green Iguana: The Ultimate Owner's Manual*, Dunthorpe Press, P.O. Box 80385, Portland, OR 97280, 1996.

Klingenberg, Roger J., D.V.M. *Understanding Reptile Parasites*, Advanced Vivarium Systems, Escondido, CA, 1993.

Milani, Myrna, D.V.M. *Preparing for the Loss of Your Pet*, Prima Publishing, 1998.

Palika, Liz. *The Complete Idiot's Guide to Reptiles and Amphibians*, Alpha Books, MacMillan General Reference, NY, 1998.

Palika, Liz. *The Consumer's Guide to Feeding Reptiles*, Howell Book House, NY, 1997.

Rossi, John M.A., D.V.M. *What's Wrong with My Iguana?* Advanced Vivarium Systems, Escondido, CA, 1998.

Slavens, Frank L. and Kate. *Reptiles and Amphibians in Captivity: Breeding, Longevity, and Inventory*, 2000.

# Appendix B: Glossary

**Adaptation:** Behavioral modifications that evolved over a period of time, usually as a response to the environment.
**Allopatric:** Occurring in separate geographic areas, as when different species do not inhabit the same area.
**Anterior:** Referring to the front part of the body.
**Arboreal:** Tree-dwelling.
**Basking:** Behavior designed to get the maximum amount of heat from the sun or a heat lamp.
**Classification:** The cataloguing of living things into systematic groups.
**Cloaca:** The chamber in reptiles where wastes discharge.
**Clutch:** A batch of eggs laid by a single animal in a single breeding season.
**Conservation:** Protecting animals and/or habitat while allowing people access to it.
**Display:** A pattern of behavior directed at other animals for purposes of breeding and courtship, territorial defense, or other actions.
**Diurnal:** Active during daylight hours.
**Dorsal:** The upper part of the body; the ridge along the backbone or spine.
**Dystocia:** Egg-bound; unable to lay eggs that have been produced in the body.

**Ecdysis:** Shedding the outer layers of skin.

**Ecosystem:** The complete environment where a reptile or animal lives; composed of all the elements that make up the system.

**Ectoparasite:** External parasite; parasite that lives on the outside of an animal, such as ticks.

**Ectothermic:** Cold-blooded.

**Egg-binding/egg-bound:** See *Dystocia*.

**Endemic:** Zoogeographically restricted species.

**Endoparasite:** Internal parasite; one that lives inside the animal, such as roundworms.

**Endothermic:** Warm-blooded.

**Family:** Classification of certain related animals; below *Order* and above *Genus*.

**Fauna:** All the animal life of a region or locality.

**Femoral pores:** Hollow scales on the inside or lower thigh which excrete a bodily substance; usually prevalent in males.

**Flora:** All the plant life of a region or locality.

**Genetic:** Pertaining to genes and inheritance.

**Genus:** Classification of certain related animals; below *Family* and above *Species*.

**Gestation:** The period between fertilization and egg laying.

**Habitat:** The environment in which an animal lives.

**Hatchling:** Animal newly hatched from an egg.

**Hemipenes:** The paired sex organ of the male lizard or snake.

**Herbivore:** An animal that eats plants and plant matter.

**Herpetology:** The study of reptiles and amphibians.

**Herptile:** Term used to refer to a reptile or amphibian.

**Hibernation:** Spending the winter months in a state of torpor.

**Incubation:** The period of time from egg laying until hatching.

**Introduced:** A species not native to an area but which now occurs there because of escaped pets or released pets, or through an accident of nature such as a storm.

**Jacobson's organ:** A scenting gland in the roof of the mouth.
**Juvenile:** Not yet sexually mature.
**Keratin:** A tough, fibrous material present in claws and scales.
**Metabolism:** Chemical or energy conversions that happen as a result of the digestion of food.
**Nocturnal:** Active at night.
**Oviduct:** The canal that carries the ova from the ovary to the cloaca.
**Oviparous:** Egg laying.
**Parietal eye:** A third eye in the middle of the forehead.
**Posterior:** Pertaining to the rear end of the body.
**Preservation:** The protection of a habitat or locality, and all the flora and fauna contained within; restricted human access.
**Sexual dimorphism:** Species that shows marked differences between male and female.
**Stress:** A condition in which psychological effects reduce resistance to disease; anything that affects the animal negatively.
**Terrarium:** A vivarium; an indoor artificial habitat; a cage with live plants.
**Terrestrial:** Ground-dwelling.
**Thermoregulation:** The manner in which ectotherms regulate their body temperature by moving from one temperature gradient to another.
**Vent:** The orifice of the cloaca.
**Vivarium:** A terrarium; an indoor artificial habitat or environment; a cage with life-like furnishings.
**Zoonoses:** Diseases that can be passed between species.

# Appendix C: The Iguana Family Tree

The family *Iguanidae* is the largest lizard family, and consists of more than 700 individual species. Unlike some reptile families, this family shows a wide diversity of form. There are slender lizards, heavy-bodied, chunky lizards, and all sizes in between. Some are small—inches in length—and others may reach seven feet long. Some are arboreal, some are terrestrial, and one is marine. Iguanas are found in North, South, and Central America; the oceanic islands of Galapagos and Fiji; and Madagascar. They are not found in Africa, Asia, or Europe. They are found in rainforests, on rocky shores, and in the desert. They swim in fresh water and salt water. They live in shrubs, grasslands, and tall treetops. Some are insectivores, some are omnivores, and some are herbivores. The variety is amazing.

Although the lizards in the iguana family do have quite a lot of variety, they also have some things in common. All have the common lizard-like shape. The body is longer than it is tall, with four legs. The tail is usually longer than the body, sometimes one and a half to two times as long. Most iguanas have teeth on the sides of the jaws and these teeth are replaceable should they be broken or lost.

Here are some of the more commonly seen members of the iguana family—those that might be kept as pets—and a few that are not suitable as pets.

# The Anoles

## American Chameleon (Anolis carolinensis)

This small lizard, also called an anole, is five to nine inches in total length and actually has no relation to the Old World chameleons in the family *Chamaeleonidae*. However, it can vary its color slightly and this ability lead to its name. It is found in the southeastern United States, from the Carolinas south through Florida and west to Louisiana. Escaped or released pets have formed small colonies in several other places, including San Diego, California. This small lizard can be found in shrubs and trees, and on walls and the sides of houses.

In captivity, a tall terrarium with branches and tall plants (or silk plants) to provide hiding places will suit this lizard well. A basking spot over one branch should heat up to 85° to 90°F. A full-spectrum fluorescent reptile light should be provided.

Feed a variety of small insects, including crickets, waxworms, and mealworms. These lizards rarely drink from a bowl, so water should be provided by misting the cage each day. The lizards will drink the droplets of water off the sides of the terrarium or off the leaves of the plants.

Males have a pinkish-white dewlap that is surprisingly large for such a small lizard. The dewlap is extended during disputes over territory and breeding rights, and during courtship. Watching the interactions between a group of these lizards can be very entertaining.

## Large-Headed Anole (<u>Anole cybotes</u>)

This anole is sturdier and heavier, but shorter than the American Chameleon. It has a larger head, is brown (medium to dark), and females have a dark brown stripe down the back. Found on the island of Hispaniola, (although there is an introduced colony in Florida), these lizards are found primarily in trees, especially on the brown bark.

These lizards have the same needs as American Chameleons, including a tall, well-planted terrarium. A hot spot warmed to 86° to 88°F is great, and a full-spectrum light is needed. These anoles will eat larger insects, including beetles.

These lizards are more aggressive than American Chameleons and should not be kept in a group. A male and female pair can be kept together.

## Knight Anole (<u>Anolis equestris</u>)

This anole grows to about 22 inches in total length, at least half of which is a long, slender tail. This green to brown lizard has a very small dorsal crest and a large white dewlap that sometimes has pink to red markings. Originally from Cuba, there are introduced colonies now thriving in Florida.

This anole is very arboreal so a large, tall cage is needed. Lots of branches and real or artificial plants can provide hiding places. A hot spot should reach 86° to 88°F during the day. Nighttime temperatures can go down to room temperature.

This lizard will eat just about any insect and will even chow down on smaller lizards. Because of this tendency, these anoles can be kept together in mixed-sex pairs, but otherwise should never be kept with other lizards.

## Giant Anole (Anolis ricordii)

This lizard is the second largest of the anoles and will grow to slightly over 19 inches, with about half of that length a long, slender tail. It is green with a small dorsal crest. The dewlap is quite variable in color but is usually white. This anole, like the Large-Headed Anole, is from the island of Hispaniola.

This diurnal lizard lives in trees, so a tall cage is needed with lots of branches and real or artificial plants. In the wild, this lizard often eats hatchling birds. Since this is not possible in captivity (unless you raise chickens), make sure you buy a captive-bred anole that is already eating insects or pinkie mice.

A heat lamp should heat one spot in the cage to 88°F. Nighttime temperatures can go as low as room temperature.

These anoles can be quite aggressive toward cagemates, so they should be kept only in male-female pairs.

## Brown Anole (Anolis sagrei)

This is a small, brown lizard—up to eight inches long. The male's dewlap is red and orange. There is a small dorsal crest. Originally from Cuba, there are Brown Anoles now living in most parts of Florida.

A tall, heavily furnished cage is best for this lizard. A hot spot to 88°F is needed during the day, although nighttime temperatures can go down to room temperature.

These lizards will eat a variety of insects. They can be aggressive toward cage mates, so should they be kept only in male-female pairs.

# The Basilisks

## Helmeted Basilisk (Basiliscus basiliscus)

Also called the Common Basilisk, this lizard is from Central and South America. It is quite unusual looking, with a prominent dorsal crest that the lizard can raise or lower at will. These slender, long-legged lizards can grow to 32 inches in length, over half of which is a long, whip-like tail. They are green with a yellowish belly.

This is an arboreal lizard always found near water. When frightened, this lizard will jump from the trees into the water. Its long toes and light body enable the lizard to run along the top of standing water.

A very tall cage is necessary, furnished with branches and real or artificial plants. A very wide but shallow water bowl is needed. Daytime temperatures should reach 88°F, although nighttime temperatures can go as low as room temperature.

This lizard can eat insects and pinkie mice. Since it can be aggressive toward smaller lizards, only male-female pairs should be kept together.

## Plumed Basilisk (Basiliscus plumifrons)

This lizard looks much like its relative, the Helmeted Basilisk, except that it has a tall, eye-catching double crest on the head, the back, and along half of the tail. This crest makes the lizard look like a dinosaur! This lizard is bright green with lighter blotches. The belly is yellow. The Plumed Basilisk lives in the rainforests of Central America.

A tall arboreal cage is needed with a hot spot that reaches 88°F during the day. Nighttime temperatures can go down to room temperature. Provide a wide but shallow water bowl bathing and drinking.

This lizard will eat a variety of insects as well as pinkie mice. Again, like the other basilisks, only mixed-sex pairs should be kept together. Smaller lizards will be tormented and eaten.

### Striped Basilisk (Basiliscus vittatus)

This basilisk is from Central America, and although it is quite attractive, it suffers in comparison to the flamboyant Plumed Basilisk. The striped version is green with striped markings and a much smaller dorsal crest.

A tall, well-planted cage is needed, with a shallow but wide water bowl. Daytime temperatures should reach 88°F, with nighttime temperatures going down to the 70s.

Baby mice and a variety of insects can make up this lizard's diet. Male-female pairs can be kept together, but this is not a community lizard. Smaller lizards will become the main course.

## Some Iguanas

### Spiny-Tailed Iguana (Ctenosaura acanthura and similis)

These iguanas are found in Mexico—*acanthura* primarily along the Atlantic coast and *similis* south to Panama. Other subspecies include *hemilopha* and *pectinata*. All are sturdy, heavy-bodied lizards with a long, whip-like tail. They are called "spiny tailed" because the tails are ringed with whorls of strongly spiked scales.

These lizards need a large cage with plenty of room to move around. Branches, rocks and cork bark can provide climbing and hiding places. One basking spot should be heated to at least 90°F, with other parts of the cage cooler. Nighttime temperatures can go down to the mid-80s, but should not be cooler than that. A reptile fluorescent light must be provided.

Primarily herbivores, these lizards are also known to eat pinkie mice, insects, some fruit, and some meat. The diet should emphasize plants. Water should be supplied in a shallow bowl or a small pool large enough for the lizard to soak in.

Males will battle and torment each other. These iguanas should be maintained separately, except during breeding season.

## Rhinoceros Iguana (Cyclura cornuta)

These large, heavy-bodied iguanas are originally from Haiti, Hispaniola, and Puerto Rico, where populations are threatened or endangered—although they have been bred in captivity for several years now. Males have three short, conical horns on their snout; this is what gives the species its name.

These iguanas can be cared for just as Green Iguanas are, with the same cage, heat, light, and environmental needs.

Although these iguanas are herbivores, like the Green Iguana, they are also known to eat insects and small rodents. In captivity a few insects or pinkie mice may be offered, but these should be fed on a limited basis. It is not known how much animal protein these lizards should have, or how much animal protein is too much.

Related iguanas include the Cuban Rock Iguana (*Cyclura nubila*), the Cayman Island Rock Iguana (*Cyclura nubila caymanensis*) and the Grand Cayman Blue Rock Iguana (*Cyclura nubila lewisi*).

## Fiji Island Iguana (Brachylophus fasciatus)

This very attractive iguana is green. Females are uniformly green while males have darker and lighter bands on the green background.

These iguanas are primarily herbivorous, although they have been known to eat insects. They need a well-planted, tall enclosure with a higher humidity level than most other iguanas would prefer.

Although these iguanas are endangered in their native land due to habitat destruction, some captive breeding is taking place.

## Collared Lizard (Crotaphytus collaris)

The Collared Lizard has recently become a quite popular pet. Handsome, brown, 12-inch-long lizards, these are hardy and easily kept. These are not slender lizards, and they get their name from their black-and-white collar. Males have a bright blue-green dewlap.

Originally from southwest United States south into Mexico, these lizards are also being bred in captivity.

This is a true desert reptile and needs a long, low, dry cage. Sand is a good substrate, and an undertank heater can warm the sand substrate. The basking area at one end of the tank should reach 95° to 100°F during the day. Nighttime temperatures can go down to 75° to 80°F. A reptile fluorescent light is necessary for good health.

Insects are the primary food for this lizard although many will also eat baby mice.

As with so many lizards from the iguana family, these lizards are not social and only male-female pairs should be kept together.

# Some Not-So-Popular Iguana Relatives

## Desert Iguana (Dipsosaurus dorsalis)

This iguana is about 16 inches long, has a plump body, a long neck, and proportionately small head. A small crest runs dorsally from the head down the back and into the tail. The body is white with stripes or bands of darker brown. The throat and belly are light.

Originally from southwestern United States and south into Mexico, this is (as its name implies) a desert lizard. A long, low, hot desert terrarium is needed to keep this lizard happy and healthy. Use sand as a substrate and an undertank heater to warm the sand. A hot lamp over the tank should heat one end to at least 95°F. Nighttime temperatures can go down to 80°F. A reptile fluorescent light is needed for good health.

This lizard is primarily herbivorous, although they also eat insects. In captivity, a varied diet should be fed, with lots of dark green vegetables. Flowers are also a favorite.

This lizard is more social than many from the iguana family and will live peacefully in a group. The Desert Iguana is protected in most of its range, although it has been bred in captivity. This is an attractive lizard—it's too bad it isn't more popular.

## Granite Spiny Lizard (Sceloporus orcutti)

This 11-inch-long lizard, also called the Blue Belly, is quite common throughout much of its range in the southwestern United States and Baja California. This lizard is sturdy rather than slender, and is usually brown to brownish-gray. A deep metallic blue shows on the belly when the lizard is basking or is excited. Males are much brighter in color than females.

Although this lizard is fairly common, it is not often kept as a pet, except perhaps for small boys who catch and bring home one or two. If you attempt to keep one or two, these lizards need a long, low cage that is quite large. If the tank is too small, the lizards will become very agitated.

Gravel or sand can be used as substrate. A few potted plants and a rock or two can furnish the cage. One end should be heated to at least 88°F, with the other end of the tank cooler. Nighttime temperatures can go down to room temperature.

A variety of insects should be fed—both commercially available insects and those found in the backyard. Water can be supplied in a shallow jar lid.

## Keel-Tailed Lizard (Tropidurus torquatus)

This small, six-inch-long lizard is gray with darker bands across the body. The tail has a dorsal keel. It is originally from northern South America, from Brazil to Venezuela.

This is a terrestrial lizard that would do well in a long, low terrarium with sand and gravel as a substrate. Furnish the tank with a couple of rocks, a small piece of cork bark for hiding and a plant or two. Water can be provided in a shallow jar lid.

A heat light should warm one end of the tank to 88°F during the day. Nighttime temperatures can be lower.

This lizard will eat a variety of insects, both commercial and those found in the backyard.

# Don't Keep These as Pets

## Horned Toad (Phrynosoma cornutum)

Many people are surprised that this spiny, squat, short-legged little lizard is related to the big Green Iguana, but it is. Although this little lizard (it's not a toad) used to be common throughout its range (southwestern USA into Mexico), today it is rarely seen and is protected. Although some of its decline could be because of habitat loss, much of it was also because of collection for the pet trade. Unfortunately, because one of its favorite foods is ants, which are difficult to provide for pets in captivity, many of these lizards died soon after being caught.

## Galapagos Marine Iguana (Amblyrhyncus cristatus)

These large (up to five-and-a-half feet long), interesting lizards are actually cousins of the Green Iguana. They are uniquely adapted to living on an island surrounded by a saltwater ocean, and dive in the ocean daily to feed on the kelp and underwater plants. Excess salt taken in via the ocean water is excreted through glands in the nasal cavity.

These lizards cannot be kept in captivity, as their food source cannot be duplicated. In addition, these lizards are endangered and protected by law.

## Galapagos Land Iguana (Conolophus subcristatus)

These large, heavy-bodied lizards live in rocky areas of the Galapagos Islands and grow to more than three feet long. They are herbivorous, eating available plants including cactus.

These lizards, like their marine cousins, are endangered and protected by law.

# Index

## A

Abscesses, 105
Absorption, 61
Accidental death, 236–237
Activity, as stress factor, 17
Adult iguanas. *See also* Aging iguanas
   babies vs., 19–20
   choosing, 20, 21
   diet for, 70
   sexing, 177–178
Age. *See also* Aging iguanas
   diet and, 69–70
   life expectancy, 8, 18, 25, 226–227
   oldest known iguana, 8, 226
Aggressiveness. *See also* Behavior and body language; Protective behavior; Taming your iguana
   biting, 15, 31, 126–127
   bluffing, 129
   breeding season and, 20, 84–85, 133–134, 182–183
   children and iguanas, 208–210
   defending territory, 131–132
   defensive fighting, 128–129
   dominance behavior, 132
   hissing, 123
   males vs. females, 20
   mating, 183, 185
   neutering to reduce, 20, 83, 176
   responding to, 84, 85, 183
   restraining your iguana, 84–86
   signs of anger, 127–128
   signs of imminent attack, 84–85, 114, 123, 127
   tail whipping, 15, 31, 124–125, 142
   toward menstruating women, 84, 182
Aging iguanas, 225–241
   appetite decrease, 229
   changes in older iguanas, 228–230
   comfort care, 229
   euthanasia, 233–236
   exercise needs, 228–229, 230
   factors affecting life span, 227
   getting another iguana, 241
   grief after death, 234–235, 239–240, 262
   illnesses in, 230–232
   increasing longevity, 225–226
   life expectancy, 8, 18, 25, 226–227
   necropsy (animal autopsy), 237–238
   saying good-bye, 233–236
   shedding, 229
   spiritual beliefs regarding death, 240–241
   weight gain, 229–230
   in the wild, 227–228
Agitation, 114
Albon (sulfadimethoxine), 113
Alfalfa pellets, 33, 51
Allergies, to iguanas, 15
Alternative actions in training, 146–147
*Amblyrhyncus cristatus* (Galapagos Marine Iguana), 279
American Chameleon (*Anolis carolinensis*), 270
Amikacin sulfate, 113
Amphibians, decline of, 247–248, 249
Anesthesia, 76
Anger signs, 127–128. *See also* Aggressiveness
Animal bites, 89–90
Animal shelters, iguanas from, 24
Anole cybotes (Large-Headed Anole), 271
Anoles, 270–272
*Anolis carolinensis* (American Chameleon), 270
*Anolis equestris* (Knight Anole), 271
*Anolis ricordii* (Giant Anole), 272
*Anolis sagrei* (Brown Anole), 272
Anorexia. *See* Appetite loss
Anti-reptile legislation, 248–250, 257
Anxiousness, 36, 114
Appetite change, 101, 229
Appetite loss, 97, 105, 110–111, 184, 186
Aquarium tanks, 14, 29, 31
Association of Reptilian and Amphibian Veterinarians (ARAV), 74, 261
Attacking behavior. *See* Aggressiveness
Awareness, iguanas', xiv, 136–137, 139

## B

Baby iguanas. *See also* Breeding
   adults vs., 19–20
   cages for, 29
   caring for hatchlings, 197–200
   choosing, 21
   color changes during growth, 112

Baby iguanas *(continued)*
  diet for hatchlings, 199–200
  diet for juveniles, 69–70
  finding homes for hatchlings, 174–175, 200
  sexing, 177
Bacterial diseases, 105–106, 113. *See also* Infections
Bark as cage substrate, 33
*Basiliscus basiliscus* (Helmeted Basilisk), 273
*Basiliscus plumifrons* (Plumed Basilisk), 273–274
*Basiliscus vittatus* (Striped Basilisk), 274
Basilisks, 273–274
Basking logs and perches
  for aging iguanas, 229, 230
  cat tree, 41, 164, 230
  cleaning, 162, 164
  picking up from, 46
  preparing, 32, 35
Bathing
  after, 161
  aging iguanas, 231
  calendar entries for, 157
  regular bath, 159–161, 204
  shedding and, 166
  water temperature, 160, 231
Baytril (enrofloxacin), 113
B-complex vitamins, 56
Behavior and body language. *See also* Aggressiveness; Taming your iguana; Training
  anger, 127–128
  attack, signs indicating, 84–85, 114, 127
  biting, 15, 31, 126–127
  bluffing, 129
  breeding season aggression, 20, 84–85, 133–134, 182–183
  courtship, 133, 184–185
  defending territory, 131–132
  defensive fighting, 128–129
  dewlap extension and color, 120–121
  dominance, 132
  eating, 132
  eyes, 122–123
  flight, 129–130
  freezing in place, 130–131
  head bobs, 85, 114, 118–120, 182
  hissing, 123
  individuality in, 134
  looking for, 125–126
  olfactory messages, 127
  problems signaled by, 114
  puffing up, 125
  spines and enlarged scales, 123–124
  tail dropping, 128
  tail movements, 124–125
  thrashing, 47, 142–143, 150–151
  tongue flicking, 121–122, 213
Belly
  hot rock caution, 37
  swelling, 108
  of well-fed iguana, 53
Bibliography, 262–263
Birds
  as dinosaur relatives, 2
  with iguanas, 212–213
Biting, 15, 31, 126–127. *See also* Aggressiveness
Bleeding, 87–88, 108
Bloating, 110
Boarding your iguana, 223
Bobbing head, 85, 114, 118–120, 182
Body language. *See* Behavior and body language
Bones
  broken, 92, 108
  metabolic bone disease (MBD), 108
Books, 262–263
Box turtles, 246
*Brachylophus fasciatus* (Fiji Island Iguana), 4, 275–276
Breeding, 173–200
  captive breeding programs, 251–253
  caring for hatchlings, 197–200
  clutch numbers, 174
  courtship, 133, 184–185
  deciding to breed or not, 174–176
  difficulties of, 173–175
  dominance behavior, 132
  egg-binding (dystocia), 107–109, 110, 189–190
  eggs described, 187
  finding homes for hatchlings, 174–175, 200
  gestation, 186–187
  hatching eggs, 196–197
  incubating eggs, 193–196
  introducing males and females, 183–184
  laying eggs, 190–192
  male aggressiveness and, 20, 84–85, 133–134
  male breeding colors, 6, 112–113, 121, 181–182
  mating process, 185–186
  nesting box for, 189, 190
  photoperiods and, 40
  physical condition for, 178–179
  planning for, 176–180
  pre-breeding nutrition, 180
  record keeping, 188
  removing eggs, 192
  season for, 181–182
  sexing iguanas, 177–178
  spaying and neutering, 20, 82–83, 176
Bringing your iguana home, 41–44
Broken bones, 92, 108
Broken tail, 46–47, 90–91, 128
Brown Anole (*Anolis sagrei*), 272
Brownish color, 113–114
Browsing outdoors, 65
Bruises, 87
Building your own cage, 30, 32–33
Bumps and lumps, 110
Burnham, Don, 8, 226
Burns, 89

**C**

Cage
  boarding your iguana, 223
  building your own, 30, 32–33
  buying, 30–31
  cleaning, 14, 32–33, 161–164, 203–204
  décor and, 210
  environmental enrichment, 206–207
  furnishings, 32–33
  heating needs, 17, 34–38, 62
  lighting needs, 38–40
  location for, 31–32
  nesting box, 189, 190
  nursery cages, 198
  outside, 16

## Index

as refuge, 16
safety tips, 214
setup, 28–31
size, 14, 17, 28–29
substrate for, 32–33
taking in and out of, 46–47, 140–141, 205, 206
toilet area, 33–34, 79, 148–150, 203
Calcium, 58, 59, 60, 69, 200
Calendar or journal, 156–159
  breeding records, 188
  daily entries, 156, 157
  importance of, 155, 156, 159
  initial information, 156–157
  quarterly entries, 159
  routine (not daily) entries, 157–158
Cancer, 230
Canned foods, 67
Captive breeding programs, 251–253
Captivity
  stresses of, 10–11
  wild-caught iguanas, 10–11, 21, 175
Carbohydrates, 54
Care. *See also* Cleaning; Feeding; Health concerns; Planning for your iguana; Training
  for aging iguanas, 229
  for baby iguanas, 197–200
  bathing, 159–161, 204, 231
  calendar or journal for, 155, 156–159
  changes in routine, 215–219
  exercise, 169, 206–207, 228–229, 230
  for ill or injured iguanas, 114–116
  reasons for unhappiness, 16–17
  requirements for happiness, 16
  routine for, 170–171, 202–204
  for shedding, 78, 165–167, 204
  sleeping needs, 169
  sunshine requirements, 16, 38–39, 170
  time required for, 202–204
  toenail trimming, 167–169, 204
  vacations, 219–223
Careers in herpetology, 258–260
Carriers, 41

Castration (neutering), 20, 82–83, 176
Cataracts, 231
Cats
  bites from, 89–90
  iguanas as pets vs., xiv, 11–12
  legislation regarding, 249
  as predators, 15–16, 43, 212
  staring by, 43
  when iguana is out of cage, 47, 212
Cat tree, 41, 164, 230
Central American iguanas, 113
Ceramic heat emitters, 36–37
Ceramic light bulb sockets, 37
Chameleons, 244, 270
Changes in routine
  guests, 218–219
  holidays, 216–218
  stress from, 215
Children
  with iguanas, 208–210
  owning iguanas, 209
Choking, 88
Choosing an iguana. *See also* Owning an iguana
  babies vs. adults, 19–20
  deciding if right for you, xiii–xiv, 13–17
  males vs. females, 20
  selecting from a group, 21
Christmas, 217
Cleaning
  after bathing, 161
  basking logs and perches, 162, 164
  bathing, 159–161, 204, 231
  cage, 14, 32–33, 161–164, 203–204
  calendar entries for, 157
  cat tree, 164
  feeding area, 163–164, 203
  for mite infestations, 100–101
  other places, 164, 204
  outside enclosure, 204
  for parasite prevention, 97
  at pet stores, 21
  as preventive medicine, 79–80, 97
  for Salmonella prevention, 81–82
  time required for, 14, 203–204
  toilet area, 34, 79, 163, 203
Cold. *See* Heat

Collared Lizard (*Crotaphylus collaris*), 276
College careers, 259–260
Colors
  aggressive, 85
  breeding colors, 6, 112–113, 121, 181–182
  changes in, 113–114
  males vs. females, 20
  protective coloration, 9, 130
  range of, 6, 112–113
  regional variations, 6
Commercial foods, 65, 66–68
Commercial incubators, 192–193, 195
Communication. *See* Behavior and body language
Companionship, iguanas vs. furry pets, 11–12
Conan (iguana)
  adoption of, xi–xii
  aggressiveness by, xiv, 74, 84, 85
  aging in, 228
  with baby iguana, 120
  breeding behavior of, 183, 185
  cage size needed by, 29
  calendar entries for, 156, 158
  in educational programs, xiii
  home accidents of, 215
  learning by, 126
  naming of, 44
  other iguanas and, xiv, 74
  personality of, xiv, 8
  reactions to, xii–xiii, 18
  toilet area of, 34
*Conolophus subcristatus* (Galapagos Land Iguana), 279
Conservation
  preservation vs., 257
  suggestions for, 256–258
Constipation, 106, 108, 110
Copper, 59–60
Corrections in training, 145–146
Costa Rican iguanas, 6
Costs
  of breeding iguanas, 175
  ownership expenses, 14
  veterinary bills, 76
Courtship, 133, 184–185. *See also* Breeding
*Crotaphylus collaris* (Collared Lizard), 276

*Ctenosaura acanthura* and *similis* (Spiny-Tailed Iguana), 274–275
Cuddling. *See* Handling
*Cyclura cornuta* (Rhinocerus Iguana), 275

## D

Daily care, 170, 202–203
DAPTF (Declining Amphibians Populations Task Force), 247–248
Dark color change, 113
Darkness, need for, 36, 169
Deafness, 231
Death. *See also* Aging iguanas; Emergencies; First aid; Safety issues
  accidental, 236–237
  baby iguana mortality rate, 19
  from cold exposure, 35, 91
  euthanasia, 233–236
  getting another iguana after, 241
  grief after, 234–235, 239–240, 262
  of imported iguanas, 11
  necropsy (animal autopsy) after, 237–238
  from overheating, 36
  from parasites, 96, 102
  from shock, 93
  spiritual beliefs regarding, 240–241
  yellow-mustard color and, 114
Declining Amphibians Populations Task Force (DAPTF), 247–248
Decorations, holiday, 216–218
Defensive behavior. *See* Aggressiveness; Protective behavior
Dehydration, 92–93, 115, 185
Dermatitis, 106–107
Desert Iguana (*Dipsosaurus dorsalis*), 276–277
Dewlap
  described, 5
  extension, 120–121
Diabetes, 230
Diarrhea, 107, 110
Diet. *See* Feeding
Digestive process, 61–63
Dinosaurs, 1–2
*Dipsosaurus dorsalis* (Desert Iguana), 276–277

Diseases and disorders. *See also* Emergencies; Health concerns; Injuries; Parasites
  abscesses, 105
  age-related illnesses, 230–232
  appetite loss, 97, 105, 110–111, 184, 186
  bacterial diseases, 105–106, 113
  behaviors indicating, 114
  cancer, 230
  care during, 114–116
  choking, 88
  color changes indicating, 113–114
  common health problems and treatments, 110–111
  constipation, 106, 108, 110
  deafness, 231
  dehydration, 92–93, 115, 185
  dermatitis, 106–107
  diabetes, 230
  diarrhea, 107, 110
  egg-binding (dystocia), 107–109, 110, 189–190
  failure to thrive, 97, 108, 109
  gout, 109
  kidney failure, 231
  liver failure, 231
  metabolic bone disease (MBD), 108
  mouth rot (stomatitis), 107, 108, 111
  oral medications, giving, 103
  parasites, 96–104
  respiratory infections, 111, 112
  *Salmonella*, 80–82
Diurnal nature of iguanas, 9, 169
Dogs
  bites from, 89–90
  with iguanas, 211–212, 213
  iguanas as pets vs., xiv, 11–12
  legislation regarding, 248–249
  as predators, 15–16, 43, 211–212
  staring by, 43
  training, 213
Doors for cages, 30
Droncit (praziquantel), 102–103
Drooling, 111
Drugs. *See* Medications
Dysecdysis (poor shedding), 111
Dystocia (egg-binding), 107–109, 110, 189–190

## E

Ears
  deafness, 231
  healthy, 77
Easter, 216
Eating. *See* Feeding
Ecdysis. *See* Shedding
Educational programs, xiii, 253–256
Egg-binding (dystocia), 107–109, 110, 189–190
Eggs. *See also* Breeding
  described, 187
  egg-binding (dystocia), 107–109, 110, 189–190
  evolution of, 3
  fertile vs. infertile, 195
  gestation, 186–187
  hatching, 196–197
  incubating, 193–196
  laying, 190–192
  record keeping, 188
  removing, 192
  weight of, 195
Emergencies, 83–93. *See also* First aid
  animal bites, 89–90
  bleeding, 87–88, 108
  broken bones, 92, 108
  broken tail, 46–47, 90–91, 128
  burns, 89
  choking, 88
  cold exposure, 91–92
  color changes indicating, 113–114
  dehydration, 92–93, 115, 185
  first aid kit, 86
  restraining your iguana, 84–86
Endangered species. *See* Threatened species
Enrofloxacin (Baytril), 113
Environment. *See* Cage; Heat; Lighting
Environmental enrichment, 206–207
Enzymes, 35, 52–53, 61–62
Euthanasia, 233–236
Evolution of reptile eggs, 3
Exercise, 169, 206–207, 228–229, 230
Expenses. *See* Costs

External parasites, 99–101. *See also* Parasites
  common drugs for, 113
  diagnosing, 98
  harm caused by, 101
  mites, 100–101
  ticks, 99–100
Eyes
  age-related problems, 231
  behavior and body language, 122–123
  closing, 123, 132
  covering to restrain, 85
  described, 5
  healthy, 77
  parietal or "third eye," 5
  sunken, 92
  swelling, 108

## F

Failure to thrive, 97, 108, 109
Familiarity, preference for, 139. *See also* Changes in routine
Families, 207–211
  children and iguanas, 208–210
  iguana ownership and, 14–15, 207–208
  spouse or roommate, 210–211
Farming iguanas, 10, 11, 175, 252
Fashion industry threats to reptiles, 250–251
Fats, 54
Fear of reptiles, 256
Feces
  blood or mucus in, 101
  calendar entries for, 157
  cleanliness, importance of, 79
  constipation, 106, 108, 110
  diarrhea, 107, 110
  frequent defecation, 101
  healthy, 77
  housetraining, 148–150
  parasite diagnosis, 98–99
  toilet area, 33–34, 79, 148–150, 203
Feeding, 49–71. *See also* Water
  adult iguanas, 70
  alfalfa pellets, 33, 51
  amounts, 71
  appetite change, 101, 229
  appetite loss, 97, 105, 110–111, 184, 186

  baby iguanas, 199–200
  basic building blocks of nutrition, 50–51
  behavior and body language, 132
  calendar entries for, 157
  carbohydrates, 54
  choking, 88
  cleaning the feeding area, 163–164, 203
  commercial foods, 65, 66–68
  digestive process, 61–63
  dishes for, 41
  enzyme needs, 35, 52–53
  evaluating results of, 71
  fats, 54
  fiber, 55
  grazing outdoors, 65
  growing your own food, 62
  by hand, 141–142, 205, 218
  heat needs and, 17, 35, 62
  hiding food, 206–207
  holiday food dangers, 216–217
  ill or injured iguanas, 115
  juvenile iguanas, 69–70
  lettuce, 22, 62–63, 65
  lighting needs and, 38
  lures and rewards, 144–145
  malnourishment, 51
  minerals, 58, 59–60
  nutritional values of foods, 64
  parasite prevention, 97
  at pet stores, 22
  place for, 70–71
  poisonous plants, 66
  pre-breeding nutrition, 180
  protein, 53–54, 109
  safe, nutritious foods, 63
  signs of well-fed iguana, 53
  supplements, 68, 200
  time for, 70
  time required for, 14, 202–203
  vitamins, 39, 55–58
  wild iguanas' diet, 49–50, 62
Feet
  described, 4
  toenail trimming, 167–169, 204
Females. *See also* Breeding
  courtship, 133, 184–185
  egg-binding (dystocia), 107–109, 110, 189–190
  handling during gestation, 187
  introducing to males, 183–184

  males vs., 20, 119, 120, 177–178
  sexing, 177–178
  size of, 7
  spaying, 82–83, 176
Fenbendazole (Panacur), 102, 103, 113
Fiber, 55
Fighting. *See* Aggressiveness
Fiji Island Iguana (*Brachylophus fasciatus*), 4, 275–276
Finances. *See* Costs
Finding
  homes for hatchlings, 174–175, 200
  the right iguana, 18–24
  veterinarians, 74–75, 261
First aid. *See also* Emergencies
  for animal bites, 89–90
  for bleeding, 87–88
  for broken bones, 92
  for burns, 89
  for choking, 88
  for cold exposure, 91–92
  for dehydration, 92, 115, 185
  kit, 86
  for mites, 100–101
  tick removal, 99–100
First night, 42
First week, 44–45
Flag Day, 216
Flagellates, 104
Flagyl (metronidazole), 104
Flight, 129–130
Fluorescent light, 38–40
Food. *See* Feeding
Fourth of July, 216
Freezing in place, 130–131

## G

Galapagos Iguanas, 4, 279
Galapagos Land Iguana (*Conolophus subcristatus*), 279
Galapagos Marine Iguana (*Amblyrhyncus cristatus*), 279
Galapagos tortoises, 245
Gatorade, 51, 92, 115, 221
Gestation, 186–187
Giant Anole (*Anolis ricordii*), 272
Gingivitis, 108
Givenchy, 250
Glass tanks, 14, 29, 31

## Index

Glossary, 265–267
Gout, 109
Granite Spiny Lizard (*Sceloporus orcutti*), 277–278
Gravel as cage substrate, 33
Grazing outdoors, 65
Green Boy (iguana), 235
*Green Iguana*, 8, 10, 226
Green Iguana Foundation, 252
Green Iguanas. *See also* Iguana family tree; Iguanas; Wild iguanas
  anti-reptile legislation, 248–250, 257
  in captivity, 10–11
  described, 2, 3–6
  furry pets vs., xiv, 11–12
  glossary of terms, 265–267
  growth rate of, 19
  life expectancy, 8, 18, 25, 226–227
  personality and temperament, 7–8
  regional variations, 6
  signs of health, 23
  size, xiii, 6–7, 19
Grief
  after accidental death, 237
  after euthanasia, 234–235
  getting another iguana and, 241
  hotlines, 262
  spiritual beliefs regarding death, 240–241
  stages of, 239–240
Grow lights, 38–39
Growth
  in aging iguanas, 229
  color changes during, 112
  failure to thrive, 97, 108, 109
  rate, 19
Guests, 218–219

## H

Habitat destruction, 9, 175, 246–247
Habitats of wild iguanas, 3, 8–9
Halloween, 216–217
Hand feeding, 141–142, 205, 218
Handling. *See also* Taming your iguana
  bathing, 160–161, 204, 231
  at the beginning, 45–46
  bringing your iguana home, 41–43
  during breeding season, 182–183
  by guests and strangers, 218–219
  kissing, 82
  pregnant females, 187
  relaxing your iguana, 47, 142–143, 150–151
  responding to aggressiveness, 84, 85, 183
  restraining your iguana, 84–86
  rubbing, 140–141
  taking in and out of cage, 46–47, 140–141, 205, 206
  thrashing behavior, 47, 142–143, 150–151
  time required for, 14
  tolerance for, 8, 13
  trimming toenails, 168–169, 204
Happy iguanas
  reasons for unhappiness, 16–17
  requirements for happiness, 16
  signs of health, 23, 53, 77–78
Harness
  introducing, 151–152
  making, 152
  walking on a leash, 153–154
Hatching eggs, 196–197
Hatchlings. *See* Baby iguanas; Breeding
Hatfield, James, 8, 10, 226
Hazards. *See* Safety issues; Stress
Head. *See also* Eyes
  bobbing, 85, 114, 118–120, 182
  covering to restrain, 85
  described, 5
  jaw deformed, 111
  mouth rot (stomatitis), 107, 108, 111
  runny nose, 111, 112
  signs of health, 77
  swelling, 108
  tongue flicking, 121–122, 213
Health concerns. *See also* Emergencies; First aid; Parasites; Safety issues; Veterinarians
  abscesses, 105
  age-related illnesses, 230–232
  anesthesia, 76
  appetite loss, 97, 105, 110–111, 184, 186
  bacterial diseases, 105–106, 113
  behaviors indicating, 114
  breeding, physical condition for, 178–179
  caring for ill or injured iguanas, 114–116
  choosing an iguana, 21–22
  color changes, 113–114
  common health problems and treatments, 110–111
  constipation, 106, 108, 110
  dermatitis, 106–107
  diarrhea, 107, 110
  egg-binding (dystocia), 107–109, 110, 189–190
  eggs don't hatch, 197
  failure to thrive, 97, 108, 109
  first aid kit, 86
  gout, 109
  metabolic bone disease (MBD), 108
  mouth rot (stomatitis), 107, 108, 111
  neutering, 20, 82–83, 176
  oral medications, giving, 103
  other reptiles with iguanas, 213
  parasites, 96–104
  preventive medicine, 78–80
  respiratory infections, 111, 112
  Salmonella poisoning, 80–82
  shedding, 78, 111, 165–167, 204
  signs of health, 23, 53, 77–78
  spaying, 82–83, 176
  veterinarians, 74–76, 93
Heat
  after bathing, 161
  for baby hatchlings, 198
  of bathing water, 160, 231
  boarding your iguana and, 223
  burns, 89
  cold exposure, 17, 35, 91–92
  color changes and, 113
  during gestation, 186–187
  heating devices, 36–38
  for ill or injured iguanas, 115
  monitoring, 37, 38
  overheating, 35–36
  requirements, 17, 34–36, 62
  for traveling with your iguana, 221
Heimlich maneuver, 88

Helmeted Basilisk (*Basiliscus basiliscus*), 273
Helmet scale, 5
Hemipenes, 178
Hemorrhaging (bleeding), 87–88, 108
Herpetological societies, 258, 261
Herpetology careers, 258–260
Hiding, excessive, 114
Hiding food, 206–207
Hissing, 123
Holidays, 216–218
Home-raised iguanas, 11
Hookworms, 98, 102
Horned Toad (*Phrynosoma cornutum*), 278–279
Hot rocks, 37
Housetraining, 148–150
Humane societies, iguanas from, 24
Hurricanes, iguanas spread by, 3

## I

Iceberg lettuce, 22, 62
Iguana family tree, 269–279
    anoles, 270–272
    basilisks, 273–274
    less popular species, 276–278
    popular species, 274–276
    species unsuitable for pets, 278–279
*Iguana iguana. See* Green Iguanas
Iguanas. *See also* Green Iguanas; Iguana family tree; Wild iguanas; *specific species*
    anti-reptile legislation, 248–250, 257
    in captivity, 10–11
    farming, 10, 11, 175, 252
    furry pets vs., xiv, 11–12
    glossary of terms, 265–267
    life expectancy, 8, 18, 25, 226–227
    personality and temperament, 7–8
    reasons for unhappiness, 16–17
    requirements for happiness, 16
    signs of health, 23
    size, xiii, 6–7, 19
    species, 2, 4, 9
Illnesses. *See* Diseases and disorders; Health concerns
Incandescent light, 36, 38, 39
Incubating eggs, 193–196

Incubators
    commercial, 192–193, 195
    making, 193–194
Infections
    abscesses, 105
    bacterial, 105–106, 113
    common drugs for, 113
    dermatitis, 106–107
    mouth rot (stomatitis), 107, 108, 111
    respiratory, 111, 112
Injuries. *See also* Emergencies; First aid; Health concerns; Safety issues
    abscesses, 105
    accidental death, 236–237
    animal bites, 89–90
    bleeding, 87–88
    broken bones, 92, 108
    broken tail, 46–47, 90–91, 128
    bruises, 87
    burns, 89
    care during, 114–116
    internal, 88
    restraining your iguana, 84–86
    toenail trimmed into quick, 168–169
Insecticides for mites, 100–101
Intelligence. *See* Mental characteristics
Internal injuries, 88
Internal parasites, 101–104. *See also* Parasites
    common drugs for, 113
    diagnosing, 98–99, 101–102
    flagellates, 104
    harm caused by, 101
    hookworms, 98, 102
    oral medications, giving, 103
    pinworms, 103
    protozoans, 98, 104
    roundworms, 102
    tapeworms, 102–103
Iodine, 60
Iron, 59–60
Irritability, 114
Isoflurane, 76
Ivermectin, 113

## J

Jaw. *See also* Head; Mouth
    deformed, 111

    mouth rot (stomatitis), 107, 108, 111
    swelling, 108
Journal. *See* Calendar or journal

## K

Keel-Tailed Lizard (*Tropidurus torquatus*), 278
Kennels, 223
Kidney failure, 231
Kissing, 82
Knight Anole (*Anolis equestris*), 271

## L

Large-Headed Anole (*Anole cybotes*), 271
Lauren, Ralph, 250
Laws, anti-reptile, 248–250, 257
Laying eggs, 190–192
Learning. *See* Training
Leash, walking on, 153–154. *See also* Harness
Legislation, anti-reptile, 248–250, 257
Legs
    broken bones, 92, 108
    described, 4
    handling, 46
    hind leg extension, 111
    swelling, 108
Lettuce, 22, 62
Life expectancy of iguanas, 8, 18, 25, 226–227
Lighting
    for baby hatchlings, 198
    calendar entries for, 158
    ceramic sockets, 37
    darkness, need for, 36
    heat from, 36
    photoperiods, 40
    requirements, 38–40
Litter for toilet area, 34
Liver failure, 231
Lumps and bumps, 110
Lures (training technique), 144–145
Lyons Electric incubator, 192

## M

Magazines, 262
Magnesium, 60

Males. *See also* Breeding
  aggressiveness during breeding season, 20, 84–85, 133–134, 182–183
  breeding colors, 6, 112–113, 121, 181–182
  courtship, 133, 184–185
  females vs., 20, 119, 120, 177–178
  introducing to females, 183–184
  neutering, 20, 82–83, 176
  physical anatomy, 178
  sexing, 177–178
  size of, 7
Malnourishment, 51
MBD (metabolic bone disease), 108
Medical care. *See* Emergencies; First aid; Health concerns; Injuries; Preventive medicine; Veterinarians
Medications
  common drugs for iguanas, 113
  Droncit (praziquantel), 102–103
  Flagyl (metronidazole), 104
  following instructions for, 115
  giving orally, 103
  Panacur (fenbendazole), 102, 103, 113
Memory of iguanas, 137
Menstruating women, aggression toward, 84, 182
Mental characteristics. *See also* Training
  awareness, xiv, 136–137, 139
  intelligence of reptiles, xiv, 13
  learning capacities, 147–148
  memory, 137
  reasoning abilities, 137–138
  stubbornness, 138–139
Metabolic bone disease (MBD), 108
Metabolism, 61–62
Metronidazole (Flagyl), 104
Mexican iguanas, 6, 113
Minerals. *See also* Feeding
  in diet, 58–60
  for hatchlings, 200
  supplements, 68, 200
Mirrors as stress factors, 17
Mites, 100–101
Monitoring
  breeding record keeping, 188
  calendar or journal for, 155, 156–159
  heat, 37, 38
  weight, 77–78, 159
Monthly routine, 171
Mortality rate. *See also* Death
  for baby iguanas, 19
  for imported iguanas, 11
Motionlessness
  from cold, 17, 35, 91
  freezing in place, 130–131
  from internal injuries, 88
  yellow-mustard color and, 114
Mouth
  breathing through, 111
  healthy, 77
  hissing, 123
  mouth rot (stomatitis), 107, 108, 111
  tongue flicking, 121–122, 213
Mouth rot (stomatitis), 107, 108, 111
Muddy color, 113–114
Museum careers, 259

# N
Nail trimming, 167–169, 204
Names
  naming your iguana, 44–45
  recognition of, 147
Native habitats of iguanas, 3, 8–9
Necropsy (animal autopsy), 237–238
Nesting box, 189, 190
Neutering, 20, 82–83, 176
Newspaper for cage floor, 32–33
Noise, cage location and, 31
Nutrition. *See* Feeding

# O
Older iguanas. *See* Aging iguanas
Olfactory messages, 127
Oral medications, giving, 103
Outdoors time, 151–154
  cautions, 65, 151, 153
  cleaning the outside enclosure, 204
  grazing or browsing, 65
  guidelines, 153
  harness introduction, 151–152
  making a harness, 152
  walking on the leash, 153–154

Oviposition (laying eggs), 190–192
Owning an iguana. *See also* Care; Planning for your iguana; Training
  babies vs. adults, 19–20
  by children, 209
  commitment required, xiii–xiv, 14, 18, 25
  companionship expectations, 12
  deciding if right for you, xiii–xiv, 13–17
  family issues, 14–15
  finding the right iguana, 18–24
  furry pets vs., 11–12
  getting another after death, 241
  learning capabilities, 13
  life expectancy, 8, 18, 25, 226–227
  males vs. females, 20
  other pets as predators, 15–16
  personality and temperament and, 7–8, 13
  reasons for unhappiness, 16–17
  requirements, 13–14, 16

# P, Q
Panacur (fenbendazole), 102, 103, 113
Paralysis, 111
Parasites, 96–104
  common drugs for, 113
  diagnosing, 98–99, 101–102
  external, 99–101
  flagellates, 104
  hookworms, 98, 102
  internal, 101–104
  life cycle of, 98
  mites, 100–101
  oral medications, giving, 103
  overview, 96
  pinworms, 103
  preventing, 97
  protozoans, 98, 104
  roundworms, 102
  symptoms, 97, 101–102
  tapeworms, 102–103
  ticks, 99–100
Parietal eye, 5
Pedialyte, 51, 92, 115, 221
Penises, 178
Perches. *See* Basking logs and perches

Periodicals, 262
Personality and temperament, 7–8.
    *See also* Mental characteristics
Peruvian iguanas, 6, 112
Pet sitters, 220–222
Pet Sitters International, 220
Pets other than iguanas, 212–213.
    *See also* Cats; Dogs
Pet stores, 20–22
Petting. *See* Handling
Phosphorus, 58, 59, 60
Photoperiods, 40
*Phrynosoma cornutum* (Horny
    Toad), 278–279
Picking up. *See* Handling
Pinworms, 103
Planning for your iguana, 27–47
    bringing your iguana home,
        41–44
    cage furnishings, 32–33
    cage location, 31–32
    cage setup, 28–31
    cat tree, 41
    first night, 41
    food and water dishes, 41
    heating needs, 17, 34–38, 62
    lighting needs, 38–40
    naming your iguana, 44–45
    toilet area, 33–34
Plumed Basilisk (*Basiliscus
    plumifrons*), 273–274
Poisonous plants, 66, 217
Praziquantel (Droncit), 102–103
Predators
    iguanas as, 213
    other pets as, 15–16, 43,
        211–212
    for wild iguanas, 9, 175
Preparations. *See* Planning for your
    iguana
Preservation, conservation vs., 257
Preventive medicine, 78–80
    cleanliness, 79–80
    details, paying attention to, 79
    for parasites, 97
    for Salmonella, 81–82
Protective behavior. *See also* Aggressiveness; Behavior and
    body language; Taming your
    iguana
    anger, 127–128
    biting, 15, 31, 126–127

bluffing, 129
breeding season aggression, 20,
    84–85, 133–134, 182–183
defending territory, 131–132
defensive fighting, 128–129
dominance, 132
flight, 129–130
freezing in place, 130–131
hissing, 123
puffing up, 125
signs of imminent attack, 84–85,
    114, 127
tail dropping, 128
tail whipping, 15, 31, 124–125,
    142
thrashing, 47, 142–143,
    150–151
in the wild, 9
Protective coloration, 9, 130
Protein, 53–54, 109
Protozoans, 98, 104
Protrusions, 111
Public education about reptiles, xiii,
    253–256
Puffing up, 125

R
Reasoning abilities, 137–138. *See
    also* Mental characteristics
Record keeping. *See* Calendar or
    journal
Reflective surfaces as stress factors,
    17
Relaxing your iguana, 47, 142–143,
    150–151
Removing eggs, 192
Reptile dealers, 22–23
Reptiles
    anti-reptile legislation, 248–250,
        257
    attitudes and behavior toward,
        243–245
    evolution of eggs, 3
    fashion industry threats to,
        250–251
    fear of, 256
    glossary of terms, 265–267
    herpetological societies, 258
    herpetology careers, 258–260
    as pets, iguanas with, 213
    public education about, xiii,
        253–256

*Reptiles and Amphibians in Captivity,* 8
Rescue groups, iguanas from,
    23–24
Resources, 261–263
Respiratory infections, 111, 112
Restraining your iguana, 84–86
Rewards (training technique), 145
Rhinoceros Iguana (*Cyclura
    cornuta*), 4, 275
Rock Iguanas, 4
Roommates and iguanas, 210–211
Roosevelt, Theodore, 17
Roundworms, 102
Routine care. *See* Care
Rubbing. *See* Handling
Runny nose, 111, 112

S
Safety issues. *See also* Emergencies;
    First aid; Injuries; Stress
    accidental death, 236–237
    birds as predators, 212
    birds as prey, 213
    cats as predators, 15–16, 43,
        212
    children and iguanas, 208–210
    cold exposure, 17, 35, 91–92
    dogs as predators, 15–16, 43,
        211–212
    foods to beware of, 62–63, 65,
        69
    grazing outdoors, 65
    holidays, 216–218
    home safety tips, 214–215
    hot rock caution, 37
    other reptiles with iguanas, 213
    outdoors time, 65, 151, 153
    overheating, 35–36
    poisonous plants, 66, 217
    removing shedding skin,
        166–167
    Salmonella, 80–82
    supplements, 68
    toenail trimming, 168–169
Salmonella, 80–82
    anti-reptile legislation and,
        249–250
    dangers of, 80–81
    educational programs and, 254
    preventing, 81–82
Sand as cage substrate, 33

Scales
  described, 5–6
  enlarged, 123–124
*Sceloporus orcutti* (Granite Spiny Lizard), 277–278
Security. *See* Safety issues
Seizures, 108, 111
Selecting an iguana. *See* Choosing an iguana
Sexing iguanas, 177–178
Shedding
  in aging iguanas, 229
  calendar entries for, 157
  care during, 78, 165–167, 204
  poor (dysecdysis), 111
  problem areas, 166, 167
  spines, 166
Shelters, iguanas from, 24
Shipping, death from stress of, 11
Shock, 93, 114
Signs and symptoms. *See also* Behavior and body language; *specific symptoms*
  of aging iguana illnesses, 230–231
  of attack impending, 84–85, 114, 123, 127
  of cold exposure, 17, 35, 91, 113
  color changes, 112–114
  common health problems and treatments, 110–111
  of dehydration, 92
  of healthy iguanas, 23, 53, 77–78
  of internal injuries, 87
  of overheating, 36
  of parasites, 97, 101–102
  of Salmonella poisoning, 80
Sitters, pet, 220–222
Size
  of cage, 14, 17, 28–29
  calendar entries for, 159
  of iguana clutches, 174
  of iguanas, xiii, 6–7, 19
  monitoring weight, 77–78
  puffing up, 125
Sizeman, Tom, 235
Skin
  bumps and lumps, 110
  dermatitis, 106–107
  healthy, 77
  poor shedding (dysecdysis), 111
  protrusions, 111
  shedding, 78, 165–167, 204
  spines and enlarged scales, 123–124, 166
  wrinkled, 92
Slavens, Frank L., 8
Sleep, 36, 169
Snakes, 244, 250, 256
Sneezing, 111, 112
Soap for bathing, 160
Socialization. *See* Taming your iguana
Sources for iguanas
  humane societies and shelters, 24
  iguana rescue groups, 23–24
  pet stores, 20–22
  reptile dealers, 22–23
Spaying, 82–83, 176
Species of iguanas. *See also* Threatened species; *specific species*
  anoles, 270–272
  basilisks, 273–274
  less popular species, 276–278
  number of, 9, 269
  overview, 2, 4
  popular species, 274–276
  unsuitable for pets, 278–279
Spine curvature, 108
Spines, 123–124, 166
Spiny-Tailed Iguana (*Ctenosaura acanthura* and *similis*), 274–275
Spiritual beliefs regarding death, 240–241
Spouses and iguanas, 210–211
Staring, 43, 218
Stomatitis (mouth rot), 107, 108, 111
Strangers
  awareness of, 139
  guests, 218–219
Stress
  bringing your iguana home, 41–43
  cage size and, 17, 28–29
  from captivity, 10–11
  causes of, 17
  from changes in routine, 215
  closing eyes, 123
  eliminating for hatchlings, 198
  guests and, 218–219
  handling recommendations, 45–47
  ill or injured iguanas and, 115–116
  from staring, 43, 218
Striped Basilisk (*Basiliscus vittatus*), 274
Stubbornness, 138–139
Substrate for cage, 32–33
Subtympanic shield, 5
Sulfadimethoxine (Albon), 113
Sunshine
  cage location for, 31
  glass tanks and, 31
  requirements, 16, 38–39, 170
  vitamin D from, 39, 57
Supervising
  children and iguanas, 208–209
  iguanas out of cage, 210–211, 215
Suriname iguanas, 6, 112
Swelling, 108
Symptoms. *See* Signs and symptoms; *specific symptoms*

T
Tail
  body language, 124–125
  broken, 46–47, 90–91, 128
  described, 4–5, 6
  dropping part of, 128
  handling, 46–47
  whipping or thrashing by, 15, 31, 124–125, 142
Taming your iguana, 139–143. *See also* Handling
  guests and, 218–219
  hand feeding, 141–142, 205, 218
  as ongoing process, 143, 201–202
  relaxing, 47, 142–143, 150–151
  rubbing, 140–141
  taking in and out of cage, 46–47, 140–141, 205, 206
  thrashing behavior, 47, 142–143, 150–151
  time required for, 204–205
Tapeworms, 102–103
Target sticks, 144, 207
Teasing, cruel, 17

Temperament and personality, 7–8. *See also* Mental characteristics
Temperature. *See* Heat
Territory
 breeding and, 183–184
 defending, 131–132
 dominance behavior, 132–133
 need for, 16
Thanksgiving, 217
Thermometers for monitoring heat, 38
Thinking abilities. *See* Mental characteristics
"Third eye" (parietal eye), 5
Thrashing
 relaxing when handling, 47, 142–143, 150–151
 tail whipping, 15, 31, 124–125, 142
Threatened species
 amphibians' decline, 247–248, 249
 box turtles, 246
 captive breeding programs and, 251–253
 by fashion industry, 250–251
 future conservation suggestions, 256–258
 Galapagos tortoises, 245
 by habitat destruction, 9, 175, 246–247
 iguana farming and, 10, 175, 252
 iguana species at risk, 4
 by pet trade, 245–246
 public education about, 253–256
Thrive, failure to, 97, 108, 109
Ticks, 99–100
Time. *See also* Aging iguanas
 bathing frequency, 159, 204
 calendar or journal for care, 155, 156–159
 for care, 202–204
 for cleaning, 14, 161, 162, 203–204
 demands on yours, 14
 diet and age, 69–70
 for feeding, 70, 202–203
 life expectancy, 8, 18, 25, 226–227
 regular attention, need for, 143, 201–202

routine for care, 170–171, 202–204
 for taming and training, 204–205
 toenail trimming frequency, 167, 204
Time out (training technique), 147
Toenail trimming, 167–169, 204
Toes, 4
Toilet area
 cleaning, 34, 79, 163, 203
 housetraining, 148–150
 moving, 149
 providing, 33–34, 148–150
 water in, 34, 150
Tongue flicking, 121–122, 213
Toys, 207
Training, 135–154. *See also* Taming your iguana
 alternative actions, 146–147
 corrections, 145–146
 fundamentals, 143–147
 housetraining, 148–150
 lures and rewards, 144–145
 mental characteristics of iguanas, 136–139
 motivation as key, 135
 for outdoors time, 151–154
 patience required for, 154
 relaxing your iguana, 47, 142–143, 150–151
 rules learned by you, 13
 taming your iguana, 139–143
 target sticks for, 144, 207
 time out technique, 147
 time required for, 204–205
 tricks, 148
 verbal cues and corrections, 143, 145–146
 what you can teach iguanas, 147–148
Traveling
 boarding your iguana, 223
 bringing your iguana home, 41–42
 bringing your iguana with you, 219–220, 221
 pet sitters, 220–222
 vacations, 219–223
Tremors, 108, 111
Trimming toenails, 167–169, 204
*Tropidurus torquatus* (Keel-Tailed Lizard), 278

Twitching, 108, 111
Tympanic plate, 5

U
Ultraviolet light, 38–39. *See also* Lighting
Undercage heaters, 38
University careers, 259–260
UVA and UVB rays, 38–39. *See also* Lighting

V
Vacations, 219–223
 boarding your iguana, 223
 pet sitters, 220–222
 taking your iguana with you, 219–220, 221
Venezualan iguanas, 6, 113
Veterinarians, 74–76. *See also* Emergencies; First aid; Health concerns
 aging iguanas and, 232–233
 careers, 260
 euthanasia by, 233–236
 finding, 74–75, 261
 questions for, 75, 76
 vacation arrangements with, 222, 223
 when to call, 87, 88, 89, 90, 93
 working with, 74, 75–76
Vitamins, 55–58. *See also* Feeding
 A, 55–56, 58, 60
 B complex, 56, 58, 60
 C, 46–47, 58, 60
 combining for best effect, 58, 60
 D, 39, 57, 58, 60
 E, 57–58
 fat-soluble, 54
 for hatchlings, 200
 K, 58
 supplements, 68, 200
Vitton, Louis, 250
Vomiting, 102, 111

W, X
Walking on the leash, 153–154
Water
 bathing in, 159–161, 204, 231
 dehydration, 92–93, 115, 185
 dishes for, 41, 52

Water *(continued)*
  need for, 51–52
  providing, 52
  in toilet area, 34, 150
Wattage
  for heat emitters, 37
  for light bulbs, 36
Web sites
  for iguana information, 261–262
  Pet Sitters International, 220
Weekly routine, 170–171
Weight
  appetite loss, 97, 105, 110–111, 184, 186
  of eggs, 195
  failure to thrive, 97, 108, 109
  gain in aging iguanas, 229–230
  loss, 97
  monitoring, 77–78, 159
Welcoming your iguana. *See* Planning for your iguana
Werner, Wegman, 252
Wild-caught iguanas, 10–11, 21, 175
Wild iguanas
  diet of, 49–50, 62
  habitats, 3, 8–9
  older iguanas, 227–228
  predation on, 9, 175, 243
  protective behavior, 9
Wildlife management careers, 259
Wire for cages, 29, 30

Worms
  diagnosing, 98–99, 101–102
  hookworms, 98, 102
  pinworms, 103
  roundworms, 102
  tapeworms, 102–103
Wounds. *See* Injuries

# Y
Yellow-mustard color, 114

# Z
Zinc, 58, 60
Zoological park careers, 259
ZooMed cages, 30